T0314256

KANTIAN ETHICS AND ECONOMICS

KANTIAN ETHICS AND ECONOMICS

Autonomy, Dignity, and Character

Mark D. White

STANFORD UNIVERSITY PRESS

STANFORD, CALIFORNIA

Stanford University Press
Stanford, California

Printed in the United States of America on acid-free, archival-quality paper

Library of Congress Cataloging-in-Publication Data

White, Mark D., 1971–
    Kantian ethics and economics : autonomy, dignity, and character / Mark D.
White.
        p.   cm.
    Includes bibliographical references and index.
        ISBN 978-0-8047-6894-8 (alk. paper)
        1. Economics—Moral and ethical aspects.   2. Kant, Immanuel, 1724–1804—
Ethics.   I. Title.
HB72.W48   2011
174—dc22

                                                            2010038590

To Anya and Andrew:
May you always live with dignity

Contents

Acknowledgments

If I have seen a little further it is by standing on the shoulders of Giants.
—Isaac Newton (1676)

My influences and debts are numerous, great, and deep. First and foremost, of course, is Immanuel Kant, as well as the Kant scholars by whose writings I have been enlightened over years of study (and whose influence is well reflected in the Bibliography), such as Roger Sullivan, Thomas Hill, Onora O'Neill, H. J. Paton, and Mary Gregor. I wish to emphasize two in particular: Christine Korsgaard, whose recent book *Self-Constitution* was such an inspiration to my views on character, and Barbara Herman, who has fired many of my recent (and still developing) ideas about judgment. John Searle, along with Jay Wallace, Richard Holton, and David Velleman, assured me that rationality is not as fatalistically deterministic as most economists (and philosophers) would have it, and confirmed my intuitions about the will. Amartya Sen showed me (and so many others) that economics and philosophy are two great tastes that taste great together. Finally, Ronald Dworkin crafted a theory of judicial decision-making based on integrity and character that I think can be even more; hints of that are in this book, and I hope to develop them more in future work. I have benefited so much from all of these scholars' work, and I hope to continue to learn from them (and others) for as long as I live.

While I have had occasional passing contact with some of the scholars above—well, maybe not Kant—I have enjoyed closer relationships with many wonderful thinkers and people who also had a tremendous influence on this book, two of whom I want to thank specifically. John

Davis has been a terrific friend, colleague, and mentor since I started doing economics-and-philosophy back in . . . oh well, that's not important. His book, *The Theory of the Individual in Economics*, opened my eyes to many new topics, concepts, and approaches, and led me to look at identity and self in my own way. Every time I open my dog-eared copy I learn something new, and I look forward to every new thing he writes. Deirdre McCloskey has been a terrific sparring partner, a generous supporter, and a shameless flatterer who nonetheless will not hesitate to take me to task when the situation merits it. She exemplifies the virtues of the economist-philosopher, and sets a high standard for the rest of us; her book *Bourgeois Virtues*, in all of its insight, wisdom, and charm, captures her essence and yet does not do this fascinating woman justice.

I would also like to thank the many people who supported me on the road to this book, which took me through many conferences, journal articles, and book chapters. My colleagues, past and present, in the Department of Political Science, Economics, and Philosophy at the College of Staten Island have been unbelievably supportive, especially the philosophers who helped guide me in my initial forays into their world, including Keya Maitra, Chalmers Clark, Barbara Montero, Peter Simpson, Amy Hannon, and Bob Chiles; the chairs who have helped to guide my career, Vasilios Petratos, Rich Flanagan, and Robin Carey; and the regulars at our monthly Philosophy Forum, particularly Linda Coull, Richenda Kramer, and the late Dan Kramer. I would also like to thank all my co-editors and contributors to my edited volumes, especially Chrisoula Andreou and Jennifer Baker, as well as my friends and colleagues in the Association for Social Economics, especially David George, Jonathan Wight, Irene van Staveren, Deb Figart, Morris Altman, John Marangos, and Wilfred Dolfsma. And finally, there are people who defy any category (Kant be damned): Steve Pressman, Jerry Gaus, Peter Boettke, Ed Stringham, Tim Brennan, and Sandy Peart.

Finally, I owe more gratitude than I can ever express to my best friends Maryanne Fisher, Bill Irwin, and Shana Meyer, and my editor at Stanford (who has become a very good friend as well), Margo Beth Crouppen. Without their support and encouragement, I would not have finished this book. Thank you.

Much of the material in this book grew from the seeds of previously published work, which has been rewritten, reorganized, consolidated, and extended between these covers. I thank the following publishers and editors for their kind permission to adapt portions of these pieces in this book: "Can *Homo Economicus* Follow Kant's Categorical Imperative?," *Journal of Socio-Economics* 33 (2004): 89–105 (Elsevier); "Preaching to the Choir: A Response to *Fairness Versus Welfare*," *Review of Political Economy* 16 (2004): 507–15 (Routledge); "Multiple Selves and Weakness of Will: A Kantian Perspective," *Review of Social Economy* 64 (2006): 1–20 (Routledge); "A Kantian Critique of Neoclassical Law and Economics," *Review of Political Economy* 18 (2006): 235–52 (Routledge); "Does *Homo Economicus* Have a Will?," *Economics and the Mind*, edited by Barbara Montero and Mark D. White, 143–58 (Routledge, 2007); "A Kantian Critique of Antitrust: On Morality and Microsoft," *Journal of Private Enterprise* 22 (2007): 161–90 (Association of Private Enterprise Education); "Social Law and Economics and the Quest for Dignity and Rights," *The Elgar Companion to Social Economics*, edited by John Davis and Wilfed Dolfsma, 575–94 (Edward Elgar, 2008); "Pareto, Consent, and Respect for Dignity: A Kantian Perspective," *Review of Social Economy* 67 (2009): 49–70 (Routledge); "Kantian Ethics and the Prisoners' Dilemma," *Eastern Economic Journal* 35 (2009): 137–43 (Palgrave); "In Defense of Deontology and Kant: A Reply to van Staveren," *Review of Political Economy* 21 (2009): 315–23 (Routledge); "Adam Smith and Immanuel Kant: On Markets, Duties, and Moral Sentiments," *Forum for Social Economy* 39 (2010): 53–60 (Springer); "Resisting Procrastination: Kantian Autonomy and the Role of the Will," in *The Thief of Time: Philosophical Essays on Procrastination*, edited by Chrisoula Andreou and Mark D. White, 216–32 (Oxford University Press, 2010); and "Behavioral Law and Economics: The Assault on Consent, Will, and Dignity," in *New Essays on Philosophy, Politics and Economics: Integration and Common Research Projects*, edited by Gerald Gaus, Christi Favor, and Julian Lamont, 203–23 (Stanford University Press, 2010).

Introduction

I love economics, I really do. And I always have, ever since my sixth-grade teacher Mr. Dalton drew a supply-and-demand diagram on the chalkboard. After he explained how it works, I thought he had revealed to me The Answer to Everything. But while I love economics, we definitely have a love/hate relationship. One way in which this book can be seen is as an exploration of that relationship, mediated ultimately by philosophy (and an unlikely choice for a marriage counselor).

As we typically teach our undergraduate students, economics has a positive side and a normative side. The former attempts to explain why the world is how it is, how it got there, and how it will be if things change; the latter tries to tell us how the world ought to be, and what should be done to get us there. Economics tries to do both in a "scientifically" or "value-free" way, which is absurd. The absurdity is most obvious in reference to normative economics, which claims to make "ought" statements with no value to support the ought (which, naturally, is all for naught). But the absurdity is also present, though less apparent, when we talk about positive economics, because economic explanations and predictions—especially in microeconomics—are ultimately based on human behavior, which is driven by an ersatz mixture of moral, amoral, and immoral reasons and desires, all processed very imperfectly (as behavioral economists keep telling us).[1]

It was this realization that introduced a crack into my relationship with economics that has only grown over the years. At the same time as I was trying to master technical mainstream economics in graduate school, I started reading philosophy on the side—picture me crouched in the back of the classroom, a dog-eared tome of contraband wisdom hidden in the dustcover of Hal Varian's micro text—in an attempt to answer some of my questions and flesh out my reservations and intuitions. And when I lit upon the moral philosophy of Immanuel Kant, I knew I had found what I was searching for. Finally, after a very prominent and respected economist told me, "you're either an economist or you're a Kantian—you can't be both," my course was set—I would be both.

Why Kant?

Of all the moral philosophers in this big world, I had to choose Kant. As many a frustrated PHIL 101 student would ask, "Why?" (This is only appropriate, since the universal response to hearing that I teach economics is, "Oh, economics was the most confusing course I took in college!" To which I say, "Go ask for your money back, then—it shouldn't have been that tough.") Let me try to explain why Kant "spoke to me," and in the process, I will also explain a little about how this book will proceed.

As usually taught and practiced, modern economics is essentially utilitarian. Normally traced to Jeremy Bentham and John Stuart Mill, *utilitarianism* is a system of ethics that judges the morality of actions by the goodness (or "utility") of their consequences, and is therefore a type of *consequentialism*. Variants of utilitarianism define utility or the good in different ways: some utilitarians hold happiness to be the good, others use a broader sense of well-being (often including income, wealth, or health), while yet others use utility more formally as a numerical index of preference satisfaction. It is this last type of utilitarianism that most closely resembles economic models of choice, in which agents act to maximize their preferences within their constraints (usually based on money or time). Originally defined over consumption goods which serve to increase one's own self-interest, preferences have since been generalized to include altruistic or interdependent impulses or drives, which led to the earliest models of altruistic economic behavior.

However, the structure of preferences in economic choice models implies trade-offs between the options over which preferences are defined. If a consumer plans to buy a certain combination of soda and juice, and then discovers that the price of soda has risen, we would expect her to buy less soda and more juice. By the same token, if an agent is deciding how to allocate her income between consumption and charitable giving, and then the tax deduction on charity is reduced (making it more costly), we would expect her to donate less to charity and spend more on herself (or her family or friends). A similar picture can be painted in terms of time: as a worker's wage rises, she would likely spend more time at her paid work and less time donating her time to a local charity. Trade-offs are everywhere in economic models of choice, and analyzing these trade-offs, made necessary by scarcity of resources, is what I consider economics' most important contribution to the world. (It may even make up for Paul Krugman.)

Nonetheless, surely there are some things we do (or devote resources to) that would not be affected by changes in their cost, and choices regarding these things would not involve trade-offs. To continue the examples of charity, we can imagine a person who promises to donate $50 to a local animal shelter every month. Even if the opportunity costs of that monthly donation go up (due to higher bills one month), it is possible that she will not change her donation, because she made a promise. Another person dedicates three hours of her time a week to the same animal shelter, and may not reduce her time even as it grows more valuable in another way (for instance, due to a higher wage or a new romantic relationship). We could say, of course, that these kind persons just have *very* strong preferences for helping this animal shelter. But this would imply that if the opportunity cost of their charity rose enough, they would reduce it. And this is reasonable to imagine in some cases, but it is not universally true; for some people, a promise is a promise, simple as that.[2] And the model of preference-satisfaction cannot explain keeping a promise just because it is a promise, except by assuming an *ad hoc* preference for keeping promises (which can itself be traded off for other things, and so on).

I soon discovered that other economists shared this concern, the most prominent of them being Amartya Sen, whose seminal work integrating economics and philosophy—particularly his succinct book *On Ethics and Economics*—was a great inspiration to me and many others in the field. Specifically, in his classic paper "Rational Fools," he wrote of *commitment*, which cuts across and often against preferences, severing the connection between preferences and choice which was considered ironclad before then (and still is, sadly, by most economists today). As I began to read Kant in anticipation of working his insights into economics, I discovered that others had done similar work in a Kantian vein. Amitai Etzioni wrote of a "Kantian socio-economics" in which agents balanced moral preferences with self-interested ones.[3] Lanse Minkler had incorporated commitment into a simple mathematical model of choice, and even cited Kant's ethics as one possible source for it (among others).[4] So I knew I wasn't crazy—and even if I were, at least I wasn't alone.

To be sure, Kant has a very particular way of conceptualizing commitment: duty. We will see how he explains and defends the concept of duty by reference to his famous categorical imperative in the first chapter of this book, but for now, suffice it to say that the strictest duties do not bend to opportunity cost, and they are not traded off or compromised when circumstances change. (Sometimes, perhaps more often than we think, a strict duty has to bend to another duty, which we will discuss later, but never to the particular consequences of an action.) This was one element of what drew me to Kant, this steadfast notion of doing one's duty, doing what's right, no matter what the cost. More generally, Kant maintained that when a duty applies to a situation, it is *the* right thing to do, regardless of contingent factors or circumstances. This is not to say that determining one's duty in any given circumstance is easy, but once you solve that puzzle, you know the right thing to do—your duty.

Aside from the limited conception of individual choice, which makes no room for concepts like duty or right, a more obvious implication of the utilitarian basis of economics is found in welfare economics. Welfare economics evaluates states of the world based on the total utility or welfare accruing to the parties involved, and actions or policies are likewise judged by their effects on aggregate utility. If everyone was made better off by a change, then there would seem to be no problem (but, as we will see in Chapter 5, things are actually not that simple). While such improvements are possible with changes in rules or institutions, they are far less common when resources have to be allocated—or, to be more precise, reallocated. When dealing with scarce resources (such as in a budgetary process), usually one group of persons can benefit only if another group loses; a municipal planner can also increase funding to the parks department by taking funds from another department or the taxpayers. Welfare economics therefore typically looks at the *net* effect of a change, accepting a certain amount or degree of harm to some as a means to the end of benefiting others by a larger amount or degree. Usually no effort is made (or even considered) to rectify or compensate for the harm done, much less secure the consent of the harmed persons; these are considered bureaucratic technicalities to be dealt with by politicians after the economists have finished their part of the job.[5]

This recalls a signature problem with utilitarianism, which treats persons as mere receptacles of utility to be summed up to arrive at an aggregate number which can—indeed, *must*—be maximized at any cost.[6] If this were true, then there would be nothing wrong with reducing the utility of one person to some degree in order to increase the utility of another by more. But if we are going to respect these persons as persons and not as objects or mere things, we cannot simply use them like this. What did the first person *do* to deserve being harmed? What did the second one *do* to deserve benefit, especially at a cost to the first? Why are economists fine with these redistributions of benefit and harm with no consideration of why persons deserve one or the other? These questions were particularly frustrating to me as I was studying economics as an undergraduate and a graduate student—and they still are.

But Kant again provides us with an alternative way of thinking about such matters, writing that every rational being—which is to say, every person—is endowed with *dignity*, an incalculable and incomparable worth, by virtue of her *autonomy*, the capacity to follow laws of her own design without undue influence from external pressures and internal desires. The dignity of a person demands respect from both other persons and herself, and provides a substantive basis for Kant's ethics, reflected most clearly in his prohibition against using persons as mere means to an end. This has obvious and potentially disastrous implications for welfare economics as it is currently practiced, since it typically endorses policies as efficient when they benefit one party to a greater extent or degree than they harm another, even though the harmed party has done nothing to deserve such treatment and is usually not compensated for her harm. And even if she were so compensated, but did not consent to the change in the first place, then the change was forced upon her, which can be considered an insult to her dignity more fundamental than a failure to rectify her harm. Welfare economics, as with utilitarianism in general, has no room for concepts of desert, rights, justice, or dignity—at least without making them contingent on, or constitutive of, utility—which is its fundamental weakness in the face of a Kantian approach.

So, to answer the question "why Kant," his approach to ethics appeals to me because of two basic ideas: that a person should, can, and sometimes *does* do the "right" thing even at the expense of his own self-interest, and that respect for the dignity of the individual can sometimes trump matters of aggregate utility. (The "trump" language comes from legal and political philosopher Ronald Dworkin, from whom we will also hear in the chapters to follow.) Furthermore, I have come to believe strongly that dignity is the heart of Kantian ethics; his is a very humanistic ethics, one concerned with both the right that persons do and the good that comes to them because of it. It reaffirms the majesty of the individual as an autonomous, free person, and also the responsibility of each person not just to look out for herself, but also to maintain constant respect for other persons, both negatively and positively, so we can also live together in harmony and prosperity. I hope all of this comes out in the pages that follow.

Why Not Virtue Ethics?

One frequent criticism of Kant's moral theory is that it is excessively cold, unfeeling, and harsh, a judgment which many Kant scholars (including me) feel is an exaggeration. This perception often results from a familiarity with just the first of his three books on ethics, 1785's *Groundwork for the Metaphysics of Morals*. This short book serves as an excellent introduction to the concept of duty, the categorical imperative, and the nature of the good will, but leaves out much of the richness of Kant's system. The *Groundwork* alone leaves the reader with the impression that Kant was solely concerned with duty and morality, and very little with happiness, pleasure, or well-being, much less virtue or character. His second book on ethics, 1788's *Critique of Practical Reason*, primarily justifies the theory presented in the *Groundwork*, but in the third, 1797's *The Metaphysics of*

Morals, Kant makes clear that he cares intensely for happiness, if only secondarily to duty; persons are worthy of happiness in proportion to their virtue. He also emphasizes that many duties, such as that of helping others, are quite flexible in their execution, and may be moderated even to pursue even one's own interests. Furthermore, he discusses his conception of virtue as strength of character, as well as factors that can support or impede the development of that strength (a theme elaborated upon in 1793's *Religion within the Boundaries of Mere Reason*).

Recently, I have come to know and debate with, in person and in print, brilliant economists and philosophers, such as Deirdre McCloskey and Irene van Staveren, who argue the case for virtue ethics as a preferable moral foundation for economics.[7] Not to put too dramatic a point on it, but I prefer to think of virtue ethicists and Kantians as allies in the eternal battle with utilitarians for the heart and soul of economics. (See, no drama.) But naturally I am asked, "Why aren't you a virtue ethicist instead of a Kantian?" So allow me to address this briefly, without trying to make a Grand Definitive Statement on the issue (as I hope to explore virtue ethics and Kant in relation to economics further in the future).

The easiest way to answer the question, somewhat of a dodge but nonetheless correct, is to argue that Kant and virtue ethics have much more in common than usually supposed.[8] So by promoting a Kantian approach to economics, by implication I am advocating the relevant parts of virtue ethics as well. But that naturally leads to the question, "What do Kant and the virtue ethicists have in common?" And I would answer, simply: *character*. Kant and virtue ethicists hold moral character to be of significant concern, though in different ways. Virtue ethics is notoriously difficult to define, as Aristotle, David Hume, Adam Smith, and Confucius have all been called virtue ethicists of one sort or another, despite the many differences in their moral philosophies. Nonetheless, virtue ethics is most commonly associated with Aristotle, and in his version moral judgment applies primarily to persons themselves, not to their actions or the consequences thereof. It is the person who is virtuous, and an act is morally good if it is what a virtuous person would do in similar circumstances. As such, virtue ethics is often contrasted with ethical systems which focus on acts, whether in regards to their intrinsic properties (such as Kant does) or their outcomes (such as utilitarians do).

But it is not so simple to characterize Kant in this way. He famously asserts, at the very beginning of the *Groundwork*, that "there is no possibility of thinking of anything at all in the world, or even out of it, which can be regarded as good without qualification, except a *good will*."[9] But a good will is not defined by the acts it performs; rather, a good will is one which is autonomous and therefore follows the moral law, and *that* is why it is good (and therefore performs moral acts). Acts can certainly be judged morally good or bad without asking if a person's will is good without qualification, but at bottom, a good will is the most important thing when evaluating a person's own morality, and this essential focus on moral character on the part of Kant parallels virtue ethics. At the same time, both Kant and the virtue ethicists are very realistic about the fallibility of human reason and morality, and they have written rich accounts of weakness of will and succumbing to impulses that compromise one's character or virtue. (In fact, Kant referred to strength of will as "virtue.") Utilitarians, on the other hand, have no such accounts; as we shall see in Chapter 2, despite much mathematical and analytic elegance, economists have not developed an account of weakness of will rich enough to explain how persons can *resist* temptation and persist in their virtue. Also, unlike utilitarians, Kant and most virtue ethicists give critical importance to the motivation behind an act. To be truly ethical, one has to do the right thing for the right reason; for Kant, this means performing one's duty for the sake of duty, and for Aristotle, this means fully internalizing a virtue, not just simulating it.

Despite their similarities, Kant has nonetheless been criticized by virtue ethicists (and others) on several grounds, two of which I will address here (as well as later in the book). One is that he is excessively formalistic and analytical. For instance, we will soon see that one version of Kant's categorical imperative, the Formula of Universal Law, reads: "act only according to that maxim whereby you can at the same time will that it should become a universal law."[10] It is both understandable and unfortunate that the universalization aspect of this formula has come to signify Kantian ethics to the exclusion of its deeper, richer elements (and Kant himself promoted the use of this formula over the others). But as I said above, I regard dignity to be the true heart of Kantian ethics, and this heart is reflected more explicitly in another version of the categorical imperative, the Formula of Respect of the Dignity of Persons: "act in such a way that you treat humanity, whether in your own person or in the person of another, always at the same time as an end and never simply as a means."[11] From this formula, we learn that each person must recognize the equal dignity and autonomy of every other person, which generates the strong sense of reciprocity that motivates, and is inherent in, the universalization requirement (and therefore unites these two versions of the categorical imperative). So while more directly useful as a test for maxims, universalization is merely an inferior reflection of dignity, which is the true meaning of Kantian ethics, although it is often obscured and distorted by near-exclusive emphasis on the Formula of Universal Law.

Another common criticism is that Kantian ethics is too rule-oriented, and as a result is divorced from context and circumstances; certainly the terms "categorical imperative" and "duty," so prevalent in the *Groundwork*, make one sympathetic to this view. For instance, van Staveren argues that virtue ethics, as opposed to utilitarianism and Kantian ethics, "acknowledges that in the real world, agents are concerned with both consequences and duties, but subject to social relations and context."[12] But Kantian ethics also takes both of these things into consideration. For instance, as we will see in Chapter 3, the importance of social relations is embodied in our perfect and imperfect duties toward other persons, based on their inherent autonomy and dignity, and the respect owed to them thereby. In fact, a third version of the categorical imperative, the Formula of the Kingdom of Ends—"every rational being must so act as if he were through his maxim always a legislating member of the universal kingdom of ends"[13]—makes clear that the overall goal of morality is to bring about a world in which every person can pursue his or her ends, consistently with everyone else doing the same, achieving a social equilibrium representing maximal freedom for all. Given this respect for personhood (in oneself and others), I maintain that Kant can be considered one of the most humanistic and socially oriented moral philosophers.

The role of context, which I take to mean the realities of human existence, social or not, is another often misunderstood component of Kant's ethics. The categorical imperative, and the duties resulting from it, are too general to apply directly to our actual lives in all of their complexity; as philosopher Barbara Herman writes, "the categorical imperative is not itself a moral rule—it is an abstract formal principle."[14] As such, the categorical imperative itself is not contextual, and cannot itself be applied directly to any real-world moral dilemma. It can help a person see what her various obligations are in any given situation, but in order to decide on a course of action, she needs to use her *judgment.* As Kant wrote, "to be sure, these laws require . . . a power of judgment sharpened by experience, partly in order to distinguish in what cases they are applicable, and partly to gain for them access to the human will as well as influence for putting them into practice."[15] Kant does derive general rules or duties from the formal moral law, but these are not to be applied mechanistically to real-life dilemmas; they merely provide guidelines for right action. To decide what we should actually do in any situation, we make choices guided by our "moral compass" and informed crucially by the context of the situation itself. And Kant gave us no rules for how to do this—not as an oversight, but in recognition that any rule that tells us how to apply another rule would in turn require a rule telling us to apply it, and so forth. Instead, he trusted in our judgment, crafted over time by recognition and appreciation of the moral law.

So if they're so similar, as I've argued, then why *do* I prefer Kantian ethics to virtue ethics? I would have to say because of its grounding in autonomy and dignity, which confirms the endless potential and intrinsic worth of every human being, as well as our responsibilities toward each other. Kantian ethics maintains a firm basis in character, and derives specific duties and obligations from that, in a more systematic way than most systems of virtue ethics. Most generally, I find Kantian ethics to be empowering, inspiring, and humbling at the same time. Consider, for instance, one of my favorite passages from the *Groundwork*:

For the pure thought of duty and of the moral law generally, unmixed with any extraneous addition of empirical inducements, has by the way of reason alone . . . an influence on the human heart so much more powerful than all other incentives which may be derived from the empirical field that reason in the consciousness of its dignity despises such incentives and is able gradually to become their master.[16]

Once you get past all the talk of duty, there is a tremendously positive message in Kant's ethics. When a person realizes what she is truly capable of, she can do anything. And if all of us do the morally right things (according to respect and concern for all persons), *we* can do anything. Through the ideal of the kingdom of ends, morality provides the foundation for prosperity, flourishing, and happiness. Kant reveals to us our limitless potential by virtue of our autonomy, which at the same time implies responsibilities to ourselves and each other. (And I think that's wonderful, in the most literal sense of the word.)

Why Should Economists Know About Kant?

So now you know why I was drawn to Kant's ethics, and why I prefer it to utilitarianism and virtue ethics. But why should other economists care? What does an understanding of Kant have to offer to them?

For mainstream economists, exposure to a Kantian approach will do (at least) two things. First, it will expose the utilitarian foundations of what they do. Certainly many economists are aware of this, but just as many—if not more—are not. Once they realize the origins of modern mainstream economics, particularly economic models of choice and welfare economics, and they have been exposed to an alternative, they can choose which one makes more sense to them. As economist John Hicks wrote, "If one is a utilitarian in philosophy, one has a perfect right to be a utilitarian in one's economics. But if one is not . . . one also has the right to an economics free from utilitarian assumptions."[17]

Let me mention here a dangerous misperception among some economists, that utilitarianism is somehow more "scientific" than Kantian (or virtue) ethics. After all, when applied by economists, it reduces everything to numbers, variables, and functions, which can then be added, multiplied, and maximized—and graphed! What could be more objective? But of course, there are very strong and controversial value judgments underlying those calculations; for instance, everyone's utility is treated equally regardless of desert, and no rights exist that are not subject themselves to utilitarian justification (and therefore are not true rights at all), except the implicit right of those in authority to execute policy in the interest of aggregate utility. Utilitarianism is neither scientific nor objective—its normative foundations are simply hidden under the veneer of mathematics. Once this fact is appreciated, economists can make a true choice among the values they choose to endorse. If they choose utilitarianism, fine—as long as they do so with eyes open. But I suspect some would choose Kant (or virtue ethics, for that matter), and this book provides one way to incorporate Kantian insights into economics.

Second, incorporating aspects of a Kantian approach into economics will broaden and strengthen the explanatory, predictive, and justificatory powers of economics. I make the case in the first two chapters of this book that the typical model of economic choice is deficient because it does not incorporate duty (Chapter 1) or willpower (Chapter 2). With an expanded perspective on human decision-making, economists can better understand, explain, and predict normal and "anomalous" behavior, which in turn will enhance the efficacy of policymaking. But more importantly, a Kantian approach will shine a critical spotlight on the ethical dimensions of economic policy itself and the utilitarian analysis that supports it. In the last two chapters, I explain that Kantian ethics poses serious problems for the typical evaluative standards of welfare economics, in particular Kaldor-Hicks efficiency (Chapter 4) and Pareto superiority (Chapter 5), by recognizing that the dignity of persons implies rights that can trump considerations of social welfare (total utility). Mainstream economists typically pay no attention to the process by which welfare is maximized, but if this can be done only by violating important rights, this represents a grave offense to human dignity.

But I did not write this book only for mainstream economists. I wrote it also for social economists, who share my concern about the ethical content of economic theory, practice, and education. Naturally, social economists tend to be more conversant in philosophical ethics, and more eager to question the assumptions of mainstream economics. Besides their support of incorporating ethics in economics, social economists, as the name would suggest, also are interested in social aspects of the economy and the connections and interdependences between economic agents. As such, they tend to be very skeptical about individualism, especially of the atomistic variety espoused by mainstream economics (often under the aegis of methodological individualism). Specifically, they often regard this individualism to be at odds with sociality, threatening to weaken the bonds that bring persons together and support a flourishing society. They typically extend this concern to criticisms of the market, which they consider an instrument of separation and isolation through which individualism corrodes those social bonds.

It was largely for social economists that I wrote Chapter 3 of this book, which also serves as a bridge between the discussion of individual ethics in the first two chapters and the discussion of policy in the last two. Through it I hope to assure them that individualism is not inconsistent with sociality and community, especially when the individual is understood in a Kantian context. I argue that the Kantian agent is individual in essence and social in orientation: while as agents, persons are very much individual as a result of their autonomy, the moral law demands a mutual concern that supports a flourishing society. This is made most apparent in Kant's "kingdom of ends," the utopian endgoal of his ethical system in which persons live in harmony, pursuing their ends consistently with each other in the support of the moral law.

CHAPTER I

Kantian Ethics, Economics, and Decision-Making

Economists have developed a very powerful model of human decision-making, often personified in the metaphor of "economic man" or *homo economicus*. While certainly not without its share of criticism, from both mainstream and heterodox economists as well as other social scientists and philosophers, this model has proven extremely useful in helping us explain countless aspects and examples of human behavior, from common business decisions to government policy-making, and from choosing a life of crime to selecting a mate. Recent developments in behavioral economics, which question some of the core assumptions of the standard economic model of decision-making, have illuminated many standard deficiencies in rational decision-making, resulting in an even richer conception of human choice.

But despite the success of these models of choice in explaining countless types of behavior, they have struggled to explain behavior motivated by ethical concerns. The simplest approach is simply to introduce a "taste for morality" into the standard set of preferences or utility function; in such a model, ethical actors are simply indulging one preference out of many. Either this approach extends the usual assumption of the self-interested agent to include other-regarding preferences, or it simply subsumes such preferences within the very concept of self-interest, which stretches and thereby weakens the term beyond all recognition. Other approaches to modeling ethical behavior involve interdependent preferences, wherein one person has preferences over another's well-being, and as a result takes that other person's interests into account in her own decision-making, or various conceptions of reciprocity, wherein altruistic behavior is strategically undertaken (consciously or not) to maximize long-term self-interest.[1]

What ties together these various approaches to modeling ethical behavior is that they all assume that the utility-maximizing agent seeks to achieve the best outcome (as measured by her preferences) out of all the possible outcomes over which she has influence (as determined by her exogenously imposed constraints). If we translate this into the language of moral philosophy, this implies that the agent is a hedonist or egoist, if narrowly self-interested; an altruist, if she takes into account the welfare of select others (such as family or friends); or a broader utilitarian, if she takes into consideration the well-being of all persons (and perhaps other species as well). In all of these cases, the agent can be described as a *consequentialist*, since she determines the moral worth of actions according to the goodness of their outcomes. This is the implicit assumption made in most economic models of individual choice, which has been extended to study behavior in the context of the law and the family, for example, as well as more traditional market transactions.

But this pervasive reliance on consequentialism in economics comes at a price. Attempts to force a utility-maximizing explanation on "sacrificing" behavior (such as voting, tipping while traveling, or heroic acts) results in unsatisfactory, *ad hoc* assumptions of new preferences. Assuming that people behave ethically only out of expectation of future benefits, or even out of an unconscious, evolved disposition toward reciprocity, seems overly cynical, and cheapens the true ethical acts of persons, whose conscious, reflective, and deliberate behavior deserves to be explained in ways that emphasize its moral nature without cynically degrading it to self-interest.

Perhaps the most important contribution toward this end came from Amartya Sen, a Nobel laureate in economics and a prominent philosopher as well, who introduced the concept of commitment into the discussion of rational choice in his classic 1977 paper "Rational Fools." By suggesting the possibility of commitment as an alternative method of motivating and explaining choice, he opened the door for deontological values and principles to be incorporated into economics. Using Sen's commitment framework, agents can act on principles, duties, or values without representing them as preferences which can be substituted for others as relative (subjective) costs dictate. Sen's approach allows for absolute considerations in economic models of choice, influences which are not subject to standard economic factors such as prohibitively high opportunity cost or diminishing marginal benefit. Furthermore, as Sen noted, commitment "drives a wedge between personal choice and personal welfare," since an agent's choices cannot be assumed to maximize her own well-being if it is possible that they were motivated by some conviction or principle.[2]

Consistent with Sen's theme, if economics strives to explain human behavior, it must recognize there are other ways for agents to behave other than according to consequentialist logic. As Vivian Walsh, another prominent economist and philosopher, writes:

It has always been thought that some actions were wrong despite their consequences. These claims must have a place in any serious moral theory, and economic theory and decision theory should not be allowed to foreclose what is properly an issue for moral philosophy, simply by adopting particular formal structures as constitutive of rational choice without explicit dialogue on the philosophical issues raised by doing so.[3]

In this chapter—and, more broadly, this entire book—I propose to construct an economic model of decision-making based on nonconsequentialist ethics, specifically the moral theory of Immanuel Kant, in which the nature of actions themselves, rather than their consequences, determines their moral worth.

This type of ethical theory is often called *deontological*, as opposed to consequentialist or teleological (goal-oriented); these terms are heavily debated among philosophers, but William Frankena's definition is often taken to be representative:

Deontological theories . . . deny that the right, the obligatory, and the morally good are wholly, whether directly or indirectly, a function of what is nonmorally good or what promotes the greatest balance of good over evil for self, one's society, or the world as a whole.[4]

Like most scholars, Frankena defines deontology negatively, in terms of what does *not* determine the right thing to do—namely, the goodness of the outcomes of actions. Understood practically, this means that deontological ethics may allow, in some cases if not all, for persons to act in ways that do not maximize the goodness of consequences, and may even demand it.[5] For instance, a deontologist may not allow the intentional killing of one innocent person to save two (or more) others; even though the number of lives lost would be smaller if the one innocent person were killed, and therefore the single killing would likely be recommended by a consequentialist, a deontologist may judge the act of killing an innocent person to be wrong regardless of the consequences.[6] Positive definitions of deontology are harder to come by, mostly because every deontologists has a different idea of what makes certain actions right, but most agree that it is not a consequential measure.

Philosopher John Broome once wrote that "if deontological moralities affect people's behaviour in important ways, then economics is in for a shock."[7] Well, among moral philosophers, Immanuel Kant is widely held to be the paradigmatic deontologist, and in this chapter, at risk of shock, I use his conception of duty to incorporate deontological considerations into the economic model of choice.[8] I begin with a summary of key aspects of Kant's moral theory, including autonomy, dignity, the categorical imperative, perfect and imperfect duty, and judgment. Next, I illustrate these ideas by applying them to the classic prisoners' dilemma of game theory. Finally, I present a Kantian-economic model of decision-making, which shows one way in which Kant's ethics can be incorporated into the economic optimization framework. My contention is that with the proper understanding of duties, preferences, and constraints, the standard economic model can describe deontological choice along Kantian lines; if I'm right, the shock should be a little less painful.

Kantian Ethics

Despite his high degree of name recognition, Kant is widely misunderstood as a moral philosopher. He is often accused of being cold, rigidly logical, and uninterested in the realities of human existence, and much of the blame for this must be laid at the feet of the great magister himself. Many people's exposure to Kantian ethics starts and ends with his slim

1785 work, the *Groundwork for the Metaphysics of Morals*, especially if it is taught as part of an introductory ethics course alongside the work of other moral philosophers.[9] The more approachable sections of the *Groundwork* detail, in a relatively straightforward fashion, the three formulae of the categorical imperative in the context of four examples of immoral behavior (making false promises, committing suicide, failing to develop your talents, and neglecting the needs of others). But the treatment of autonomy, dignity, and the will in the *Groundwork* is much more abbreviated, incomplete, and difficult for students to grasp without lengthy elaboration from their teacher (or secondary readings), and topics like strength, virtue, and judgment are all but ignored. It is not until 1797's *The Metaphysics of Morals* (especially the second half, known as the *Doctrine of Virtue*) that Kant explains the real-world implications of following the moral law. There, alongside lengthy discussions of the nature of virtue, vice, and other general ethical topics neglected in the *Groundwork*, he provides a systematic listing of duties to others and to ourselves, along with "casuistical questions" for the reader to ponder.

Furthermore, Kant himself regarded the more formalistic universalization formula of the categorical imperative as more applicable than the other two more humanistic versions, given its more technical, algorithmic nature: "One does better if in moral judgment he follows the rigorous method and takes as his basis the universal formula of the categorical imperative."[10] I regard this as unfortunate, because it is from the other formulae—especially the Formula of Respect for Humanity—that what I consider the "heart" of Kant's ethics emerges, and it is with this heart, namely dignity and the autonomy from which it derives, that I begin.[11] After explaining these more general aspects of Kantian ethics, only then do I turn to the categorical imperative, which operationalizes autonomy and dignity, and then to the nature of the duties that result from it and the role of judgment in moral decision-making. Duties will then be the main focus of the remainder of the chapter, which lays out a Kantian model of decision-making, and the next chapter will emphasize autonomy and the will at length, at which point the model of decision-making—or what I will call judgment—becomes a true model of choice.

Autonomy and dignity

Kant's moral philosophy is ultimately based on *autonomy* (or *inner freedom*), the capacity of every rational agent to make choices according to laws that she sets for herself, without undue influence from either external pressures or internal desires. Thus considered, autonomy has equally important and interrelated negative and positive aspects. The agent is not bound to either internal desires or external authority, and therefore she is free to make choice according to her moral judgment. Nonetheless, she is bound by the laws she determines for herself (and which will rationally accord with the moral law), but since these laws are imposed on the agent *by* the agent herself, she is acting freely. If she sets herself the rule "I shall not lie," then she is not limiting her freedom or autonomy—rather, this is the ultimate expression of her autonomy, because the rule is of her own making and imposition. To put it another way, we are free to restrict ourselves. "In one sense," philosopher Christine Korsgaard writes, "to be autonomous . . . is to be governed by principles of our own causality, principles that are definitive of your will. In another, deeper, sense to be autonomous . . . is to *choose* the principles that are definitive of your will."[12]

Of course, the word autonomy has a number of meanings, in both the personal and political realms, and in common usage as well as philosophy.[13] Perhaps the most familiar usage comes from international politics, in which national autonomy is roughly synonymous with sovereignty, which applies when no other power can legally compel a nation-state to action (or inaction). While the United States (for example) can be persuaded or given incentive to enter into a treaty with another nation, whether to do this is the choice of the appropriate government official or body in the U.S., not the other nation. By contrast, its fifty constitutive states have limited sovereignty or autonomy, given that their actions are limited by the U.S. Constitution; for example, the states cannot enter to treaties with foreign countries, and to some extent must follow the policies of the federal government. But the U.S. itself in not subject to other nations' laws, so it is autonomous in this sense. Nation-states, particularly those with constitutional legal systems, are autonomous in the other sense as well, that of determining the laws or principles by which they will operate. Constitutions are laws that a nation sets for itself, to set procedural guidelines for its activities (such as setting up legislatures, executives, and judiciary), as well as to limit those activities more substantively (such as the Bill of Rights in the U.S. Constitution).

Kant's use of the word "autonomy" in relation to an individual agent is very similar to the meaning from international politics.[14] An autonomous person does not allow external factors—especially outside authority—to determine her choices or actions. This is not to say, of course, that she cannot be influenced by external factors, or even decide to do what someone tells her; both happen all the time, and neither by itself implies any lack of autonomy. But she cannot cede her own decision-making authority to another, and if she chooses to follow someone's direction or order, she must make a conscious, deliberate choice to do so. In this way, the ultimate decision is hers, not the other person's, for she must endorse the external reason for action and thereby make it her own.[15]

This aspect of autonomy, that of resisting external compulsion when making decisions, is familiar to most, and corresponds fairly closely to how we think of autonomy in personal situations (and in fields like medical ethics). While we take this aspect for granted most of the time, the other aspect, that of resisting one's own preferences and desires, is more particular to Kantian ethics, and also more counterintuitive. Most of the time, following one's desires and preferences—or *inclinations*, to use Kant's term—is unproblematic, since there is no moral conflict involved. (Even so, one must make a conscious choice to follow them, rather than do it unthinkingly.[16]) But in an ethical choice situation, Kant held that one's preferences are not a reliable guide to proper decision-making; what we want to do, even if it may seem ethical, is not necessarily the right thing to do. When the moral choice differs from our preferred choice, autonomy grants us the power to deny our inclinations and do the right thing instead; in fact, autonomy implies the *responsibility* to follow the dictates of one's own moral judgment. This is in clear opposition to Hume's famed position that "reason is, and ought only to be the slave of the passions," a view against which Kant aligned himself from the start.[17]

While Kant held that all rational agents have the capacity for autonomous choice, exercising this capacity is not automatic, nor it is always easy. If an agent allows either her preferences or desires, or the wishes or commands of other persons, to influence her choice without adequate reflection and endorsement, she is said to have acted *heteronomously*: she has allowed her will to be co-opted by a force other than her own judgment. But even in such cases, the agent *has* made a choice—she has chosen to sacrifice her autonomy or inner freedom. As Irwin puts it, "the difference between heteronomy and autonomy does not consist in the difference between compulsion and free acceptance, but in the source of the principles that we freely accept. We become evil not by being overcome by an evil principle, but by freely incorporating such a principle in our maxim."[18] Korsgaard, drawing from Kant's *Religion*, writes that "we learn that a bad person is not after all one who is pushed about, or caused to act, by his desires and inclinations. Instead, a bad person is one who is governed by what Kant calls the principle of self-love. The person who acts on the principle of self-love *chooses* to act as inclination prompts."[19] Finally, according to Thomas Hill, Kant held "that all have autonomy, that this implies commitment to certain rational constraints, and that some live up to these commitments while others do not."[20] In this way, autonomy is not just a property of rational beings, but also, in a normative sense, a goal: a person *should* always try to assert her judgment and her will without blind obedience to either her internal desires and preferences, or external authorities and influence. Only by doing so can she be true to herself, preserving her integrity and respecting her dignity.[21]

According to Kant, rational beings are imbued, as an implication of their autonomy, with *dignity*, an "unconditional and incomparable worth" that in turn demands respect from all persons (as codified in the second version of the categorical imperative discussed below).[22] Kant famously contrasted things and persons, the former having a price and the latter possessing a dignity above price: "whatever has a price can be replaced by something else as its equivalent . . . whatever is above all price, and therefore admits of no equivalent, has a dignity."[23] Things are instrumental, simply means to an end, and therefore their value is contingent on their usefulness; whereas persons, who are to be regarded as "ends in themselves," possess an intrinsic worth which is incalculable and incomparable, resisting summation or substitutability, and which "admits of no equivalent."[24]

Kantian dignity is a relatively simple concept, and a very appealing one to the modern person (though shocking in his day).[25] As Hill puts it, "the root idea of dignity is simply that virtually everyone, regardless of social station, talents, accomplishments, or moral record, should be re-garded with respect as a human being."[26] Despite its simplicity, the Kan-tian conception of dignity has very strong implications for how persons may be treated, by other persons as well as by the state (and themselves). This is of paramount importance to mainstream economics, where the concept of trade-offs is a central one, because Kantian dignity cannot be "exchanged," since it has no price. Furthermore, one source of dignity—in other words, a person—cannot be traded off against another source of dignity, even if the latter seems to represent "more" dignity (such as two persons). As Hill writes,

> this may seem to imply that there can never be a justification for impairing the ra-tionality or sacrificing the life of any human being, but this is not necessarily so. What is implied, strictly, is only that one may not sacrifice something of dignity *in* exchange for something of greater value. Thus, if the sacrifice of something with dignity is ever justified, the ground for this cannot be "this is worth more than that" or "a greater quantity of value is produced by doing so.[27]

This may seem to be only a symbolic difference—a person's dignity may be sacrificed, but not "in exchange"—and to some extent it is, but nonethe-less it is an important one, for when we find we have to impose harm on someone undeserving of it, we want to ensure that it is done with regret and stark acknowledgment of what is being done, not the cold, smug sat-isfaction of efficient exchange.[28]

As I said above, despite the formalistic gloss with which it is pre-sented in the *Groundwork*, I maintain that the true heart of Kant's ethics lies in his belief in the essential dignity and autonomy of rational beings. The categorical imperative and the duties that are derived from it, which I discuss next, ultimately can be traced back to dignity and autonomy, and thereby can be understood as simply operationalizing the respect that is owed every person due to his or her capacity for free choice. And as we shall see below, real-world ethical decision-making often cannot be con-ducted by straightforward recourse to duties or rules, but is rather a matter of judgment. Such judgment depends not on an encyclopedic knowledge of Kantian duties (wonderfully caricatured by Deirdre McCloskey as eth-ics by "pocket-sized, three-by-five inch card"),[29] but rather on a more ho-listic appreciation of dignity and autonomy, and the responsibilities which they imply for persons in an ethical community.

The categorical imperative

Based on the autonomy of rational agents, and the equal respect it demands persons pay to each other (and themselves), Kant developed the *categorical imperative*, his version of the "moral law" that all rational agents freely impose on themselves. Kant maintained that the categorical imperative merely formalized the ethical decision-making of the common person: "The ordinary reason of mankind in its practical judgments agrees completely with [the categorical imperative], and always has in view the aforementioned principle. . . . To be sure, such reason does not think of this principle abstractly in its universal form, but does always have it actually in view and does use it as the standard of judgment."[30] In Kant's view, a person is to apply the categorical imperative—preferably the universalization formula—to her plans of actions or *maxims*; if a maxim "fails the test," then that planned action is rejected as immoral, and if it passes, it is judged as permissible (not necessarily moral, and never demanded).[31] This belies an all-too-frequent characterization of Kant's ethics, that it is excessively demanding and rigorous. As I will explain later in this chapter (and further in Chapter 3), Kantian ethics are demanding only in what one must *not* do, not in what one must do instead; there is much room for judgment in what the agent actually chooses to do in fulfillment of her duties.

Kant laid out three formulations of the categorical imperative, which he claimed are equivalent ways of stating the basic principle from difficult angles.[32] The *Formula of Autonomy or of Universal Law* (henceforth the "Formula of Autonomy") is the most commonly known version of the categorical imperative—and perhaps, as I mentioned above, the most misrepresentative. It is based on the universalization of maxims: "act only according to that maxim whereby you can at the same time will that it should become a universal law."[33] The standard illustration of this formula deals with lying: suppose I propose a maxim of lying to promote my interests. If I will that everyone may do the same, as the Formula of Autonomy demands, that would promote lying to such an extent that no one would believe anything anybody said, which would thereby defeat the goal of the lie (to benefit my interests). Despite its apparent reliance on logic and noncontradiction (as Kant explained it),[34] the Formula of Autonomy is ultimately based on the equal dignity of all persons, and the implication thereof that no one person should claim special allowances for herself that she cannot grant equally to everybody.[35] Understood this way, the problem with lying is not that it defeats my interests once universalized, which would imply an egoist ethic. Rather, in order for lying to work, I must be the only one (or one of very few) lying, which means I must not grant everyone else the same license I grant myself. Since I have no grounds on which to do this, given the equal dignity of all persons, I cannot will that a maxim of opportunistic lying be universalized.

Technically, there are two understandings of consistency in Kant's ethics: consistency-in-conception and consistency-in-the-will. *Consistency-in-conception* is the well-known test of logical consistency discussed above, which rules out lying because a universalized maxim of lying would destroy the trust on which successful lying depends. *Consistency-in-the-will* stems from a variant of the Formula of Autonomy commonly known as the *Formula of the Law of Nature*: "Act as if the maxim of your action were to become through your will a universal law of nature."[36] The unique feature of this version is that it extends the teleological (or goal-oriented) basis of natural laws (including those based on human nature) to maxims; as Paton explains,

When we ask whether we could *will* a proposed maxim as if it were to become thereby a law of nature, we are asking whether a will which aimed at a systematic harmony of purposes in human nature could consistently will this particular maxim as a law of human nature.[37]

The word "will" is stressed above for a reason; the consistency-in-the-will test asks if the agent can *rationally will* that her maxim be universalized, not simply whether such universalization is logically inconsistent.

This test generates duties such as beneficence by ruling out a maxim of indifference to others: since everyone will need aid at some time, no one can rationally will that everyone neglect the well-being of others. Rather than logical consistency, the consistency-in-the-will test demands that universalized maxims not contradict "objective ends, which depend on motives valid for every rational being,"[38] such as our humanity (based on dignity) and our own survival (based on the teleology of human nature), but not our everyday preferences and inclinations. Universal indifference endangers our own survival, so it fails the consistency-in-the-will test. As we shall see in our discussion of the prisoners' dilemma game below, this version of consistency is often misunderstood (when recognized at all). It introduces considerable vagueness into the universalization formula (since logical consistency is no longer enough), and also compromises its formalism (which is exaggerated anyway), with the effect of humanizing one of the aspects of Kant's ethics which most often draws accusations of coldness and inhumanity, but at the cost of additional ambiguity.

Based on these first formulae, we can see exactly how Kant does, and how he does not, allow consequences, circumstances, and context to enter into moral considerations. It is true that specific, personal consequences of actions have no influence on their moral status, because such features cannot, by definition, be universalized without denying the equal dignity of all in order to carve out exceptions just for oneself; this is Kant's version of the "impartial spectator" or "disinterested viewpoint" of Smith and Rawls, and it justifies universalization (not the other way around).[39] Some take this too far, claiming that Kant pays absolutely no attention whatsoever to consequences or context, but this is a distortion, because some empirical knowledge of human behavior (and the consequences thereof) is necessary to derive the results of universalizing a maxim. For instance, to say that universal lying is self-defeating, we must know what a lie is, what its purpose is, how people react to it, how it affects the trust they have in communication, and so on. Also, context can be incorporated into a maxim; while a maxim of killing for advantage is forbidden, a maxim of killing in self-defense would not be. In Paton's words, "if Kant had said merely that we must not allow our desires for particular consequences to determine our judgment of what our duty is, he would have avoided a great deal of misunderstanding."[40] The categorical imperative itself can be derived *a priori*, but the duties derived from them depend on empirical knowledge of human life: even in the *Groundwork*, Kant wrote that "all morals . . . require anthropology in order to be *applied* to humans."[41] As we shall see later in this chapter, judgment is essential to derive specific moral commands from the categorical imperative, even after general duties like "do not lie" are derived from it, as well as to settle conflicts among obligations, and empirical facts are indispensable in this judgment.

While, as we saw above, Kant recommended the Formula of Autonomy as the most easily applied version of his moral law, I believe it is the second version of the categorical imperative, the *Formula of Respect for the Dignity of Persons*, that better captures the heart of his moral philosophy:

"act in such a way that you treat humanity, whether in your own person or in the person of another, always at the same time as an end and never simply as a means."[42] As is evident from both the title and language, this formula is explicitly grounded in the essential dignity possessed by rational, autonomous persons, and is a much more humanistic formula than the Law of Autonomy (and more clearly so than the Formula of the Law of Nature). To continue with the example of lying, when a person lies, she is using the person to whom she lies, as well as the humanity in her own person, as a means to the end of this deception (whatever she stands to gain for it). She is using the other person as a means to her end because she is not treating him as an end-in-himself; she is not treating him with the respect he is owed as a rational, autonomous person. To look at it another way, the other person is not an equal participant in the situation, because he literally cannot agree to be lied to (a lie, by its nature, must be concealed). It is for this reason that coercion and deception are considered the two paradigmatic ways that one can be treated merely as means (while not at the same time as an end). Furthermore, the liar is also using herself as a means to her end, relying on her good name and the trust the other person has in her to further her ends; she thereby fails to respect the dignity in her own person, demeaning herself for the sake of momentary advantage.

A common misunderstanding regarding the Formula of Respect (for short) is that it prohibits using other persons under *any* circumstances. If taken this way, the categorical imperative would forbid all commerce, whether market-based or informal, in the form of contracts, promises, or favors—in short, any transaction in which one person makes use of another for any reason. But Kant's wording is masterfully precise: one must never use persons *simply* as means, without *at the same time* treating them as ends. So we are free to use each other for our own ends, provided that in doing so we treat each other with respect, since we are all rational, autonomous agents possessed of dignity.[43] More precisely, it must be possible (not necessarily likely) for any person with whom we deal to consent to the way in which we use them. On this understanding, coercion and deceit are the paradigmatic ways in which persons can be used merely as means: coercion obviously denies the person any opportunity to consent or dissent, and deceit implies that the person is not aware of the deceiver's true intentions, and therefore does not have the chance to agree with them.

The Formula of Respect rules out these actions, but leaves enormous room for mutually voluntary and honest transactions.[44]

Finally, the Formula of Respect is not merely a negative principle that commands us to refrain from using persons simply as means; it also instructs us to take other people's ends as our own, and thereby generates duties such as beneficence. As Kant wrote, "It is not enough that he is not authorized to use either himself or others merely as means (since he could then still be indifferent to them); it is in itself his duty to make man as such his end."[45] As we will see below when we discuss the two types of duty, this type is different than that which prohibits using persons merely as a means, as it is much more general and "wide," allowing of more latitude than the latter. Also, in our discussion of sociality in Chapter 3, the negative and positive conceptions of respect invoked in the Formula of Respect will help us frame the stages of human sociality. While the negative aspect of the formula is much better known, and is certainly an important first step to civil relations, the positive aspect is needed if human society is to flourish in any meaningful sense.

Our later discussion of sociality also invokes the third version of the categorical imperative, the *Formula of Legislation for a Moral Community*. While not used for judging maxims, the Formula of the Kingdom of Ends (as it is also known) is usually considered to be a combination of the first two, but with a unique emphasis on legislation and the teleological nature of Kant's broader ethics: "every rational being must act as if he were through his maxim always a legislating member of the universal kingdom of ends."[46] This version reminds us that each person sets the moral law to and for herself, keeping in mind that that law must also be universalizable to all rational persons. It also makes clear the ultimate goal of ethical behavior: the attainment of the "kingdom of ends," an ideal state of the world in which every person's individual ends coexist in a harmonious, moral community.

Kant contended that the three formulae of the categorical imperative were equivalent: "the aforementioned three ways of representing the principle of morality are at bottom only so many formulas of the very same law: one of them by itself contains a combination of the other two."[47] However, he neglected to explain exactly why or how this is true (as occasionally was his wont). Certainly, the third formula is easily reconciled with the first two, as it can be seen as a combination of them, but the relationship between the first two may be more difficult to grasp. Such esteemed Kant scholars as Barbara Herman and Christine Korsgaard (just to name two) have questioned the consistency of the first two formulae in judging even basic moral concepts such as murder and lying, finding that the Formula of Autonomy is much more "flexible" than the Formula of Respect and even the former's close cousin, the Formula of the Law of Nature.[48] In large part, this is due to the fact that the Law of Autonomy (and its consistency-in-conception test) is much more sensitive to the way maxims are stated, which directly affects their logical consistency when universalized. For instance, Korsgaard attempts to reconcile the blanket prohibition on lying that stems from the Formula of Respect with the more elaborate constructions of maxims of lying that can "not so much pass as evade universalization."[49] The more general duty not to lie seems more in line with the spirit of Kant's ethics, where the possibility of cleverly crafted maxims that can slide by the consistency-in-conception test abuses the concept of equal dignity that is at the core of the Formula of Autonomy (and which should make it equivalent to the Formula of Respect).

Also, some maxims, even those that describe acts which are clearly immoral in commonsense terms, may not be logically inconsistent when everyone adopts them. Herman gives the example of the maxim "to kill whenever that is necessary to get what I want," which I hope the reader will agree is an immoral plan of action.[50] If this maxim were universalized, the world would definitely be a worse place in which to live, but that is hardly inconsistent as a matter of pure logic; certainly such states of the world have existed through human history (and even today in some parts of the world). The Formula of the Law of Nature (which demands consistency-in-the-will) would judge this maxim immoral, since no one—not even a opportunistic murderer—could will a world in which her life is constantly imperiled by (other) opportunistic murderers. Herman flatly admits that "this result surprised me," as she had earlier regarded the consistency-in-conception test as more demanding, and its prohibitions more important, than the consistency-in-the-will test.[51] But this result supports my contention that, even though the Formula of Autonomy is ultimately grounded in equal dignity, the more clearly humanistic versions of the categorical imperative better represent the heart of Kant's ethics, even though they are less formulaic and deterministic in their judgments.

Duties perfect and imperfect

As we know from above, when a maxim is rejected by the categorical imperative, the result is a duty prohibiting such a plan of action. (If the maxim is not rejected, it is judged to be permissible but not required, and not necessarily moral in any affirmative sense.) For instance, a maxim of opportunistic lying is rejected by the categorical imperative, resulting in a duty not to lie. Similarly, a maxim of indifference to the suffering of others would be rejected, resulting in a duty not to be indifferent to suffering (often understood as a duty of beneficence).

These are standard examples of the two types of Kantian duties, perfect and imperfect. A *perfect duty* (also called *narrow* or *due* duty), such as the duty not to lie, is one "which permits no exception in the interest of inclination,"[52] and is usually negative in nature, such as "do not kill" or "do not steal." Generally, perfect duties are derived from the Formula of Autonomy (based on the logical inconsistency of universalization), and also from the negative portion of the Formula of Respect (which forbids using humanity merely as a means).[53] An *imperfect duty* (also called a *wide* or *meritorious* duty) is one that the agent has some latitude in executing, both in degree and method: "the law cannot specify precisely in what way one is to act and how much one is to do."[54] Such duties are mostly represented in positive terms, such as the duties of beneficence and cultivation of one's talents, but technically they are negative—do not be indifferent to others, do not neglect your natural abilities—because, like perfect duties, they too result from the rejection of maxims. Imperfect duties demand that we include certain ends in our decision-making processes, but they do not require any particular action in service to those ends (or inaction, as perfect duties normally do).[55] Imperfect duties are most easily derived from the positive part of the Formula of Respect (treat humanity always as an end), and also the Formula of Law of Nature (requiring consistency with ends-in-themselves).

Another understanding of this distinction is that perfect duties are duties of action, while imperfect duties are duties of ends: "the distinction which Kant has in mind is that between a law commanding (or prohibiting) an action and a law prescribing the pursuit of an end."[56] Perfect duties are precise in their requirements regarding forbidden acts: do not lie, do not kill, and so forth. Perfect duties, insofar as they are negative duties (as most are), constrain the agent from using certain means in pursuit of her inclinations. Imperfect duties are less precise, merely spelling out attitudes (such as beneficence) that should be adopted, with no specific instructions on how to express them in action.[57] Kant leaves the rational agent some discretion regarding how heavily to weigh these dutiful ends against other duties, and even against one's self-interested ends, and he suggests that they should be pursued only when doing so would not lead to excessive hardship or sacrifice on the part of the agent: "How far should one expend one's resources in practicing beneficence? Surely not to the extent that he himself would finally come to need the beneficence of others."[58]

Though the substantive content of perfect and imperfect duties ensures that actions performed according to them are moral, Kant holds agents to an even higher standard to be moral themselves: they must perform dutiful acts not merely *according* to the moral law, but *out of respect* for it. This adds an essential motivational standard for Kantian agents that parallels classical virtue ethics (as described in the Introduction above): doing the right thing for the wrong reason does not make an agent moral or virtuous.[59] A bad person can do a good thing—unintentionally or for the wrong reason—just as a good person can do something that turns out badly. This accords fairly closely with common intuitions about morality, where intentions are seen as more important (in terms of moral evaluation of character) than results or consequences. The common sayings "you tried to do the right thing" and "it's the thought that counts" are two common reflections of this point of view.

This requirement is a reflection of Kant's doctrine of the good will; as the first line of the *Groundwork* reads, "there is no possibility of thinking of anything at all in the world, or even out of it, which can be regarded as good without qualifications, except a *good will*."[60] Many other human capacities are useful, or even admirable, but nonetheless they can be used for ignoble ends; a good will is necessary to ensure those capacities are used correctly. Kant believed that intentions are the only things that are completely under an agent's control; once an action is initiated, the laws of the physical world take over, as well as possible intercessions from other persons. "A good will is good not because of what it effects or accomplishes, nor because of its fitness to attain some proposed end; it is good only through its willing, i.e., it is good in itself."[61] So ethically correct intentions formed out of respect for duty, even if they fail to culminate in the intended actions or results, still earn the person moral acclaim, but good actions done with impure intentions do not: "if with the greatest effort it should yet achieve nothing, and only the good will should remain . . . yet would it, like a jewel, still shine by its own light as something which has its full value in itself. Its usefulness or fruitlessness can neither augment not diminish this value."[62]

Even moral sentiments cannot ensure the good will, as Kant explained in a particularly notorious passage:

> There are many persons who are so sympathetically constituted that, without any further motive of vanity or self-interest, they find an inner pleasure in spreading joy around them. . . . In such a case an action of this kind, however dutiful and amiable it may be, has nevertheless no true moral worth.[63]

In another part of the *Groundwork*, Kant even says that although we have a duty to preserve our own lives (and not commit suicide), most of us do so not out of duty, but rather out of an obvious inclination (to live!) which only happens to be in accordance with duty.[64] Only those who refrain from committing suicide because they believe it to be wrong are truly moral. Of course, this does not imply that following one's inclination to live is immoral, but merely amoral or not deserving of merit or esteem. But, on the other hand, we would safely say that a person whose only desire was to end her life, but nonetheless did not, was moral, since her respect for the moral law outweighed her (presumably very strong) inclination to die.[65]

This is a rare case where we may be able to infer the true motivations behind an action: when it is clearly in opposition to a person's inclination. But most of the time, Kant recognized, we very rarely know the true motivation of our actions—whether they were performed out of duty, inclination, or both—much less anybody else's. If someone sacrifices something of value to herself to act dutifully—say, running into a burning building to save a stranger's child—then it is fairly safe to assume that action was done out of duty rather than out of an inclinational motive. However, if the person were hoping for adulation and a six-figure book deal, that would change our assessment of his motivation and character—as I think it would for most people, not just Kantians. It seems much more likely that we act with mixed motivations in most cases: partly to do the right thing, but also because we want to help others, be honest, and so forth. Kant's position, partly in response to sentimentalists like Hume and Smith, was that persons should not behave morally because it feels good, but rather it should feel good that they behave morally. In other words, the moral assessment of the act comes first, and the "warm glow" or satisfaction (as long as it does not lapse into vanity) derives from that assessment.[66]

Judgment

It is unfortunate that, with regard to his ethical system, Kant developed the reputation of being demanding, uncompromising, rule-obsessed, and insensitive to context and circumstances. Once again, if one reads only the *Groundwork*, it is clear why this impression is so pervasive; indeed, even a wider reading of Kant's ethical writings tends to reinforce this. But in truth, none of these characterizations is deserved, because the categorical imperative and the duties that result from it provide merely a basic framework for ethical deliberation in real-world contexts, with significant room for flexibility to accommodate the context of individual decision-making situations. As Onora O'Neill explains:

Discussions of judgment . . . are ubiquitous in Kant's writings. He never assumes agents can move from principles of duty, or from other principles of action, to selecting a highly specific act in particular circumstances without any process of judgment. He is as firm as any devotee of Aristotelian *phronesis* in maintaining that principles of action are not algorithms and do not entail their own applications.[67]

A related critique is that Kant's moral theory is excessively focused on rules, but Kant opposed rule-worship as the enemy of true freedom and autonomy: "Dogmas and formulas, those mechanical instruments for rational use (or rather misuse) of [man's] natural endowments, are the ball and chain of his permanent immaturity."[68] As O'Neill writes, in her response to virtue ethicist Alasdair MacIntyre's criticisms of Kant along these lines, "Kant provides us primarily an ethic of virtue rather than of rules," in part because "Kant offers us a form of rationalism in ethics that . . . does not generate a unique moral code, but still provides fundamental guidelines and suggests the types of reasoning by which we might see how to introduce these guidelines into the lives we lead."[69] At most, the categorical imperative, and the duties it generates, are intended to provide rough guidelines for moral intention and action, a sort of moral "compass"[70] that we rely on to help us through the trickier ethical corridors of life.

Despite the apparently rule-oriented nature of the *Groundwork*, Kant had tremendous respect for judgment: "though understanding is capable of being instructed . . . judgment is a peculiar talent which can be practiced only, and cannot be taught. It is the specific quality of so-called mother-wit; and its lack no school can make good."[71] Sullivan emphasizes the never-ending development and growth of our judgment:

> Through simply living, facing ordinary moral problems day by day, we all accumulate a store of moral experience to help us judge how to act; we all develop some sensitivity to the features to which we should attend. Moreover, most of the situations in which we find ourselves are familiar ones, and we do not need to deliberate over how to act. We simply act on maxims that reflect our long-standing commitments and values.[72]

Kant refuses to elaborate on judgment in terms of higher-order principles or rules, arguing that doing so would lead to infinite regress: since no rule, even higher-order rules, will be determinate in all situations, one would need yet higher rules to show how apply them, and then even higher-order rules for those, and so on.[73]

Judgment proves essential to moral decision-making in several ways. For one, judgment is necessary to apply the general guidelines provided by the categorical imperative to day-to-day decisions. Of supposed "universal decision procedures" that are imputed to Kantian ethics, Allen Wood writes that "human life and moral deliberation are too complex for any such procedure ever to exist."[74] Robert Louden argues that moral anthropology is need to "strengthen agent's powers of judgment," which it does by "organizing and presenting relevant aspects of human experience to agents to reflect on under controlled circumstances."[75] Barbara Herman refers to this function of judgment as providing "rules of moral salience," which allow the agent "to pick out these elements of his circumstances or of his proposed actions that require moral attention."[76] Then, because the categorical imperative "is not itself a moral rule—it is an abstract formal principle,"[77] judgment is required to understand exactly how to construct a maxim, itself "a principle that expresses a complex volitional judgment,"[78] and also how to determine its validity vis-à-vis that formal principle, as it is rarely obvious (even, as we saw above, in the supposedly straightforward and logical contradiction-in-conception test). And after the relevant moral aspects of a situation have been determined, judgment is necessary to determine how to act dutifully in accordance with moral laws—especially with regard to imperfect duties—for "to be sure, these laws require . . . a power of judgment sharpened by experience, partly in order to distinguish in what cases they are applicable, and partly to gain for them access to the human will as well as influence for putting them into practice."[79]

Perhaps most important for practical purposes, judgment is essential for solving the problem of conflicting obligations or rules. Obligations often conflict through no fault of the conflicted person: she may be called suddenly to help a family member at the same time she has promised to meet a friend. Kant believed that a person only had one operative duty at any given time, so one obligation must be pronounced to be of "stronger ground of obligation" than the other.[80] As he sometimes did, Kant elaborated little on what exactly he meant by this, but rather than reflecting oversight on his part, this may have been intentional. He may have meant to imply that the agent must use her judgment to decide which obligation is more important, based on her knowledge of, and respect for, the moral law, as opposed to deterministically following an established set of rules. It is entirely possible that two people, both dedicated Kantians facing identical circumstances, would make two different judgments regarding the best action in that particular case, because each person's judgment, based on previous experiences and choices, is unique to her.[81] In other words, each person will make the choice, based ultimately on the moral law, that preserves the integrity of her character.[82]

While, as in the case with judgment in general, Kant provided no definite rule or algorithm for comparing the "pull" of conflicting obligations, the outcome in some cases may seem clear: when a perfect (narrow) duty is at odds with an imperfect (wide) one, the latter would seem to give way, since it is flexible in its execution whereas the perfect duty is not. But recall that all duties are essentially negative, so "do not x" is roughly comparable with "do not y," even if the first command generates a strict obligation (such as "do not lie") and the second a wide one (such as "do not be indifferent to others"). Consider this example: Alicia makes a promise to Bill to drive him to a blind date, but while en route to pick him up, Alicia sees Carl by the roadside, in urgent need of assistance because his wife Debbie is in labor. The duty to keep promises is a narrow one while the duty to offer assistance is a wide one, but favoring the former does not seem right in this case: most would agree that Carl and Debbie are in much direr straits than Bill (no matter long it has been since he last had a date). It is not hard to imagine that, whatever "stronger ground" may mean, it could certainly mean the more important obligation, where "importance" may be defined in terms of consequences (helping deliver a baby will likely do more good than furthering Bill's love life), social proximity (saving a friend rather than a stranger when both are in danger), and so on.[83] Of course, none of these empirical factors enter into the determination of a duty itself, but since there is no rule to pick the more important obligation, such aspects of the situation, filtered through the faculty of judgment, may be necessary to break the logjam.

We can go even further and recognize that conflicts among obligations are very common in real life, in which case even perfect duties are often not as rigid and demanding as they appear in isolation. There may be many obligations facing us in any given choice situation, and the responsibility for balancing their pull, or comparing the strength of their grounds, falls to judgment.[84] In a discussion of moral dilemmas, Barbara Herman cites "the hard work of moral deliberation that is central to a moral life: the engagement with multiple moral considerations present in an agent's current or anticipated circumstances of action."[85] This is the sense in which the categorical imperative and the various duties that come from it are merely guidelines for ethical behavior, reasons for action that we must take into account when facing moral dilemmas, but ultimately must be weighed and balanced by our judgment. If Kantian ethics were truly a strict rule-based system, none of this would be necessary.

The Prisoners' Dilemma

At this point, it may be useful to provide an example applying much of what was presented above, so we will now unleash Kant's ethics on the most famous and widely discussed situation in game theory, the *prisoners' dilemma* game.[86] The essence of the prisoners' dilemma game is that both players have dominant strategies (actions that earn them the highest pay-off regardless of the other player's action), but when they both choose their dominant strategies (as it is assumed they will), they both end up with lower payoffs than if they had both chosen the dominated strategy instead. The game derives its name from a tale of two criminal suspects (or "prisoners") being interrogated in separate rooms; if they both kept quiet about their recent activities, they would get a small jail term, but each has the opportunity to sell the other out (and receive no jail time) if he or she confesses (and implicates the other as the mastermind), whether or not the other is likely to confess, which is therefore each suspect's dominant strategy. In the end, both suspects confess, earning them both longer jail terms than if they had both kept quiet. The prisoners' dilemma stands as the prototypical example of conflict between individual and collective rationality: through mutual pursuit of self-interest, all players end up worse off than if they had behaved otherwise.

It has been suggested that ethical behavior, as opposed to self-interested decision-making, would help solve prisoners' dilemma problems. Most prominently, Amartya Sen, referencing the classic interpretation of the game, has written that "it is indeed easy to see that it will be difficult to find a moral argument in favor of confession by the prisoners," implying that any ethical system (other than ethical egoism) would demand cooperative behavior in prisoners' dilemma situations, including Cournot oligopolistic competition, private contributions to finance public goods, and arms races, to mention just a few.[87] As an example of such an ethical system, many scholars (including Sen) have focused on Kant, arguing that the application of Kantian ethics would require that the players in such games cooperate rather than deviate, and therefore reach the Pareto-superior outcome. But I will argue against this, based on the description of Kantian ethics given above.

To begin, we can simply follow Kant's own advice and apply the Formula of Autonomy to the players' behavior in the game. I will use the term "deviation" to refer to the dominant strategy in a prisoners' dilemma game (which leads to the suboptimal outcome), and "cooperation" for the dominated strategy (which leads to the optimal outcome).[88] Can a maxim of deviation be universalized without inconsistency? First, we will apply the consistency-in-conception test: is one player's deviation logically

inconsistent with the other player doing the same? Certainly both players can, and often do, deviate simultaneously—that is the crux of the
problem, after all—so there is nothing logically inconsistent there.[89] (Of
course, this behavior results in inferior payoffs, but that does not affect the
logical consistency of mutual deviation.) But, as we saw above, consistency-in-conception does not rule out occasional murder either, so we turn
to consistency-in-the-will, which asks if the agent can *rationally* will that
her maxim of deviation be universalized. Certainly, universal indifference
to suffering cannot be willed rationally, but unless serious harm is threatened, it is difficult to see how universal deviation is inconsistent with any
ends-in-themselves. So if we rule out such extreme circumstances, neither
understanding of consistency derived from this formula of the categorical
imperative prevents deviation in the prisoners' dilemma game.

Sen comes close to the contradiction-in-the-will test when he writes
that "certainly neither prisoner would *like* that confessing becomes a universal practice, and the only universal law that each prisoner would *like* is
that everyone should refuse to confess."[90] But here he conflates "willing"
with "liking" or "wanting," introducing inclination into the universalization procedure.[91] A similar misunderstanding of the universalization
formula of the categorical imperative has been repeated often in the literature on altruism and public good financing. For instance, Bilodeau and
Gravel understand Kantian ethics to mean "compelling an individual to
undertake any action which we would *want* everyone else to undertake,"[92]
and cite many papers that share this conception, including Laffont's
"Macroeconomic Constraints, Economic Efficiency and Ethics," one of
the earliest attempts to integrate Kantian ethics explicitly into economics. But Bilodeau and Gravel recognize that this understanding of Kant's
moral theory may not be accurate; in fact, they point to other papers that
emphasize the frequent misuse of Kantian ethics in economics (an august
grouping to which your author would add this humble monograph).[93]

Perhaps we should look at the nature of duties themselves for a different perspective on the problem. Is there a perfect duty not to deviate in
prisoners' dilemma games? We saw above that such action cannot be ruled
out by the consistency-in-conception test, which normally results in perfect duties, so "do not deviate" is likely not one. But what about imperfect
duty: could a duty not to deviate in prisoners' dilemma games be a specific

instance of the duty of beneficence? Not deviating will increase the other player's payoff regardless of her action, so it would certainly be considered helpful, and may even be considered a virtuous act. But at the same time it comes at a sacrifice to yourself (since you would be choosing the dominated strategy), and you are not required to make any given sacrifice to perform a wide duty. So while cooperation in a prisoners' dilemma game may be nice, kind, admirable, or noble, it is not required; even a concern for the other player based on treating her as an end (as the Formula of Respect dictates) does not mandate that one sacrifice his own well-being by avoiding the self-interested dominant strategy of deviation. This highlights the essential problem with relying on Kantian ethics to prevent prisoners' dilemma outcomes: while the categorical imperative rules out many actions as immoral, it does not specify any precise actions that *must* be taken otherwise. Since imperfect duties do not demand specific action, we cannot thereby derive a strict moral obligation to cooperate in prisoners' dilemma games based on them.

But if we expand the strategies available to the players, there may be a way to imply a perfect duty to cooperate, specifically by allowing both players to promise cooperative behavior before the game is played. Kant uses promise-keeping as one of his four examples of using the categorical imperative, and the argument based on consistency-in-conception is straightforward: as with lying, if promises are not kept, trust will be compromised and promises will lose their efficacy.[94] So if the players make promises to each other to cooperate, then they are bound by their duty to keep these promises, thereby avoiding the prisoners' dilemma outcome. However, there is no duty to make such a promise in the first place (because such a duty would be based on a perfect duty to cooperate, which as we have seen does not exist), so there is still no perfect duty that requires the players to choose the cooperative action in prisoners' dilemma games.

Even though we have ruled out a perfect duty to make cooperative promises, such a practice can nonetheless provide a way for players to avoid the prisoners' dilemma outcome: if each player promised to cooperate, contingent on the other player making the same promise, then both players would be bound by their promises and would therefore cooperate. But such a promise to cooperate is effective in eliciting similar behavior from other players only insofar as the player making the promise is known to be a

Kantian—after all, anyone can promise to cooperate, for doing so is "cheap talk" in a single-play game (and may be generated by purely self-interested behavior in an infinitely repeated game). For these reasons, the Kantian duty of promise-keeping cannot be relied upon to ensure cooperative behavior in prisoners' dilemma games, but it can provide a method for Kantian agents to resolve prisoners' dilemma games in their own self-interest.

Maybe we need a more general, humanistic perspective, one given by the Formula of Respect. Is there any sense in which deviation in a prisoners' dilemma game treats the other players simply as a means while not at the same time as an end? It is true that one player's deviation always raises his payoff and lowers the other player's payoff (regardless of the other player's action), but does that imply that the first player *used* the second simply as a means to his benefit? If it did, it would imply that one firm uses its competitor when it lowers its price to gain market share, increasing its own profit "at the expense" of the other firm's profit; or that a firm in a imperfectly competitive industry uses its customers due to its ability to raise price above marginal cost. Would these actions be forbidden by Kant's injunction to respect the dignity of persons (assuming we can extend this concept to firms as well)?

While these actions may fall into some readers' personal conception of using someone, Kant had a much more precise notion of what it means to use someone merely as a means and not at the same time as an end. To respect another person's dignity, Kant wrote that you must treat her as an autonomous, rational being; specifically, as we saw above, she must be able to—though not necessarily *want* to—rationally assent to your ends. For instance, in the context of the duty not to make false promises, Kant described what it means to treat someone otherwise:

[T]he man whom I want to use for my own purposes by such a promise *cannot possibly* concur with my way of acting toward him and hence *cannot himself hold the end of this action*. . . . [A] transgressor of the rights of men intends to make use of the persons of others merely as a means, without taking into consideration that, as rational beings, they should always be esteemed at the same time as ends, i.e., be esteemed only as beings who must themselves *be able to hold the very same action as an end*.[95]

Note the emphasis on possibility and ability, not preference or desire: the other person does not have to actually share my end or agree with it, and can in fact abhor it. Kant requires only that she be able to rationally assent to it, even if she chooses not to, for it is the fact that she *can* choose to, not whether she would, that is essential.

For this reason, as I mentioned above, coercion and deception are the primary examples of using someone simply as a means, because they both render her incapable of making a choice regarding the other person's end.[96] Coercion obviously rules out choice altogether, and deception keeps the other person unaware of my true end, denying her the ability to assent to it. But if she can make a choice without coercion or deceit on my part, then I have treated her as a rational, autonomous person, and have considered her as an end as well as a means.[97] So the firm that, without engaging in coercive or fraudulent behavior, lowers prices to steal business from a competitor treats that competitor with respect (even while lowering its profit). Asymmetry of power, as in the imperfect competition case, does not imply violation of respect, either; though she may be resentful of the higher price charged, the customer has the choice whether or not to participate in a transaction with the company and recognize its end of profit-maximization, as long as it has not acted fraudulently.[98] The same goes for the prisoners' dilemma game: each player's end is assumed to be his or her own self-interest, a goal to which the other player can certainly assent (even if the players have no regard for each other, or if they despise each other). Since the standard definition of the prisoners' dilemma game rules out coercion (through free choice of actions) and deception (through common assumptions on information), it is implied that the players are treating each other with the respect due to rational, autonomous persons.

So while Kantian ethics may *encourage* some degree of cooperation in a prisoners' dilemma game, it does not *require* it. The categorical imperative permits players in prisoners' dilemma games to choose their dominant strategies of deviation despite the resulting suboptimal payoffs for both. Because the categorical imperative does not demand specific actions, but only forbids certain actions (in the case of perfect duty) or requires the adoption of general attitudes (in the case of imperfect duty), it does not support a strict duty of beneficence toward the other player. Furthermore, deviation does not involve treating the other player simply as a means and not at the same time as an end, because it does not impair her autonomy or choice through coercion or deceit. At bottom, Kantian ethics is not strict enough to guarantee cooperation in prisoners' dilemma games, supporting the broader point that Kantian ethics provides a framework for moral judgment rather than definite, ready-to-apply rules.

Kantian-Economic Model of Decision-Making

Having discussed Kant's moral philosophy, we are now ready to incorporate these ideas—particularly his distinction between perfect and imperfect duties—into the standard economic model of decision-making. This model assumes that the agent has fixed, stable preferences, which she maximally satisfies within given constraints and information (or beliefs). If the agent's preferences are complete and transitive, they can be represented by an ordinal utility function, which assigns higher levels of utility to more preferred options. It is important to note that in this context, the word "utility" does not refer to a mental state such as pleasure or happiness, but simply a numerical index or ranking of options.[99] Accordingly, an agent's preference ranking is not assumed to be based on any psychological sense of desiring one option over another; instead, the ranking can be based on another person's well-being, a faith-based way of life (reflected in observance of dietary restrictions, for instance), or any other source, whether or not it is based on self-interest (however widely or narrowly understood). By denying a mental-state conception of utility, economists are freed from having to place substantive restrictions on preferences, allowing agents to be self-interested or altruistic, narrowly hedonist or broadly utilitarian, all-loving or misanthropic.[100] The constraints in the standard model of choice are traditionally given less attention, but are also assumed to be exogenous, and of a financial, physical, or temporal nature.[101]

For the purposes of this chapter, we will accept the broad terms of the constrained preference-satisfaction model of economic choice, and go on to explain how this model can incorporate Kantian ethics as summarized above. We will approach this in two steps. First, we will assume that the agent has determined her duties as they apply in a given decision-making context, and sees how those duties fit into the model. Once we have done that, we will explore the details regarding the determination of her "best" action, which will complete the Kantian-economic model of decision-making. Both steps necessarily involve judgment, emphasizing the point that this is the central faculty involved in modeling and practicing Kantian ethics.

Incorporating duties into preferences and constraints

The most apparent difficulty with our task is that there seems to be no room in the standard economic theory of choice for duties, especially duties that, by definition, cannot be performed because an agent *wants* to (for any reason, selfish or altruistic). But recall that the term "preference" in modern economic theory does not imply any basis in a mental state such as happiness and pleasure, but merely an ordering or ranking of states of the world over which the agent has some influence. So, in theory, preferences can also be based on Kantian duty as derived from the categorical imperative; the agent could rank states of the world in which she performed her duty higher than ones in which she did not, without implying any "desire" for the former over the latter. Furthermore, if the agent can rank some duties higher than other duties as well as her "normal" preferences, and can do so completely and transitively, then these duty-based "preferences" can be included in a ordinal utility function alongside any others. The resulting utility function can then be maximized within the agent's constraints, involving marginal adjustments in response to changes in prices and income, just as in standard choice theory.

But can all duties be represented in terms of preferences in this way? This is where the distinction between perfect and imperfect duties becomes crucial. Plainly, perfect duties cannot be included among preferences, since they take precedence over inclinations and cannot be traded off amongst them if performing them becomes too expensive. Rather, perfect duties constrain the pursuit of inclinations, spelling out the means we may not use to achieve our ends. This is most clearly seen in terms of the Formula of Respect, which forbids a person from doing anything that uses other persons (or herself) merely as means while not at the same time as ends. With this understanding, we can model perfect duties as constraints, in the same way that budget constraints limit a consumer's spending. A Kantian agent is free to pursue her own ends (including the ends imposed by imperfect duties, to be discussed next), as long as she acts within the constraints given by perfect duty: do not lie, do not steal, do not kill, and so forth.

Certainly, explicit consideration of moral constraints such as these is not the norm in economics, but economists often implicitly assume these constraints in the background. In standard models of trade and commerce, for instance, economists normally assume that buyers and sellers make voluntary transactions, free from fraud and deceit, and with no threat of theft from either side. While such factors have certainly been added—in the literatures on corruption and crime, for instance—they are represented as aberrations, modifications of the basic modeling structure which assumes such exceptions away. Since the agents in these standard models are not free to resort to such immoral means to achieve their ends, they are behaving as if they were Kantian agents observing their perfect duties. Ironically, the nature of perfect duty seems to be the tallest hurdle to overcome when integrating Kantians ethics into the economic model of choice, but in a way, it has been there all along.

Another way to model "unusual" constraints on decision-making is to use lexicographic preferences, preferences that must be satisfied before others can be considered (similar to the stepwise process of alphabetical ordering). In other words, an agent could have a lexicographically superior preference for not-lying, such that she had to satisfy that "preference" before acting to satisfy any others. But this technique is descriptively inaccurate and practically unwieldy. It is inaccurate because it represents actions we feel are wrong as inactions which we prefer to "take." But it is not that we rank "not lying" as a higher option than all the rest; it is something we simply will do or not do in trying to satisfy our normal preferences—a constraint. It is unwieldy because it violates the spirit of the preference-satisfaction model: to model trade-offs among preferences according to prices and income. Lexicographic preferences, by definition, cannot be traded off, and are unresponsive to prices or income—which is true of perfect duties and constraints, but not of preferences as usefully understood.[102] So why model such aspects of choice as any sort of preference when they do not function as preferences, especially when we have the concept of constraints conveniently available? While perhaps an interesting theoretical construct, lexicographic preferences misrepresent the purpose and role of moral duties and principles in decision-making, which is rather to constrain preference-satisfaction for ethical reasons.

A more moderate suggestion is to model strict moral duties and principles as preferences which can be traded off with other preferences as prices and income dictate. For instance, Gintis writes that "one might be tempted to model honesty and other character virtues as self-constituted constraints on one's set of available actions in a game, but a more fruitful approach is to include the state of being virtuous in a certain way as an argument in one's preference function, to be traded off against other valuable objects of desire and personal goals."[103] While this maintains a preference ordering allowing trade-offs, which is methodologically more workable (theoretically and empirically), there is still the problem of representing something we feel we should not do as something we want to avoid doing—this may be part of the story, but not the entire tale.

Consider a weary traveler who has arrived home after a long business trip, and the only thing on her mind, the only desire or inclination she cares about, is to see her beloved fiancé (or dog—your choice). She spots a cab, rushes towards it, but a feeble elderly man gets there just before she does. She could easily push the man aside to get the cab and satisfy the only preference she cares to act on, but does not; she recognizes one of the most basic rules of civilized behavior—"wait your turn"—and catches the next cab. Which explanation sounds more natural: that she indulges a stronger preference to not push aside senior citizens—or, at least, that particular senior citizen—to the detriment of her preference to see her fiancé a little sooner, or that she recognizes a duty not to push aside senior citizens (even if she may not particularly like them) that constrains her actions taken to see her fiancé? Again, framing moral duties or principles which tell us what not to do as preferences over what we want not to do (I dare you to say that three times quickly) obscures what is going on in such situations.[104]

But what if persons do not regard their duties or principles as absolutes, and do in fact trade them off in response to opportunity costs? Citing common sense and experimental evidence, Gintis writes that "if the cost of virtue is sufficiently high, and the probability of detection of a breach is sufficiently small, many individuals will behave dishonestly."[105] The curt response is that such persons do not recognize moral duties or principles at all, reminding one of the old joke in which a man asks a woman, "Would you sleep with me for a million dollars?" When the woman says yes, the man then asks, "Would you sleep with me for five dollars?" The woman indignantly replies, "Absolutely not—what kind of woman do you take me for?" The man answers, "We've already established that—now we're just bargaining over the price." It does not take a Kantian to see that duties or principles which are subject to compromise for mere goods or money (rather than other duties or principles) are no duties or principles at all. And if we rule true, priceless duties and principles out, we are left with persons whose virtue can be bought, which is not an attractive picture of morality (or politics, for that matter). But, of course, persons do compromise their duties or principles for self-interested reasons, but I do not think that such behavior should be treated so casually (especially in the context of modeling moral choice!), but rather as the aberration it is (or should be). (Accordingly, we will discuss it in such terms in the next chapter.) Let us not compromise our agents' morals before we even begin to understand them.[106]

Some may agree with the interpretation of duties as moral constraints, but object that such factors are "merely" normative constraints, and are less binding in a physical or logical sense than the typical budget or technological constraints in economics. But, as Goldfarb and Griffith recognize, even those constraints may not be binding unless they are reinforced by normative constraints; for instance, a consumer's budget constraint is less binding if he is open to shoplifting, and a producer's technological constraints can be loosened by compromising workplace safety or the quality of the final product.[107] But nonetheless, it is true that moral constraints, especially if self-imposed and enforced as the result of autonomous processes, can be violated just as voluntarily; we will address this in the next chapter when we discuss weakness of will and character and their role in ensuring dutiful action in the face of human weakness. But to rule out self-imposed constraints altogether is to deny an essential component of autonomy and self-determination, which must include not only what one wishes to do, but also the lengths to which one will *not* go to achieve one's goals.

While perfect duties must be modeled as constraints, imperfect duties can easily fit alongside other preferences in an overall ranking. Unlike perfect duties, imperfect duties do not demand specific performance of action (or inaction), but instead only mandate general ends that should be adopted, allowing latitude with respect to inclination and other duties. So an agent can order the ends imposed by imperfect duty, such as beneficence, among her inclination-based preferences in her overall ranking, since the modern economic sense of "preference" does not necessarily imply true desire in the psychological sense. Furthermore, Kant was clear that the agent's own happiness and well-being can and should be taken into account in her decision-making, if only because she herself, as a person with dignity, is to be treated as an end along with all other persons: "lawgiving reason . . . *permits* you to be benevolent to yourself on the condition of your being benevolent to every other as well."[108] Seeing this, we can model the economic agent as following the categorical imperative by incorporating perfect and imperfect duties into her choice framework as constraints and preferences, respectively. Once the imperfect duties have been "chosen" by judgment in accordance with, and out of respect for, the agent's duty, an ordinal utility function can be constructed from them, which she will maximize as usual. Therefore, Kantian economic agents differ from consequentialist ones not so much in how they optimize, but *amongst what* they optimize (rankings of imperfect duties and inclinations), *against what* they optimize (perfect duties and exogenous constraints), and *how they choose* what to optimize (autonomous judgment).

Deliberating on action

There are several problems with the simplistic model just described. First, we have not explained how the agent orders her imperfect duties against her inclinations, much less against her other imperfect duties. Second, we need to confront the possibility of a conflict between perfect duties, in which one constraint may cancel out another. Finally, there may be conflict between perfect and imperfect duties that cannot be resolved by simply compromising the performance of the imperfect duty (such as being less helpful if a lie were required to be more helpful). As we saw earlier, perfect duty cannot be assumed always to take precedence over imperfect duty, for this ranking depends on the strength of their respective grounds of obligation, not simply on their relative strictness.

As we saw above, Kant gave no definite answers regarding these matters; the agent must use her judgment to resolve these issues, and in this way judgment plays an integral role in crafting an agent's overall "objective function." Once judgment has determined the operative duties, as well as their relative importance, in any given choice situation, the agent can then maximize her objective function as usual (pending the issues of will and character to be discussed in the next chapter). Furthermore, judgment is not reducible to an algorithm; as we said above, the agent must make choices consistent with her understanding of the moral law, based ultimately on the inherent dignity and equality of every person, to maintain the integrity of her character.

Nonetheless, we can expand on how this process of judgment might play out in each of the following circumstances:

1. Ranking imperfect duties against inclination and other imperfect duties. Imperfect duties, even if they generally fit nicely among inclinations in the agent's preference ranking, must nonetheless be ordered somehow amongst them, as well as against each other. While there is no one "right" ordering that every agent must follow—as there would be for the simple case of perfect duty over inclination—we can suppose that there is such a "right" ordering for any given agent in any given choice situation. But from where does this "right" answer come? Again, it comes from the agent's judgment, which can be understood as her personal interpretation of the moral law above and beyond the formality of the categorical imperative, stemming from an appreciation of the essential dignity and autonomy of human beings (from which the categorical imperative is derived).

In his theory of judicial decision-making, Ronald Dworkin argues that there is a "right answer" to any legal dispute, as determined by the principles inherent in the legal system and rights implied by them, and it is the judge's responsibility to find it and declare it in her opinion.[109] But this is not an ontological claim to legal certainty, for two judges may each think she has the "right answer" though they differ on what that is. Dworkin's point is that a judge must be confident that she has taken all of the relevant factors into account, weighed them properly against each other, and found the answer she believes to be "right." Accordingly, the

Kantian agent follows the same process, weighing all the facts of the situation and her moral obligations to arrive at the answer she feels is right—in other words, consistent with her understanding of the moral law and the concept of dignity upon which it is based. Of course, two agents may come to different decisions when facing the same dilemma, but each one must feel comfortable that he or she has made the best judgment possible, and should stand ready to defend that decision with reason.

2. *Ranking perfect duties against each other.* Understood as constraints, perfect duties pose less of a problem for our model of decision-making, simply prohibiting certain actions we might otherwise take to further our ends. The moral agent does not lie to gain advantage, does not cheat to win a game, and does not kill to eliminate romantic competition. In a sense, perfect duties shrink the "action space" available to a moral agent: they foreclose all the actions that involve deception, coercion, and so forth. Perfect duties always take precedence over mere inclination, perhaps the only clear ranking in this picture of Kantian decision-making. But what if several perfect obligations conflict with each other? To continue with a visual analogy, what if all actions (including inaction) are foreclosed by one duty or another, but a course of action must be chosen all the same? This is what philosophers call a *tragic dilemma*, a choice from which the agent cannot emerge with "clean hands." To be more precise, one perfect duty (or more) must be compromised, beginning with the one with the weakest ground of obligation. And once again, this decision comes down to judgment: the agent must judge which action is most consistent with preserving respect for dignity and autonomy.[110]

Whichever perfect duty (or duties) the agent judges to be most important constrains her action as described above, and then her decision-making continues as before, maximizing her objective function within the remaining constraints. Of course, she should not "take advantage" of the relaxation of the compromised perfect duty; it is not a perpetual license to do wrong. If it becomes possible to act in accordance with that perfect duty again, then the conflict is no longer an issue, and the duty once again becomes operative. But while it remains in "suspension," the agent should regret that she cannot follow it, though she should not feel guilty, for she literally could not fulfill that obligation while maintaining the other one (or ones) which she judged more important.

3. Ranking perfect duty against imperfect duty. By now, the reasoning should be clear. When perfect and imperfect duties come into conflict, two things may happen. If the perfect duty is judged to be more important, then the imperfect duty is compromised *to some degree*—an option not available to us in the case of the compromise of perfect duty. If you planned to donate $1,000 to charity, and then realized you had forgotten a debt of $500 that you have to repay, you can always reduce your donation without forgoing it altogether. More generally, you still hold the end of charitable giving, but you decide that the planned, specific execution of the corresponding duty must be compromised to some extent. The apparent ease of accommodation in this case may have contributed to the presumption that in the case of such a conflict, imperfect duty always bends a knee to perfect duty.

But it may not always be the case that imperfect duty is judged less important; despite Kant's unfortunate rhetoric in pronouncing the supremacy of the duty to not lie to the murderer at the door who seeks to kill your friend hiding inside, the duty to help your friend to escape the murderer's wrath almost certainly does take precedence, as our judgment easily confirms.[111] So here we have a case of perfect duty being relaxed, for just as long as this particular conflict continues, to make room for proper execution of the imperfect duty judged to be of more importance. And to be sure, again this does not give the agent license to lie to just anybody, but only when a more important end or duty is at stake, and not without a certain amount of regret. In each of these cases of conflict, the agent uses her judgment, based on her appreciation of the moral law and its basis in the dignity and autonomy of human beings, to resolve the conflict to what must be her satisfaction (if not her presumptive confidence). And from such use of her judgment, she determines her operative duties in any given choice situation, and choice continues from that point as if she were an ordinary economic decision-maker.

In this chapter, we have been presuming an agent who embodies perfect morality and rationality, one who never wavers in her devotion to the moral law, whose will is unquestionable. Since such a person has never existed outside the realm of fiction, in the next chapter we further refine the model of Kantian decision-making to incorporate the will, in all its strength or weakness, and only then will we have a model of true choice.

CHAPTER 2

A Kantian-Economic Model of Choice

In the first chapter, I proposed a basic model of the Kantian economic agent, showing how perfect and imperfect duties can be incorporated into her objective function and how she can then choose an action based on them, reflecting her best judgment based on her understanding of the moral law. But up to now, I have implicitly assumed that once her objective function is "set" according to her best judgment, she would follow it with unswerving devotion and fortitude. But this is hardly realistic, nor is it faithful to the picture of human rationality that Kant himself painted. In this chapter we will work to rectify that, incorporating Kant's less formalistic ethical thinking about strength, virtue, and character into our model, which will result in a description of morally imperfect agents who must exert willpower in order to stay on the moral path and show true respect for the moral law. We will also describe the nature of the agent's character, combining her judgment and will, which foreshadows the discussion of the Kantian individual and her identity in Chapter 3.

As Christine Korsgaard wrote at the beginning of her book *Self-Constitution*, "human beings are *condemned* to choice and action."[1] Economics is often described as the science of choice, but the typical economic agent in fact has no true choice—her decisions are determined by her preferences and constraints. This may be sufficient for normative purposes, demonstrating how agents "should" make choices if they want to adhere to the economic conception of instrumental rationality by maximizing their utility or degree of preference satisfaction (at least according to what an outsider takes to be their preferences). But it has little connection to how real persons make decisions: we believe that we have true, free choice. As Korsgaard put it so well, we *have* to believe we have free choice in order to act in the world:

> Maybe you think you can avoid it, by resolutely standing still, refusing to act, refusing to move. But it's no use, for that will be something you have chosen to do, and then you will have acted after all. Choosing not to act makes not acting a kind of action, makes it something that you do.[2]

We can make the "right" choice or we can make the "wrong" one, attributions of right and wrong being a personal, subjective judgment. We can let principles and commitments reign over our most intensely felt preferences, sometimes choosing to endure great sacrifice for our beliefs, as described in the previous chapter, or we can succumb to our basest temptations, even ones that our judgment clearly counsels against, as we will see below.

To support such free choice, some would say that each of us has a *will*, a distinct faculty of choice that operates between judgment and action, and can either follow the dictates of one's best judgment or not, according to its strength. I begin this chapter with a basic discussion of the will, explaining why I believe this concept is essential to understanding human agency and rationality (based on the philosophical approach known as volitionism) and how economists have dealt with (or, more often, avoided) the issue of the will. Then we will return to Kant, describing his views on fortitude or strength (which he referred to as virtue), and then how the Kantian-economic model from the last chapter can adapt to include a will. Next, we will discuss a specific instance of weakness of will, procrastination, in light of the Kantian-economic model of choice, highlighting its correspondence with Kant's conceptions of choice and strength. The chapter concludes with a look forward to the next, in which we will see how an individual's character defines who she is and where she stands in relation to the world—and most important, to the people—around her.

Determinism, Volitionism, and the Will

As we saw in the last chapter, the standard picture of economic decision-making portrays an agent as choosing the most preferred option
available within her constraints. This is essentially the traditional view of
action theory in philosophy, that desires (preferences) and beliefs (information) determine both the decision made and the action taken. Among
the most famous proponents of this view is Donald Davidson, who held
that desires and beliefs together completely determine and cause an action.[3] This general perspective on the nature of choice is often traced back
to David Hume, for whom reason was slave to the passions, or Thomas
Hobbes, of whom philosopher Roderick Chisholm writes that "according to Hobbism, if we *know*, of some man, what his beliefs and desires
happen to be and how strong they are . . . then we may *deduce*, logically,
just what is it that he will do."[4] J. David Velleman describes the Humean
model like so:

There is something that the agent wants, and there is an action that he believes
conducive to its attainment. His desire for the end, and his belief in the action as
a means, justify taking the action, and they jointly cause an intention to take it,
which in turn causes the corresponding movements of the agent's body. Provided
that these causal processes take their normal course, the agent's movements con-
summate an action, and his motivating desire and belief constitute his reasons for
acting.[5]

In a simple way, the desire-belief model seems perfectly rational, and indeed, if the agent's preferences are consistent (and fulfill other technical
considerations, especially in cases of uncertainty), this process defines rationality as far as most economists, philosophers, and decision theorists
are concerned.

This may be sufficient for a prescriptive model of rational choice, albeit one of a somewhat tautological nature: setting aside issues of principle
(from last chapter), *if* persons are concerned solely with satisfying their
given preferences, *then* they should choose the most preferred option available. But does this suffice as a positive, descriptive theory of choice? Do
agents always and everywhere, reliably and without fail, choose the most
preferred option available? Of course, there are many critics of simple rational choice models that would say no, based on theories of bounded

rationality and cognitive biases.[6] While acknowledging their validity and importance, I am neither making nor disputing those arguments here; indeed, everything I will say here is compatible with such ideas, though I set them aside for the purposes of this discussion.[7]

More essentially, I am not questioning whether individuals consistently come to the best decisions given their ability to acquire and process information, but whether they always follow through on that decision when the time comes to act on it. The main problem on which we will focus is that most economists (and philosophers) make no distinction between decision (based on judgment) and action. Once an agent comes to her decision based on her best judgment, of course she acts on it—why would she not? The action is seen as little more than an afterthought, the physical manifestation of her choice, the playing out of a formed intention. This is one reason that most economists and philosophers have had so much trouble explaining cases of weakness of will, or *akrasia*, in which a person acts against his best judgment. In the traditional view of choice, this is paradoxical: if the agent decides that doing *A* is the best option available, why would he then choose to do something other than *A*? It seems nonsensical, and in this simplistic view of choice, it certainly is.[8]

Mainstream economists have had little to say regarding the determinism of the standard model of decision-making; as psychiatrist George Ainslie has written, "the straightforward simplicity of utility theory seems to have put it out of the business as an explanation for irrational behavior," which would include making choices against one's better judgment.[9] But some heterodox economists have been very forthright about the neutered faculty of choice accorded to the agents we model. Mark Lutz laments the fact that "economic choice takes the real choice out of economics,"[10] and quotes G.L.S. Shackle to the same effect: "conventional economics is not about choice, but about acting according to necessity."[11] John Davis laments that "on the standard view in economics, an entity only 'acts' because it is determined to do so as the result of some antecedent cause in a cause-and-effect process," and therefore "neoclassical economics lacks a true concept of an individual economic agent."[12] David George argues that the economic agent, as usually represented, is "more animal than human," as it simply reacts to stimuli and does not reflect on them.[13] Timothy Brennan asks in what sense choices are ever voluntary in an economic model of choice that cannot consider free choice, which "presupposes the possibility of a dichotomy between what a person does and what they want to do."[14] Most recently, Lanse Minkler bemoans the determinism of economic modeling because it "does not permit truly free choice by individuals."[15] This is merely a sampling, to be sure, but sadly the population of economists who realize this foundational shortcoming of traditional economic modeling is too small.

Philosophers have provided more criticism on this front, aimed at the Humean desire-belief model in general. R. Jay Wallace derides this model as the "hydraulic conception," which "pictures desires as vectors of force to which persons are subject, where the force of such desires in turn determines causally the actions the persons perform."[16] Wallace links this conception with *psychological determinism*, which "leaves no room for genuine deliberative agency. Action is traced to the operation of forces within us, with respect to which we as agents are ultimately passive, and in a picture of this kind real agency seems to drop out of view."[17] Velleman also maintains that the standard model "fails to include an agent . . . reasons cause an intention, and an intention causes bodily movements, but nobody—that is, no person—*does* anything."[18] He adds that "what makes us agents rather than mere subjects of behavior—in our conception of ourselves, at least, if not in reality—is our perceived capacity to interpose ourselves into the course of events in such a way that the behavioural outcome is traceable directly to us."[19]

In his 2001 book *Rationality in Action*, John Searle refers to the Humean picture as "the Classical Model," which he (like David George above) claims "represents human rationality as a more complex version of ape rationality" (referring to experiments that showed apes to be rational decision-makers).[20] Searle argues that rationality requires a true act of choice or agency, and he locates this agency in "gaps" in the decision-making process, one of which exists "between the reasons for making up your mind, and the actual decision that you make."[21] In other words, the gap "occurs when the beliefs, desires, and other reasons are not experienced as causally sufficient conditions for a decision,"[22] a description reminiscent of Wallace's and Velleman's criticisms of psychological determinism.[23] But obviously, the activity in the gap is not itself reducible to desires, beliefs, or other reasons, so Searle asks (and answers), "What fills the gap? Nothing.

Nothing fills the gap: you make up your mind to do something, or you just haul off and do what you are doing to do."[24] According to Searle, an "irreducible notion of the self" is necessary for understanding "our operation in the gap," "a self that combines the capacities of rationality and agency," where agency implies "consciously try[ing] to do something."[25]

These criticisms lead some philosophers to postulate a distinct faculty of will, the true seat of choice which operates separately from, and possibly contrary to, one's judgment formed on the basis of desires and beliefs.[26] Discussion of the will as a distinct faculty has been rare in recent action theory and philosophy in general, with most philosophers adhering to the position of Gilbert Ryle, who declared the notion of a separate will "an inevitable extension of the myth of the ghost in the machine" (referring to his characterization of the more general idea of Cartesian dualism), and of Donald Davidson, who wrote of "mysterious acts of the will."[27] More recently, economist and philosopher Don Ross discussed the implications of cognitive science for the idea of an autonomous will, concluding that "the very idea of a will as a specific causal engine is not a very helpful idea."[28] And of course, the term "will" is often used in different senses; for instance, Harry Frankfurt discusses will in his famous work "Freedom of the Will and the Concept of a Person," but in the context of being able to follow one's higher-order preference, not as a faculty of choice that is invoked once those preferences are recognized. Like Ross, George Ainslie questions the existence of a separate faculty named the will, and instead uses the term to summarize his theory of choice arising out of intrapersonal bargaining between subsequent "selves" to overcome the time-inconsistent preferences resulting from hyperbolic discounting: "I argue that this intertemporal bargaining situation *is* your will."[29] And understandably, the will has received even less attention in the economics literature, rarely mentioned even in the relatively sizable literature on self-control.[30] (I survey the sparse but important contributions to the study of the will by economists later in this chapter.)

But in recent decades there has been a renewed discussion of the will as a "psychological phenomenal something whose existence philosophers have in recent years tended to deny."[31] Wallace is a leading proponent of this view, naming his theory the "volitionist conception of rational agency":

On the volitionist conception, there is an important class of motivational states that are directly subject to our immediate control. Familiar examples from this class of motivations are such phenomena as decision and choice. Ordinarily we think of decisions and choices not merely as states to which we happen to be subject. Rather they are states for which we are ourselves directly responsible, primitive examples of the phenomenon of agency itself. It is most often in our power to determine what we are going to do, by deciding one way or another. Furthermore, when we exercise our power of self-determination by actually making a decision, the result is something we have done, not something that merely happens to us.[32]

Elsewhere, Wallace writes that "rational agents are equipped with a capacity for active self-determination that goes beyond the mere susceptibility to desires and beliefs."[33] Along the same lines, Richard Holton holds that "the agent's decision is determined not just by the relative strength of the conative inputs, the desires and the intentions. Rather, there is a separate faculty of will-power which plays an independent contributory role" and "that the agent actively employs."[34] Furthermore, in Holton's conception, the exertion of willpower involves effort, leading into a discussion of strength and weakness of will which will influence the Kantian-economic model discussed below.

Finally, elaborating on his concept of "gaps" in the decision-action process, John Searle writes that "we presuppose that there is a gap between the 'causes' of the action in the form of beliefs and desires and the 'effect' in the form of an action. This gap has a traditional name. It is called 'the freedom of the will.'"[35] Due to this freedom, actions do not result directly and deterministically from antecedent causes such as desires (or preferences) and beliefs, even when the action corresponds to these factors, and to the outside observer they seem determinate of the action taken. But sometimes agents do not follow their best judgment or decision; your "decision is not causally sufficient to produce the action. There comes the point, after you have made up your mind, when you actually have to do it. And once again, you cannot let the decision cause the action" without an act of true choice, which occurs in the gap mentioned previously.[36] Furthermore, the operation of the will within this gap is inexplicable, for this is where free choice occurs.

Searle also holds that this gap is a necessary condition for true rationality. Actions taken as a direct result of antecedent causes are no more sophisticated than actions taken by animals or computers (hence the "ape rationality" comment); it is humans' ability to choose to act on our beliefs and desires—or not to—that defines our rationality, which is very different from the standard definition of strictly following one's judgment based on desires and beliefs. This idea is also very Kantian, and it is to Kant that we now return.

Kant on the Will, Virtue, and Weakness

In the last chapter, we discussed Kantian autonomy or freedom, the capacity by which agents can follow laws of their devising without undue influence from external and internal factors. In the context of the model of Kantian decision-making or judgment, autonomy is reflected in the self-determination of perfect and imperfect duties, as well as their placement in the agent's objective function alongside (or constraining) her inclination-based preferences. More generally, the agent is autonomous because she is free to—and does—subsume her preferences to the requirements of duties which she has determined are more important, based on her understanding of the moral law.

Because of the formalism of the categorical imperative and the strict requirement that agents adhere to the duties that result from their judgment, it is easy to conclude that Kant was naïve regarding the moral fortitude of normal people in real-world situations. But this would be grossly inaccurate. In fact, Kant understood that human beings are never perfectly rational and moral; this is why the moral law presents itself as an imperative, not merely a description of normal behavior. As he wrote, "the perfect fit of the will to moral law is holiness, which is a perfection of which no rational being in the world of sense is at any time capable."[37] Only God (and the angels) can be perfectly moral, and for Kant, this defines His holiness (not the other way around): "Even the Holy One of the gospel must first be compared with our ideal of moral perfection before he is recognized as such."[38] Kant's term for human agents' moral fallibility is contingent rationality, and he uses virtue to denote one's strength of will or steadfastness to the moral law in the face of such potential lapses.[39]

A point that deserves particular emphasis is that an agent's strength of will is distinct from her judgment, which helps determine one's operative duties and obligations; her strength of will affects how well she fulfills those obligations after she determines them. My usage of these terms corresponds roughly to Kant's two aspects of the will, *Wille* and *Willkür*, the first determining the moral law and the second serving as the seat of agency and choice.[40] Another way to think of the distinction is that *Wille* is the legislative aspect of the will, setting the laws the agent should follow, while *Willkür* is the executive aspect, (ideally) carrying out the dictates of *Wille*.[41] Autonomy comes into play both in *Wille's* determination of the agent's moral duty without prior cause (negative freedom), and also when *Willkür* takes action, whether based on *Wille's* "command" or not (positive freedom). According to this distinction, the agent acts immorally (but nonetheless freely) when her *Willkür* deviates from the dictate of *Wille*, which is normally understood to represent pure reason, incorruptible by material impulses. While every person, by virtue of her rationality, has the capacity for autonomy (or inner freedom), her strength or virtue in this regard can vary: "For while the capacity to overcome all opposing sensible impulses can and must be simply *presupposed* in man on account of his freedom, yet this capacity as *strength* is something he must acquire."[42] And when the agent's strength falters and she allows inclination to affect her choice, she has become heteronomous.

There are several ways in which a person can be heteronomous. One is "the general weakness of the human heart in complying with the adopted maxims, or the *frailty* of human nature."[43] I will henceforth call this *simple weakness*, which describes the person who is generally of strong will but occasionally lapses in her moral duty; picture the person who cheats on his diet once in a while (assuming he regards dieting to accord with duty), but for the most part sticks to it. As the term implies, this is merely common weakness, due to the imperfect rationality and morality of human beings and the constant, relentless pull of inclination, which no person can resist all of the time (although some are more successful, or stronger, than others). As Kant writes, "I incorporate the good (the law) into the maxim of my power of choice; but this good, which is an irresistible incentive . . . is subjectively the weaker (in comparison with inclination) whenever the maxim is to be followed."[44] More precisely, this weakness does not imply any viciousness on the part of the agent, but "only a *lack of virtue* . . . which indeed can coexist with the best will."[45]

In cases of simple weakness, inclination has not influenced the determination of the person's maxim, but has only interfered with executing the maxim itself. More troubling is the other version of heteronomy, the *impure will*, which describes the person who allows consideration of inclination to influence her very deliberations over maxims.[46] Impurity of the will involves a conscious choice to be heteronomous, a surrender in the endless fight against inclination, as opposed to simple weakness, which represents merely a temporary loss of control. Since an impure will allows inclination to participate in the determination of maxims (and, through them, actions), such a person is much less virtuous than the merely weak one, sliding dangerously close to vice and letting inclination take over completely.[47]

Kant emphasizes the distinction between simple weakness and impurity of the will in his discussions of affect and passion. To Kant, *affect* (sometimes translated as "emotion") is more akin to a momentary impulse, representing feelings which, "preceding reflection," are temporarily powerful enough to interfere with the execution of our maxims, but which then pass quickly ("this tempest quickly subsides").[48] *Passion*, on the other hand, is a "sensible *desire* that has become a lasting inclination," and therefore more stable and pervasive.[49] Simple weakness can be understood as an agent succumbing to affect (such as a sudden, irresistible craving for chocolate, or a burst of anger) which overwhelms her intended action on a lawful maxim, while the impure will is based on a strong, persistent taste or passion (such a lifelong love of chocolate, or perpetual anger), which the agent admits—even welcomes—into the determination of her maxims.[50] In other words, while affects overwhelm our rational faculties, passions become an intrinsic part of them, corrupting the very process rather than just the result. The impure will involves a deliberate submission, a choice to admit the influence of inclination—as evidenced by the fact that "the calm with which one gives oneself up to it permits reflection and allows the mind to form principles upon it"—and is therefore more blameworthy than simple weakness (which nonetheless must be fought).[51] Ultimately, the ideal "state of health in the moral life," which Kant derives from the ancient Stoics, is "moral apathy," which disregards affect (and rejects extreme passions) to achieve a "tranquil mind," which is thereby the "true strength of virtue."[52]

Judgment and Will: A Kantian-Economic Model of Choice

In this section we combine the Kantian-economic model of decision-making or judgment from the previous chapter with a representation of the operation of the will, based on Kant's distinction between *Wille* and *Willkür* described above.[53] But before we begin, let me mention that the new aspect of this model can be applied more broadly than in a Kantian context; any decision-maker who faces a conflict of interests, weakness of will, or lack of resolve can be modeled as explained below, whether the content of her conflict is ethical or not. (For instance, I conclude this chapter with an application of this model to procrastination, which does not rely on the Kantian frame, although it can be interpreted within it.)

Choosing a path and sticking to it

To model conflicted choice situations, I make use of multiple preference rankings or utilities, but in a different way than they are normally used in economics. In "Rational Fools," Amartya Sen presents the rationale for alternative preference structures:

The economic theory of utility, which relates to the theory of rational behaviour, is sometimes criticized for having too much structure; human beings are alleged to be "simpler" in reality. If our argument so far has been correct, precisely the opposite seems to be the case: traditional theory has *too little* structure. A person is given *one* preference ordering, and as and when the need arises this is supposed to reflect his interests, represent his welfare, summarize his idea of what should be done, and describe his actual choices and behaviour. Can one preference ordering do all these things? A person thus described may be "rational" in the limited sense of revealing no inconsistencies in his choice behaviour, but if he has no use for these distinctions between quite different concepts, he must be a bit of a fool. The *purely* economic man is indeed close to being a social moron. Economic theory has been much preoccupied with this rational fool decked in the glory of his *one* all-purpose preference ordering. To make room for the different concepts related to his behaviour we need a more elaborate structure.[54]

Since Sen's paper was published, there have been numerous proposals suggesting ways to construct and use multiple utilities or preference rankings (which I treat as identical, given the technical definition of utility used by most scholars), particularly for the purpose of modeling ethical behavior.[55] Some of these elaborate preference structures assume parallel preference orderings that are invoked in different situations, while others posit hierarchical systems in which higher-order preferences have an imperfect supervisory role over the lower-order preferences.[56]

But as we saw in the last chapter, we can model agents who can balance the needs of morality with the pull of inclination with no need for multiple utilities, assuming they have sound judgment which allows them to structure their objective functions to include perfect and imperfect duties, and wills strong enough to follow their judgment in the face of temptation. However, multiple utilities do become necessary when this will fails or, in other words, when we wish to model self-control problems. In such cases, the issue becomes not how to combine multiple utilities or preference rankings to arrive at a single choice, but rather how to distinguish between two radically different methods of making choices, each with their own unique motivational force, and with no overarching method to guarantee that the "best" choice is made.

For the simplest case, we assume two qualitatively different rankings, representing different "paths" the agent can follow. In the situations we are interested in modeling, these paths will be in some sort of conflict, with each having a qualitatively unique allure, as well as its own ethical implications. For instance, one path may lead to a giving life characterized by a altruistic moral code, while the alternative path may be one of pursuing one's narrowly defined self-interest. Perhaps, one may represent living a healthy lifestyle of proper diet and exercise, and the other may be a easier life of sloth and gluttony. Or, one path may involve long-range planning and commitment to one's chosen goals, while the other may represent myopia and acting on impulse. In any case, I will assume that from a moral point of view, the agent has a preferred ranking, the set of options from which she would choose if she could, reflecting a metapreference over her constrained preference rankings.[57] When we adopt a long-term view, or an impersonal one (in acknowledgment of the equal dignity of all persons), we would rather behave altruistically or ethically, pursue "higher" pleasures, or focus on long-term goals (though the particular choice of preferred path is as not important as that there be one). But the opposite in each pair has its own unique pull as well: thinking only of yourself, indulging in "base" pleasures, or living for the moment (to the detriment of future plans) all seem undeniable impulses from time to time. Because of this force, we do not always follow these preferred paths, and in fact we cannot do so perfectly, due to natural human weakness; explicit inclusion of the concept of will in the economic choice model will help explain this.

As I have described it so far, the only Kantian aspect of this part of the model is the role that autonomy plays in allowing the agent to resist following her "lower" path in favor of the "higher" one. If an agent judges that pursuing excellence in gymnastics would be a better way to cultivate her talents than becoming a world-renowned authority on reality television, her autonomy allows her to suppress her desire for television in service of the more difficult-to-achieve goal of Olympic success. But neither choice is dictated or ruled out by considerations of duty; to tie the model of the will to our model of Kantian decision-making from Chapter 1, we can assume that the "higher" path is the one dictated by her judgment out of respect for the moral law and following the applicable duties derived from the categorical imperative, and the "lower" path represents inclination (self-interested or otherwise). In a less direct way, however, setting oneself a task and then sticking to it, regardless of any ethical import accruing to the task itself, can be considered a duty of self-respect, which "would require that one develops and lives by a set of personal standards by which one is prepared to judge oneself even if they are not extended to others."[58] So even a higher path which does not correspond directly to Kantian duty may be supported by duty if it represents a commitment to oneself.

Once we determine the general paths between which the Kantian agent must choose—one based on duty, the other on inclination—the one she follows when confronted with an ethical dilemma will depend on her strength of will rather than deliberate choice. We can represent this strength of will with a simple probability distribution, in which p_H is the likelihood that the agent will follow the "higher" path (corresponding to duty), while p_L (defined as $1- p_H$) is the likelihood that the agent will follow the "lower" path (corresponding to inclination). It is important to note that the agent does not simply "choose" one path or the other like choosing the left or right fork in a road; she would rather follow the higher path, and she tries to follow it, but whether she is successful depends on her strength of will, which is represented by the term p_H. This term can also be interpreted as Kant's virtue, which he defines as "the strength of a human being's maxims in fulfilling his duty."[59] However, a stronger will does not guarantee making the right choice; even the strongest among us fails to do the "right" thing in every instance. But a person with a stronger will is more likely to make the right choice in any given situation; correspondingly, a stronger will would be associated with a higher p_H. Furthermore, as strong as a person may be, even she, on occasion, fails to pursue the right path; for human beings, p_H can never equal one, though it can approach it.[60]

One point regarding the role of the probability terms cannot be emphasized too much (although I will certainly try). The agent does *not* maximize utility over this probability distribution as she would in standard models of choice with uncertainty regarding states of the world (such as a firm choosing its price or output level while facing uncertain market demand or cost conditions), because the probability term p_H does not enter into her process of decision-making.[61] Instead, it represents the outcome of a free *choice* as seen by an outside observer: how likely the agent is, based on her strength of will, to make the right choice of morality over self-interest. This choice, in turn, influences what type of decision she will eventually make, one based on duty or one based on inclination. Also, these probabilities cannot be influenced by the relative "benefits" from using either ranking, in which case higher payoffs on the inclination side could sway the agent's choice between morality and inclination. If this were possible, the entire choice framework would then collapse to a self-interested decision, which would eliminate any true autonomy on the part of the agent.

It is very important to note also that the use of a probability distribution in this model also should not be taken to imply that the agent's choice is random, although it may appear that way to the outside observer (or behaviorist), who sees the dieter walk past the bakery, say, 75 percent of the time, but does not know why.[62] And there is no way to model the choice process that results in this rate of avoidance of tasty pastries, because this probability term represents the outcome of a free, autonomous choice, one in which the dieter somehow manages to walk by the bakery three-fourths of the time, but is weak the other quarter. The "somehow" is meant to invoke that this choice cannot be modeled as the outcome of determinate factors: "what makes the action a psychologically free action is precisely that the antecedent psychological causes were not sufficient to cause it."[63] The use of probabilities is necessary only because there is no way to model the operation of the will in a deterministic fashion; it is a matter of truly free choice—not random, but rather merely inexplicable in psychological terms.[64]

Of course, when we are considering decisions without a moral distinction (even an indirect one such as self-respect), such as what flavor of ice cream to order, the relevant preferences and constraints would be the same in both rankings, in which cases the issue of strength of will is moot.[65] Yet many of our decisions do have a moral component, of course, and this is no less true in the realm of economics. If the reader will forgive me for picking from the low-hanging fruit, I will provide an example from the economic analysis of crime (on which much more to come in Chapter 4). Given the opportunity to commit a crime (which we will regard as immoral), a person who strictly follows duty would not even consider it, while one usually inclined towards self-interest, much like the standard economic agent of mainstream economics, would calculate the costs and benefits according to his preferences (as elaborate and benevolent as they may be). I would like to believe that most of us would not even consider committing a serious crime (such as murder), but as we know all too well, some have and do, either in moments of weakness or as the result of deliberate planning and execution. Those of us with stronger wills, who put more weight on the duty-based ranking, are less likely to commit crimes, even when it is in our "interest" to do so, because we do not even consider it.[66]

Another crime-related topic this model can help us understand is the different effects on behavior of prices and sanctions, wherein prices are charged for legal transactions and sanctions are imposed for illegal activities. An example would be the choice between paying $10 to park your car in a garage or incurring an expected fine of $10 to park in a forbidden area. The typical economic decision-maker would treat the price and the sanction identically, since the expected cost represented by both is equivalent, and the normative aspect of the sanction has no effect on his behavior. To the Kantian agent, the price would be a factor in both the duty-based and inclination-based rankings (being amoral), but the sanction has influence only on the self-interested aspect of the person, whereas the dutiful aspect would not even consider doing it since such action would be blocked by perfect duty. Therefore, in the Kantian model of choice, prices and sanctions become qualitatively different because of the ways that they "speak" to the pursuit of the different paths.[67]

Precedents

Before we examine the probability terms in more detail, I would like to point out some precedents in the literature to this approach of modeling the will and the Kantian individual. In terms of the Kantian literature itself, the Kantian-economic model of choice is generally consistent with other approaches to weakness of will and *akrasia*. Thomas Hill considers weakness of will to be a defect of character, in which the agent displays a lack of self-respect in not fulfilling her own goals, not to mention lapsing in duties and obligations to herself and others.[68] In their paper "Kant and Weakness of Will," Broadie and Pybus understand weakness of will primarily in the sense of contingent rationality, even mentioning a "wedge" between respect for the moral law and subjective determination of the will, very similar to the gap that Searle argues exists in the process of rationality. Finally, Baumgarten may come closest to Searle's language when he writes of akratic action: "Kant understands man as a principally free being who determines his own actions . . . Man is to be regarded as a being who is diverse and complex, and who can therefore decide *even against himself.*"[69]

Turning away from the Kantian literature, the "two paths" component of my model is similar to Steedman and Krause's description of a "Faustian self," a conception of the self which includes many different aspects that must ultimately be integrated to reach a single decision.[70] They assume that an agent has a ranking for each aspect of his person, and a "character formation rule" that picks out one ranking out of the many alternative preference rankings to be the one that is followed. They suggest several formal character formation rules, based on the work of Amartya Sen, John Rawls, and others, but it seems the Kantian model described herein could fit as well. One significant difference between their conception and the one I present here is that the character rule in the Kantian model has an uncertain nature, whereas the examples Steedman and Krause are deterministic. But in the Kantian context, if the agent could always choose which "aspect" to follow, she would follow the moral one, and her will would be perfect by implication. However, Steedman and Krause never explicitly rule out character formation rules that are not conscious or deliberate; it may be up to chance that an agent follows a Rawlsian character rule, for instance. So it seems that their model may have an implicit nondeterministic side also, and therefore may be compatible with my Kantian interpretation of choice.

Sociologist Amitai Etzioni uses a "bi-utility conception" to model moral action in a broadly Kantian framework, with two separate rankings (similar to mine) based on self-interest and morality.[71] In Etzioni's framework, moral and self-interested action provide qualitatively incomparable types of utility (akin to Mill's dichotomy of higher and lower pleasures), rendering them incommensurable and therefore impossible to combine into a single ranking or utility function. In Kantian terms, the troubling aspect of Etzioni's model is that, rather than the purely formal interpretation of utility used here, he assumes that moral behavior provides an agent with psychologically meaningful utility, which he calls "affirmation." Kant recognized this feeling also, of course, but he held that a moral agent can never be motivated by such feeling, but must only experience such a "warm glow" as a result of knowing she acted out of respect for the moral law.[72] As we know from Chapter 1, if moral feeling or satisfaction actually motivates action, then the agent is acting from inclination, not morality (though the act may still be a good one).

A small number of economists have also written (positively) on the will, and in ways that bear some resemblance to my approach. Perhaps the closest is David George, who gives an account of the will similar to that of philosopher Harry Frankfurt: being willful consists of aligning your basic, operative preferences with your higher, preferred ones (or metapreferences).[73] Suppose that, on the simplest level, a person wants to smoke, but on a higher level she wishes she didn't want to smoke. In Frankfurt's terms, she has "freedom of the will" if she can accord her actions with her preferred, higher-order preferences, exhibiting self-control or autonomy (in the general sense). George elaborates on this, speaking instead of a "freer or less free will," a conception which admits various degrees of self-control, which could easily be translated into the probability terms used in my model.[74]

Other papers attempt more formal models of the will, but all paint an exogenous and deterministic picture of it. In a paper subtitled "Towards an Economic Theory of the Will," Robert Cooter analyzes motivational conflict and strength of will with a model that includes a probability term, albeit over risk aversion.[75] Once the agent's risk preference is revealed, she decides deterministically whether to commit a risky act, and weakness of will is inferred when she draws a low risk preference by chance. An exogenous willpower term is also incorporated by Lanse Minkler in his model of commitment integrity, which features "conscious reflection on principles, a commitment to those chosen, and the will."[76] In his model, willpower is a fixed value commensurate with the agent's cardinal utilities that serves to counteract the utility gain from acts that would compromise her commitment integrity, serving as a sort of psychic roadblock to immoral action. George Loewenstein considers including willpower, which he defines as "attempts to suppress viscerally-motivated behaviors that conflict with higher level goals," as a decision variable in behavioral models, and judges that it would "considerably complicate decision-theoretic analyses of behavior." But he adds that "when visceral factors propel behavior in directions that are not commensurate with self-interest . . . decision making models that do not incorporate willpower will be *fatally incomplete*."[77] Finally, Jeong-Yoo Kim includes an exogenous term representing strength of will in his paper on hyperbolic discounting and self-control, which I discuss further in the section on procrastination below.[78] But since all of these conceptions of willpower model it as exogenous to the agent, and as just one more determinant of choice, they do not represent the will as I describe it here: a faculty of true, free choice.[79]

Strengthening or weakening the will

Now we return to the probabilities themselves: what can affect them and how do they change over time? An example may help: suppose Bill has resolved not to eat donuts for health reasons even though he craves them regularly. Bill has a p_H of 75 percent (and a p_L of 25 percent), implying that when in a donut shop to buy coffee, he successfully resists buying donuts three-quarters of the time, but succumbs to temptation one-quarter of the time. When faced by this temptation, he has a dutiful reason not to eat donuts (to improve his health), and an inclination-based reason to eat them (to provide immediate gratification). His best judgment is to abstain, and if his will were perfectly strong, he would always follow the better reason and thereby abstain 100 percent of the time. But as he is human, his will is not perfectly strong, and he resists the donuts only 75 percent of the time.

Is there any way Bill can improve on his p_H of 75 percent? As some would advise, in an attempt to reinforce his ability to follow his better judgment, he may engage in a meta-strategy or coping strategy, such as trying not to be in situations in which he would be tempted (such as being near a donut shop). But the problem is that following such a strategy is no less a matter of will than avoiding donuts; as Elster writes, "to take cold showers in order to develop the strength of will to stop smoking is not a very good strategy if stepping under the cold shower requires the very willpower it is supposed to develop."[80] But it is nonetheless a successful strategy in reducing his consumption of donuts: using the same value of p_H, he successfully chooses to avoid donut shops altogether 75 percent of the time, but wanders into them the other 25 percent; and once there, he succumbs to eating donuts one-quarter of the time. Such a self-restraining strategy would cut his incidence of donut-eating down to 6.25 percent (25 percent of 25 percent). This is where a behaviorist will misinterpret Bill's strength of will; it is not that his p_H is now 93.75 percent, but rather that he takes measures to compensate for his true p_H of only 75 percent. Also, his will has not strengthened; he has merely worked around or accommodating the weakness he has (more on this near the end of this chapter).

This strategy would be even more effective if, as seems natural, Bill's resolve not to go into donut shops is stronger than his resolve to avoid buying donuts once in one (when the sights and smells become strong affects). Accordingly, we can elaborate on the basic framework, allowing people to have a different amount of resolve (different levels of p_H) in some situations than others.[81] One can easily imagine a person who would never think of embezzling money from his employer but may be tempted to have an extramarital affair with a co-worker (or the other way around); some drivers would never think to run a red light, but may exceed the speed limit with impunity. Nor must all decisions be binary in nature; a person may choose between staying sober, indulging in a beer (mild intoxicant), or imbibing hard liquor (heavy intoxicant). However descriptively accurate such a model may be, this formulation would sacrifice the dichotomy of resolve and temptation that I believe is more intuitive. (Also, this decision could easily be transformed into a series of binary choices: the agent chooses whether or not to drink, and if she chooses to drink, she then chooses what to drink.)

But as mentioned above, such strategies do not actually strengthen the will—but is there anything that may? And what about weakening the will? In terms of the Kantian-economic model, how might an agent's probability terms change? We can imagine that Bill's 75/25 percent split holds for "normal" temptations, and as long as only normal temptations are faced (and he resists them 75 percent of the time), these probability terms will remain fairly stable. We would also expect him naturally to succumb more often when faced with relatively great temptations (a fresh batch of his favorite donuts left on his desk), and resist relatively minor ones (a stale, half-eaten donut sitting in the trash bin under discarded coffee grounds and . . . well, you get the idea). But what if the opposite happens: suppose that, against our natural expectations, Bill resists the fresh donuts on his desk—or he raids the garbage can for the stale one. We can call these "extraordinary" temptations (in the literal sense of "unusual," not "large"), and some (including Kant) would say that extraordinary temptations are the true test of our virtue or strength.[82] Succumbing or resisting extraordinary temptations would imply a change in one's will, and this would be reflected in one's p_H and p_L. If Bill succumbs to a relatively insignificant temptation (the stale donut in the trash), that would indicate a weakening of his will (reflected by a fall in his p_H), implying that he is more likely to give in to normal temptations in the future. On the other hand, if he resists the unusually high temptation (the box of fresh donuts left on his desk), that would mean his will has strengthened (reflected by a rise in his p_H).

How exactly would the probabilities change—linearly, proportionally, exponentially, or randomly? There seems to be no obvious answer.

On the one hand, it seems plausible that if someone starts with strong will (high p_H), succumbing to the first extraordinary (weak) temptation she faces would not affect her resolve much, and she may even "snap back" to her original strength of will fairly quickly. But repeated lapses would indicate a significantly weakening will, which be reflected in increasing declines in her p_H.[83] Looking at it from the other direction, if a person with low p_H successfully resists an extraordinary (strong) temptation, this would not likely represent a drastic, sudden strengthening of her resolve (or significant change in her p_H), but if she persistently resisted them, it would gradually and significantly increase her strength (and thereby her p_H). This conception visualizes the will as having a sort of inertia, so an agent's probabilities remain fairly constant until she changes her behavior continuously for a period of time (in a process similar to Bayesian updating).

But it would seem that one can just as easily think that the process may also work the other way: consider a proudly resolute person, who suddenly succumbs to what would normally be a very small temptation. One could imagine that this transgression would have significant effects on her resolve, as it may imply that she had misunderstood and overestimated her own strength of will; she is simply not the person she thought she was, and insofar as her perceptions of her strength affect her actual strength, this realization could be potentially devastating.[84] Along the same lines, a person who is very weak-willed may, upon resisting a significant temptation, experience a significant improvement in her virtue or strength of will, and see her probabilities change accordingly. Rather than displaying inertia, this conception seems to lead toward a equilibrium state between extreme strength and weakness of will, with agents at each extreme eventually heading toward the middle after (inevitably) succumbing to or resisting extraordinary temptations. It may be the case that we cannot solve this problem *a priori*; empirical evidence may be necessary.

We *can* describe, however, how the two types of heteronomy distinguished by Kant—simple weakness and impurity of the will—affect p_H in this model. To be sure, each one lowers resolve, but each in its own way, which will become particularly relevant when we turn to procrastination below. The degree to which an agent is "simply weak," insofar as this is a determinant of p_H, would seem to be more stable, since the impulses (affects) that trigger it are transitory, and do not signal a permanent change in the agent's strength of will or her process of moral deliberation. Nevertheless, maintenance of a certain p_H involves effort, and a relaxation of moral resolve would result in more frequent lapses and thereby a lower p_H. To use the dieting example again, take a person with a p_H of 80 percent, whose 20 percent rate of lapses is based only on simple weakness. We can consider this p_H his "baseline" strength of will, although maintaining it, even in face of simple weakness only, does take a constant exertion of will; otherwise, he would give in every time. As Kant wrote (see below), strength of will develops through practice (as well as contemplation), so if the agent with a p_H of 80 percent can manage, through increased exertion of willpower, to avoid temptations more often, his will may strengthen, and if so his p_H would rise. One's will is only as strong as the obstacles it overcomes, which we can interpret as the frequency, as well as the degree, of each temptation.[85]

Compared to simple weakness, impurity of will, based on the influence of passions, poses a more serious threat to strength of will based on its essential corruptive nature; while affect "produces a momentary loss of freedom and self-control," passion "surrenders both, and finds pleasure and satisfaction in a servile disposition."[86] To some extent, impurity overrules—and eventually lowers—an agent's strength of will (and thereby p_H).[87] There are several ways to think of the impure will in the context of the model developed here. The more complicated (and problematic) way is to hold that the deliberate consideration of inclination in moral choice weakens the strict separation of the higher and lower paths. Rather than representing the likelihood of the agent choosing one path or the other, p_H may instead become somewhat of a linear combination term with which the agent chooses her maxims along some combination of duty and self-love. But blending the two paths is more difficult than it may seem, primarily because the constraints based on perfect duty would have to be weakened and either made commensurate with the agent's preferences (as Minkler does in his model of willpower) or remain probabilistic.

If we want to maintain the separation of the two paths or aspects while modeling the impure will, we can say that as a result of admitting inclination into the determination of her maxims, the agent simply chooses the lesser path more often. As strength "can be recognized only by the obstacles it can overcome, and in the case of virtue these obstacles are natural inclinations, which can come into conflict with the human being's moral resolution," an act of impure will would be one that lacks strength, because it does not even try to restrict the obstacle of temptation by passion.[88] In other words, the impure will gives up or submits to inclination, not even exerting willpower, which would be reflected in a fall in p_H; to the outside observer, the effects of either way of modeling the impure will should be the same, as the agent will be seen to choose along self-interested lines more often. Furthermore, Kant wrote, in reference to virtue or strength, "if it is not rising, [it] is unavoidably sinking."[89] As soon as the agent stops trying to resist inclination, it expands its grasp on her will; as she is more likely to succumb to temptation in the future, her strength has fallen (and her p_H with it). But by the same token, her will can also be made stronger; as Kant also wrote, "the way to acquire [strength] is to enhance the moral *incentive* (the thought of the law), both by contemplating the dignity of the pure rational law in us and by *practicing* virtue."[90] The basic point is that we can never stop fortifying our resolve, or it will atrophy—much like a muscle which is long neglected.

The dynamics of willpower in the Kantian-economic model have much in common with the physiological development of muscle, an analogy developed in the groundbreaking work of psychologist Roy Baumeister and his colleagues.[91] This concept was brought into the philosophical discussion by Richard Holton, who repudiates the Humean desire-belief model primarily on phenomenological grounds, arguing that explaining strength of will by strength of desire does not correspond to our experiences: "It certainly doesn't feel as though in employing willpower one is simply letting whichever is the stronger of one's desires or intentions have its way. It rather feels as though one is actively doing something, something that requires effort."[92] In a survey of the psychological research, Baumeister and Mark Muraven write that "controlling one's own behavior requires the expenditure of some inner, limited resource that is depleted afterward," but also "shows long-term improvement, just as a muscle gets stronger through exercise . . . gaining strength with practice,"[93] and (Heatherton and Baumeister add), "which if left alone becomes flaccid."[94] This theory complements the Kantian analysis above in that it provides psychological support for the dynamics of strength of will, in particular the implication that the will can be strengthened with continued use.

There are other aspects of this literature that resemble the analysis of the will herein. For instance, Baumeister and Heatherton write of "transcendence . . . a matter of focusing awareness beyond the immediate stimuli (i.e., transcending the immediate situation)," which may be considered analogous to the Kantian/Stoic concept of moral apathy (or, more generally, autonomy).[95] In the same paper, they also write of "acquiescence," of persons giving in to undesirable impulses rather than fighting them, similar to the actions of an impure will versus simple weakness.[96] These parallels suggest that the Kantian model of will can fruitfully be integrated with the research based on the work of Baumeister and his colleagues.[97] But for now, we turn our focus to one specific behavior in which most of us regularly experience problems with strength and weakness of will: procrastination.

Procrastination: An Application

To illustrate the Kantian-economic model of choice, and especially its handling of strength and weakness of will, we will think about procrastination, which George Ainslie calls the "basic impulse" and "as fundamental as the shape of time," and which may be the most common and widespread instance of weakness of will.[98] Many of us, if not most of us, procrastinate with respect to particular tasks some of the time, and some of us persistently procrastinate at certain tasks most of the time. Other common cases of weakness of will or *akrasia* can also be understood to incorporate features of procrastination: one component of the failure to control one's eating, for instance, can be considered procrastination with regard to starting a diet or exercise program.

In general terms, weakness of will has been discussed and debated by philosophers since Plato and Aristotle, but modern debate over the phenomenon is generally dated to Donald Davidson's classic 1970 paper "How Is Weakness of Will Possible?"[99] Though precise definitions differ, weakness of will is generally considered to describe or explain actions taken against one's better judgment: Judy has one more drink when she has to drive later, Jack has dessert against his doctor's orders, and Josephine cheats on her husband even though she knows it is wrong. In each of these cases of akratic action, the person knows which is the better action, but fails to do it, succumbing to another drive, passion, or urge; there is "a coming apart of the motivational force of the agent's wants from his assessment of the objects of those wants."[100]

Nonetheless, there are significant disagreements among philosophers regarding the deeper aspects of weakness of will, especially concerning whether actions resulting from weakness of will are irrational, intentional, or free. Most agree that acting against one's best judgment is always irrational, almost by definition, though some disagree, based on different understandings of rationality itself.[101] There is also debate over which act was actually intended—the one that was judged best but not taken, or the one taken but judged to be inferior.[102] Jack may have intended to skip dessert but indulged nonetheless; did he change his intention, or just act against it? And if he acted against his intention, was his action free, or was it compelled?[103] This last question has obvious implications for moral responsibility, and also reflects the large amount of overlap between weakness of will and addiction (as well as other instances of practical irrationality).[104]

Numerous economists and scholars from related fields have also weighed in on weakness of will, usually presenting it in terms of problems of self-control or self-management.[105] Their goals are not as much to conceptualize or analyze it as to model its causes and effects and then devise methods to help cope with it. However, despite frequently brilliant insights into human behavior, all such explanations fail to capture the central aspect of weakness of will, for one simple reason: as he is commonly understood, the economic agent has *no will to be weak*. As we discussed earlier in this chapter, "choice" in standard economic models is wholly determined by the agent's preferences, information, and (exogenous) constraints. Once he processes all of this information, he acts on it, period. But in cases of weakness of will, there is a disconnect between reason (or judgment, also absent from economic models) and action; the two do not coincide, as they do in economic models by construction. This is made evident by the fact that economists' recommendations for enhancing self-control involve modifying preferences and payoffs (such as the establishment of reward or punishment mechanisms) or restricting choice sets (like Ulysses' ordering himself tied to the mast), but never strengthening the will itself, because their models lack such a concept. But in the Kantian-economic model of choice developed in this chapter, weakness of will is a characteristic of choice, reflected in the extent to which the probability term p_H is less than one. As such, we were able to think about how to influence willpower itself, rather than accommodate and work around an agent's present strength (or weakness) of will.

As we saw above, most philosophers also share a disdain for the concept of a dedicated faculty of the will; as with economists, this stands in the way of an accurate conception of weakness of will. But there are dissenters; for example, John Searle argues, based on his idea of necessary gaps in rationality where true choice resides, that weakness of will occurs in the gap between intention and action: "because of the inevitability of conflicting desires and other motivators, for most premeditated actions there will be the possibility that when the time comes to perform the action the agent will find himself confronted with desires not to do the thing he has made up his mind to do."[106] Weakness of will is only a problem in traditional action theory because the desire-belief model (like the constrained preference-satisfaction model of economics) holds that reasons must lead directly and deterministically to action.

Consistent with their approaches to weakness of will in general, economists and philosophers have also written extensively and brilliantly on the causes of procrastination. But I argue that they have dealt with only one side of the problem, describing, often in excruciating detail (especially the economists), the reasons why procrastination is attractive to us at the time we choose it: salience, hyperbolic discounting, and so on. But while such scholars can explain why agents do or do not have incentives or preferences to procrastinate, they cannot explain why, in the face of such incentives, agents nonetheless sometimes manage to resist the urge to procrastinate. As Korsgaard writes, "sometimes to our own pleasant surprise . . . we find ourselves doing what we think we ought to do, in the teeth of our own reluctance, and even though nothing obvious forces us to do it."[107] But this suppression of preferences and inclinations is only possible if we recognize the existence of the will as an independent faculty of choice.

In terms of combating the urge to procrastinate, most economists and philosophers make the same recommendations as they do for weakness of will or self-control problems in general: manipulate the relevant costs and benefits, often through changes made in the choice environment, so that delay against better judgment is no longer "chosen" through myopic decision-making processes. But as we saw above, this does not solve weakness of will as much as it avoids or sidesteps it altogether. Someone who locks her refrigerator to block late-night binges has not exhibited a strong will—she has merely accounted for the weak will she will have later by changing the payoffs now, before temptation strikes, and when her will is somewhat stronger.

Based on the Kantian-economic model of choice and the faculty of will it assumes, I suggest an alternative to the various coping strategies suggested in the literature.[108] Rather than circumvent or account for her weakness of will, the agent can exercise her strength of will; simply put, she can *try harder.* In the same way that modern labor-saving devices have made us physically weaker (and heavier) compared to previous generations, I argue that the proliferation of coping mechanisms has made our wills weaker. This is not entirely a negative thing, of course; technological and institutional developments that economize on effort can be very beneficial, but only if they allow effort to be redirected to a more productive use. Most of us have little need for significant physical strength in our everyday lives; those of us who exercise do so primarily to improve our health or appearance. But we have no gyms or health clubs for our will, and I would argue that in the modern world we have occasion to need strength of will more often than muscular strength. If we ever lose access to our coping mechanisms, our willpower is all we have to fall back on, and we will be sorely disappointed if we find it lacking due to repeated neglect.

Economists' perspectives on procrastination

Previous work on procrastination by economists has focused on the structure of preferences that leads to such behavior, and they have analyzed a fair range of possible circumstances in which procrastination will arise.[109] The first prominent economist to address procrastination directly was George Akerlof, who based his understanding of procrastination on the *salience,* or vividness, of the costs of the arduous present task: "Procrastination occurs when present costs are unduly salient in comparison with future costs, leading individuals to postpone tasks until tomorrow without foreseeing that when tomorrow comes, the required action will be delayed yet again."[110] Akerlof emphasizes the costs of delaying the task, due to the exaggerated weight given the salient costs.

In a series of papers since 1999 which elaborated on Akerlof's conception, Ted O'Donoghue and Matthew Rabin have examined procrastination in several new contexts. To explain procrastination, they focused on *present-biased preferences*, which they consider "a more descriptive term for the underlying human characteristic that hyperbolic discounting represents,"[111] and which are functionally equivalent to Akerlof's salience (with less of an implication that they are not "real" preferences). Consistent with hyperbolic discounting, "when considering trade-offs between two future moments, present-biased preferences give stronger relative weight to the earlier moment as it gets closer."[112] In another paper, they analyzed principals' options for countering their agents' tendencies to procrastinate, basically arguing that penalties for delay must be increased for such agents to counteract their present-bias effects.[113] In a later paper they elaborated on their basic model by introducing multiple tasks and tasks of varying importance.[114] They argued that introducing a new task with higher long-run benefit may prompt the agent to switch to that task, but if it also has high present costs, the agent will procrastinate with respect to it; this is based on the observation that task choice and timing choice are made differently, and can counteract each other. This also implies that more important projects, which may have higher upfront costs, invite more procrastination. Most recently, they discussed procrastination in multi-stage projects, arguing that projects with high start-up costs but lower finishing costs never get started (due to procrastination), while projects with low start-up costs but high finishing costs get started, but not finished (again due to procrastination).[115]

In her paper "Read This Paper Later," Carolyn Fischer eschews time inconsistency, developing a model of procrastination with time-consistent preferences, using simple marginal analysis of the trade-off between work and leisure.[116] Given a fixed amount of time to perform a task, such as writing a paper, and a (time-consistent) preference for present leisure, the agent will postpone the task until there is just enough time to finish the task; furthermore, this is utility-maximizing. The problem, however, lies in interpreting this behavior as procrastination, rather than rational time-allocation (based on time preference), as a later paper of Fischer's acknowledges.[117] In that paper, she utilizes time-inconsistent preferences instead, focusing on hyperbolic discounting and "differential discounting," by which the utility from leisure is discounted at a higher rate than returns from work. (She links this to Akerlof's salience, as well as arguing that preferences based on differential discounting can appear hyperbolic.)

This is just a sampling of economists' work on procrastination, but I think they represent the dominant approach to studying the phenomenon. The problem with all of these explanations is that they focus on preferences or utility; in these models, it is the conflict among different sets or types of preferences that leads to the self-control problem. These models provide truly fascinating insights into the motivations behind procrastination, but they cannot escape the tyranny of preferences, and therefore cannot explain how the agent may resist the pull of his preferences and *choose* not to procrastinate. For that, we need a model that acknowledges that agents can somehow override their preferences—for instance, by exerting willpower.

Procrastination and the Kantian-economic model of will

For our purposes, I regard procrastination as a temporally oriented variation of weakness of will or *akrasia*, in which an agent is likely to put off performing (relatively) disagreeable tasks against her better judgment, rather than enduring the displeasure now; or, as Andreou defines it, "those cases of delaying in which one leaves too late or puts off indefinitely what one should—relative to one's ends and information—have done sooner."[118] As summarized above, economists also see procrastination as a variation of weakness of will, representing it as a self-control problem and explaining it by detailing the nature of the preferences that make procrastination attractive to the agent. Either their choice situation leads them to procrastinate or it does not—if it does, then they can manipulate the choice situation ahead of time such that they are no longer led to procrastinate when the time comes. But none of these scholars (with one qualified exception noted below) incorporates the role of the will in their models of procrastination, and therefore none of them can explain how people, while facing these strong incentives to procrastinate, nonetheless sometimes resist the urge to do so. As Christine Korsgaard writes, rather stirringly (and recognizably),

> Suppose I decide to get some work done on my book today. At this moment, now, I decide, I *will*, to work; at the next moment, at any moment (importantly, maybe even at *this* moment), I will certainly *want* to stop. If I am to work I must *will* it—and that means I must determine myself to stay on its track. Timidity, idleness, and depression will exert their claims in turn, will attempt to control or overrule my will, to divert me from my work. Am I to let these forces determine my movements? At each moment I must say to them: "I am not you; my will is this work."[119]

In the context of the Kantian-economic model of choice with its "higher" and "lower" paths, procrastination (with respect to a generic task or goal) takes the form of the lesser path, and timely action is the higher path. But why is this so? If procrastination delays the performance of an act required by duty—especially if the timing of the act is crucial, as in keeping a promised appointment—the ethical status of procrastination is clear, but it derives from the duty itself, not from procrastination with respect to it. But what if the potential delay involves something trivial, such as starting piano lessons, or dropping in on an old friend?

We can consider procrastination with regard to even such amoral tasks as a failure of duty of self-respect. According to Thomas Hill, weakness of will in general represents a violation of duty to oneself insofar as one fails to follow through on one's goals and plans (at the appropriate time) as previously deliberated upon.[120] As he writes, "in their characteristic pattern of making and breaking resolutions, the weak-willed do not display full respect for themselves as rational deliberative agents."[121] By definition, rational agents make plans for a reason, and self-respect demands that these plans be followed through on, unless there are rational arguments—not weak-willed rationalizations—for reconsidering them. "Respecting oneself as a rational agent does not require blindly following prior resolutions in all circumstances; but also it does not require, and may even rule out, trying to deliberate anew in each situation one faces."[122] This lack of self-respect, in addition to the effects on the agent's self-esteem and possibly on other people, lead Hill to conclude that weakness of will (and procrastination) often "interfere with living by the demands and ideals of morality."[123]

Understood this way, the Kantian-economic model implies that an agent has a certain likelihood of resisting procrastination based on her strength of will. Regardless of the incentives she faces, procrastination represents the lesser path, the choice favoring inclination (to delay performing the task) over duty (not to procrastinate), and therefore the perfectly autonomous agent would never choose to procrastinate. Even if circumstances change to make procrastination more attractive, the ideal autonomous agent would not be tempted, though the heteronomous agent may be.[124] Of course, as Kant was well aware, none of us is a perfectly autonomous agent, for we are all at least weak to some degree, if not impure of will. Most of us, at one time or another, have succumbed to momentary impulse—our favorite television program is on (again), the task at hand just seems particularly unbearable at the moment, and so forth. If one's will is strong (p_H is high), this will occur only occasionally, and it occurs more often if the will is weaker. Furthermore, if the "rational" incentives to procrastinate do not enter into our decision-making formally, simple weakness is all there is to it. The agent still has a duty to strengthen her will or virtue, but she is not a bad person for her weakness.

However, deliberate rational consideration of the incentives to procrastinate—the factors identified in so much detail by economists—would signal an impure will, for these elements would never be considered by an autonomous agent, or even a merely weak one, in determining her maxim.[125] Admittedly, if an agent with an impure will can manipulate her environment in such a way as to render procrastination less attractive, she will procrastinate less, and no one will deny that this is a good outcome. Kant's original description of an impure will focuses on one whose inclinations are oriented toward good, in which case inclination and duty lead to the same action. But the practical danger remains, as with any instance of mixed motivation, that inclination will sometimes dominate choice, and it will not always correspond to duty. So, morally speaking, it is preferable to resist procrastination through an act of will, rather than to rely on one's inclination based on deliberate manipulation of the choice environment. A person's will, being a core aspect of her character or identity (as I will argue in Chapter 3), is more essential to her "self" and less contingent on the details of a particular situation or environment, and exerting it will develop it further, so future exertions will not seem so difficult (though they will be no less necessary).

So far, we have only discussed isolated incidents of procrastination, which are troubling enough. But of even greater concern is persistent or chronic procrastination, the type that we find so hard to combat and to dig out from under, and which poses the greatest threat to the achievement of our goals. There are two ways to explain persistent procrastination within the context of the Kantian-economic model. The simpler theory is to posit a simply weak will—someone with a p_H of 80 percent will procrastinate in one-fifth of the relevant choice situations, independent of whether she procrastinated previously (or how often). Suppose such an agent faces the possibility of procrastination today, and there is a 20 percent chance she will succumb to it. If the possibility arises again tomorrow, she will face the same chance of procrastination (20 percent) regardless of her action the day before.[126] Looking forward from the start of her series of actions, the likelihood of a longer procrastination diminishes—the agent will experience two subsequent days of procrastination 4 percent (20 percent x 20 percent) of the time, three subsequent days 0.8 percent of the time, and so forth. Therefore, the Kantian-economic model of choice implies that the chances of a simple weak-willed person succumbing to persistent or chronic procrastination is relatively small, though it will happen on occasion. Therefore, we may want to look for another explanation for chronic procrastination within the model, and we find it in the impure will.

The dynamics of willpower in the Kantian-economic model (and the willpower-as-muscle conception discussed above) would suggest that procrastination (or resistance to it) would be self-reinforcing, so succumbing to procrastination in one situation would lower one's strength of will (and p_H) before encountering the next similar situation. For example, putting off grading exams to watch one TV show leads to higher chances of doing it with the next show, and possibly even the next time exams need to be graded. For the merely weak person, it seems unlikely that this would occur; such a person may repeatedly exhibit weakness, as described above, and may even experience a "slide" in strength of will due to an occasional increase in lapses. But I have argued that, insofar as p_H is due to simple weakness, in which the will is less corruptible by outside factors, strength or virtue is fairly robust. However, if an agent's procrastination is based on the influence of an impure will, which corrupts itself, then we would expect her resolve (and her p_H) to fall as the agent continues to procrastinate, leading to a "procrastination trap." Recall that the impure will represents laxity in resolve; the will (which is to say the agent herself) simply gives up trying to resist the pull of inclination, and instead admits its influence into her decision-making when she constructs her maxims. In other words, impurity of the will implies that the influences identified by economists hold sway—influences which, as described above, may lead to less procrastination, but for reasons that will disappear if the incentives change for the worse.

In either case, in the context of the Kantian-economic model, the agent still has a way out of the procrastination trap, no matter how long she has been in it—she can choose to break it through an act of will or volition. She can exercise her autonomy or inner freedom and choose to resist the temptation, perhaps stronger than ever, to continue to procrastinate. This is bound to happen eventually; as long as p_H does not diminish completely, there is always some willpower left, some reserve of strength the agent can summon up to resist inclination and follow the dictates of duty. But obviously, the sooner she does this, the less time she will spend in a procrastination trap.

Precedents

There are several scholars whose analyses of procrastination have much in common with the ideas presented herein. George Ainslie argues that willpower properly refers to the ability of agents to link their present actions to their future ones, so that procrastination today will be seen to lead to repeated procrastination in the future through a process of recursive self-prediction.[127] Rather than rely on external manipulation of the choice situation, Ainslie advocates an internal restructuring of the relevant costs and benefits of acting at the prudent time rather than procrastinating.[128] The formation of personal rules—preferably with bright lines precisely demarcating approved and disapproved behavior—is one example: a person establishes a rule for herself, which motivates her to resist the temptation to violate it if she believes that failing to resist this time will make future resistance less likely (a preemptive use of the procrastination trap logic). If I believe that a donut eaten today, in violation of a personal rule against eating donuts, will lead to eating donuts every day thereafter, I vest today's decision with the enormous consequences of continuous failure, and will more likely pass up the donut today.

In order to achieve some degree of self-control, Ainslie does recommend that agents reassess their incentives internally rather than rely on manipulation of the external environment, with which I am in accord.[129] However, it falls short of the Kantian ideal, because the agent is still making decisions based on her incentives or inclinations (albeit consciously and strategically manipulated ones) rather than making choices based on duty alone. Granted, this manipulation of incentives may have been done out of duty—as, too, external manipulations may be—but this is nonetheless an indirect way to act out of respect for the moral law. Such effort would not have to be invested in manipulation of incentives, whether internal or external, if agents would devote effort instead to increasing their strength of will or volition, and thereby their capacity to transcend the impact of incentives and inclinations altogether.

Among economists studying procrastination, Jeong-Yoo Kim is unique in that he does employ a version of willpower to explain resistance to it, as well as the persistence of procrastination when resistance fails.[130] He posits an "unconscious working of will, an automatic process of pre-programmed mechanism (will) that tends to resist yielding to temptation," a mechanism which "is like a machine that only responds stochastically" to incentives to procrastinate.[131] This fixed measure of willpower, together with a person's imperfect perception of her own willpower (which is determined by past actions), contributes to a probability function, the "success function," a random draw from which determines her actual resolve. Because of this understanding, "the actual choice cannot be viewed as the result of a conscious mental process," but is instead simply random.[132] Therefore, whether one procrastinates or resists is just a matter of luck, and also has an effect on the probability of success in the future through a change in her perception of her strength of will.

While the model presented in this chapter does present the actual choice as a conscious and free one, Kim's explanation of perpetual procrastination bears significant similarity to mine, in that both of our models depict a progressive decline in willpower. Where I differ from Kim is in the nature of willpower; he regards the basic measure of willpower as fixed, with the agent's success at resolve influenced also by her self-percep-tion. As a result, her realized willpower (taking into account her self-per-ception) can be stronger or weaker than her fixed willpower, which never changes. While I recognize the possible relevance of self-perception in the operation of the will, I would argue that any influence of it would be on a person's willpower itself—in other words, I see no relevant distinction between actual, self-perceived, and effective willpower. If a person loses faith in her willpower, her willpower declines, period. As she succeeds in exerting her willpower, her belief in herself grows, and her willpower grows as well. But I see no reason why Kim's model could not be modified to make the effect in willpower more direct in this way.

It has been my contention that procrastination can be avoided, not only by indirect measures such as externally manipulating the choice en-vironment or internally reconceptualizing the costs and benefits of acting now, but directly by exerting one's willpower. Willpower is certainly not omnipotent, but it is nearly omnipresent, unlike contingently available external crutches, and its exercise serves to strengthen it for future use, making one less reliant on costly external coping mechanisms in the long run. In such cases of insufficient resolve, we must rely on such mecha-nisms, as most economists, philosophers, and psychologists recommend. But we must also recognize that sometimes these extrapsychic tools are not available, feasible, or cost-effective. It is then that we find we must rely on our willpower, but if we have let our "muscles" wither through neglect, we will find them missing when we need them most.

In this chapter, we discussed the importance of the will, the agent's faculty of choice, without which she is merely a vessel through which her desires and beliefs cause actions, leaving the "agent" with no more indepen-dent influence in the world than a computer. That is what I find lacking and dehumanizing in situationism, which holds that the particular details of a choice situation play a much larger role in explaining the resulting behavior than consistent character traits do.[133] But without character traits to describe how we process and react to situations, who are we, and what remains to make each of us unique? Are we just biological machines, reacting to exter-nal stimuli according to our evolutionary programming? I hope not, but if we are more than that, then what is that extra something that makes me *me* and you *you*? I believe that something is each person's unique capacities of judgment and will, which together make up what I call her *character*. As I argue in the next chapter, it is an agent's unique character that identifies her as an individual, both in the metaphysical sense of identity (which demands that individuals be individuated from each other as well as identified through time) as well as practical identity, or who we are when we act.

CHAPTER 3

Individual in Essence, Social in Orientation

The first two chapters of this book focused on the more technical details of Kant's moral philosophy, such as the categorical imperative, the nature of duties, and the operation and strength of the will. In this chapter, I want to pull back a bit from the trees and bring the forest into view, eschewing the technical details and focusing instead on *character*, which I regard as including both judgment (from Chapter 1) and the will (from Chapter 2). I do this in order to steer the discussion toward a general Kantian view of the economic individual, and explain how this individual differs from both the *homo economicus* of neoclassical economics and other conceptions brought forward by philosophers, sociologists, and heterodox economists (especially social economists). The thesis that I defend in this chapter is that the economic agent is *individual in essence* and *social in orientation*. A person's autonomy implies that she is an individual who makes choices of her own judgment and will, and, recognizing the equal dignity of other persons, she is led to take those other persons into account in her autonomous decision-making. To that end, the first part of the chapter will focus on individualism, and the second will focus on sociality, both implied by the same reading of Kantian dignity and autonomy that I emphasized in the first two chapters (and which continues throughout the book).

Individual in Essence

I have three goals for this part of the chapter. First, I will defend the way in which the Kantian-economic model represents the individual and compare it to atomism, an aspect of the standard economic individual which is widely derided by heterodox economists, and its opposite, social embeddedness. I will defend a limited sense of atomism as an implication of autonomy that itself implies sociality rather than an asocial orientation in which the agent has no regard for other people. True to autonomy, an agent's decision is her own, independent from any inside or outside controlling influence, but she may—and often should—allow influences from many sources, especially a concern for her fellow human beings. In other words, atomism describes *how* you make choices, and sociality comes from *what* choices you make. Properly understood, atomism describes the process of choice rather than its content; the Kantian-economic agent autonomously and atomistically makes socially oriented decisions (consistent with a specific understanding of social embeddedness).

Second, I will discuss several concepts of identity as they apply to the Kantian individual. In 2003, John B. Davis published *The Theory of the Individual in Economics*, a groundbreaking work in which he analyzes and rejects the neoclassical conception of the individual. Using concepts of identity theory from philosophy, Davis argues that this neoclassical conception, which identifies the individual with his preferences, can neither individuate agents at any given time (because two persons may share the same preferences) nor identify an agent throughout time (because, contrary to standard heuristic assumptions, preferences can and do change over time). More constructively, he argues for an essentially socialized conception of the individual and argues that, ironically, social embeddedness provides a better basis for identifying the economic individual than the atomistic conception of neoclassical economics.

I agree with Davis that an agent's social bonds and roles are very important, particularly to her sociality (to be discussed in the second part of this chapter), but they fall short of defining her identity. Rather, building on the discussion in Chapter 2, I argue that an individual is defined, individuated, and identified over time by her unique character, made up of her judgment and will; after all, what can be more intrinsic to a person than her faculties of deliberation and choice? In the final section of this part of the chapter, I will borrow from the recent work of philosopher Christine Korsgaard on practical identity and self-constitution to explain how an individual's character is self-created and maintained by her choices and actions, and how this interacts with her preferences as well as the social aspects of her identities in a reflexive process, which leads into the discussion of sociality in the second half of the chapter.

Individualism, atomism, and social embeddedness

As we know, Kantian dignity endows persons with an immeasurable, incomparable value or worth, which demands respect from others as well as from themselves. But dignity is not primary; it derives from autonomy, the capacity for self-governance that separates humans from beasts. An autonomous person is a self-aware agent: she acts in the world, she knows she acts in the world, and she chooses how she acts in the world. More precisely, she determines for herself the laws that guide her decisions and her actions, without undue or unreflective influence from either external or internal factors, and then chooses to act according to those laws. To the extent that others deceive or coerce her, they are failing to respect her dignity; to the extent that she allows "alien" influences to corrupt her judgment or her will, she fails to respect her own dignity (and therefore herself).

Based on this sense of autonomy, I maintain that the Kantian economic agent is strictly individual in terms of her capacity for free choice, which in turn must conform to the laws of her own cognition and conation, and through which all other influences must be filtered. These influences, the myriad factors that may affect her choice, may be deeply social in nature. She may consider the feelings and wellbeing of her family, her friends, her co-workers, the members of her community—and indeed, in the appropriate context, she should (as we shall see in the second part of this chapter). She may consider how she herself fits into the web of sociality which she has woven around her; she may value her family ties more than her work-related ties, or seek to strengthen her community ties at the risk of weakening some ties with friends from "back home." And she may be urged by various persons in her circle to do certain things and refuse to do others. But regardless of the salience of these aspects of choice, the moral law must be supreme, and she must make a choice which is consistent with her judgment, whether it is in conformity with these social factors or in opposition to them. Particularly in the case of perfect duty, she cannot allow any other considerations to affect her resolve to perform that duty (except when it indicates a conflicting obligation). Only in cases of imperfect duties (such as beneficence), which do not demand a specific act but rather a general but sincere attitude, or an apparent conflict of duties, can these obligations be fulfilled with a mind to empirical social factors.

Autonomy demands that we reflect on our preferences and incentives, subjecting all the various aspects of them to our judgment (based on the moral law) when appropriate, and endorse them only when they are not in opposition to our moral character.[1] When a person makes a choice, she must be sure that the choice is truly hers, and that she has made it in the best way she can, consistent with the spirit of the moral law. If someone asks her to do something, she cannot automatically do it like an animal following a command or a computer executing a program. If the request is innocuous—"please pass me the sports section"—then her judgment is not invoked; but if the request is morally questionable—"if my wife asks, don't tell her you saw me here"—she must reflect on whether the requested action is something she could do in good conscience. If she blindly "obeys," she is allowing herself to be used as a tool, a mere means to another's end. If, after reflection, she chooses to go along with the planned ruse, then she has made her own choice, voluntarily inserting herself into the causal chain of events, and she is therefore responsible for the consequences. Autonomy implies responsibility, not just to make the right choices, but for the consequences of the bad ones.

The Kantian-economic person's choice is hers and hers alone, and in this sense she is an individual agent. How does this conception compare with *atomism*, which John Davis describes as "the idea that individuals are fully autonomous beings in the sense of possessing independent choice sets"?[2] If atomism is taken to deny any other-regarding preferences or inclinations, where external factors are limited to impersonal constraints (prices, opportunities, and the like), then this does not apply to the Kantian-economic individual at all. She is certainly not blind to others, their pleasures and pains, their needs and desires—nor is she blind to her own desires and needs concerning others. But she does put these needs and desires, others' as well as her own, in the proper context, and does not let them unduly influence her choices when they conflict with the moral law. Part of this is a matter of judgment—knowing when such factors should count and when they should not—as well as her will—being able to resist such factors when they threaten the execution of her best judgment. But the Kantian-economic agent is not atomistic in the sense of making choices in isolation from the concerns of (or regarding) other people.

Nonetheless, there is an essential atomistic element to the Kantian individual implied by autonomy: the *process* of choice is atomistic in that, at bottom, the individual makes her own choices, making use of outside factors only when she judges it appropriate. Furthermore, the second part of this chapter emphasizes that Kantian duty *requires* that external influences and concerns play an important role much of the time, orienting the essential individualistic agent in a very social way. Remember that even the universalization procedure based on the Formula of Autonomy depends on social knowledge; for example, lying is shown to be self-defeating because of the effect of universalized lying on trust, an inherently social concept. Social knowledge is also essential for the proper operation of judgment in choosing applicable duties (or resolving conflicts between obligations) and then tailoring the chosen action to the particular (social) situation. Finally, as Andrews Reath writes, autonomous action in the world "presupposes a background of rules and social practices, or better, a system of reasoners able to exercise the same capacities, and limited only by the principle of using their reason in ways that other agents can accept while at the same time continuing to view themselves as autonomous."[3] But regardless of the social context of any specific decision situation, and how much the agent may incorporate social information about it into her deliberation, at the end, her choice is hers and her alone—by virtue of her autonomy, it is essentially and necessarily atomistic.[4]

Atomism is often contrasted with social embeddedness; these are the two opposing views of the individual analyzed by Davis in *The Theory of the Individual in Economics* and other work, representing the views of mainstream and heterodox economics (especially social economics). In Davis's words, "the difference between these two conceptions rests on whether individuals and their behavior are explained 'externally' in terms of their social relationships or 'internally' in terms of their private tastes and preferences."[5] But I regard this as a false dichotomy, or at least a non-exhaustive pair. Choices, behavior, and actions can certainly be explained, at least in part, by social factors such as relationships, roles, and norms, as well as by the agent's own preferences, beliefs, and values, which themselves may be influenced by social factors.[6] But the process by which all of these enter deliberation, as implied by Kantian autonomy, is strictly internal. For instance, Mark Lutz, another prominent social economist, writes that "persons as *social individuals* are embedded in a constitutive web of social relations: they value persons and evaluate institutions as to their responsiveness to people."[7] Once again, this is no problem for the Kantian individual, since it does not address the process of decision-making, but only its domain, which can (and should) include social factors, subject to endorsement by judgment.

There are obvious dangers in failing to exercise judgment in the face of social factors. Economic sociologist Mark Granovetter, in a seminal paper on social embeddedness, cautions that this concept can be taken too far, and can result in just as much atomistic choice as under-socialized individualism can:

A fruitful analysis of human action requires us to avoid the atomization implicit in the theoretical extremes of under- and oversocialized conceptions. Actors do not behave or decide as atoms outside a social context, nor do they adhere slavishly to a script written for them by the particular intersection of social categories that they happen to occupy.[8]

Granovetter's point is very Kantian in spirit: persons can certainly take their social roles and relationships into account when making choices, but to be autonomous they must make these choice themselves, after adequate reflection, rather than blindly following what is expected of them by others. Davis agrees, writing that "the idea of pure embedding is an unsustainable conception," as does Lutz, who writes that social economics properly "includes decision makers who function neither as mechanical atoms nor as subordinated cells nourished and controlled by social processes."[9]

But perhaps the process of judgment is not so atomistic after all; we have seen that social factors inform judgment, but they may go even deeper than that. As Hodgson writes,

Individual choice requires a conceptual framework to make sense of the world. The reception of information by an individual requires a paradigm or cognitive frame to process and make sense of that information. The acquisition of this cognitive apparatus involves processes of socialization and education, involving extensive interaction with others. The means of our understanding of the world are necessarily acquired through social relationships and interactions. *Cognition is a social as well as an individual process. Individual choice is impossible without these institutions and interactions.*[10]

The ideal would be for the autonomous person to reflect on these social factors as they are incorporated into her cognitive processes, but doing so is clearly unrealistic: many if not most of this activity occurs at a subconscious level, and long before we reach any level of mental maturity. Nonetheless, once maturity is reached, the autonomous agent will reflect on her ways of thinking, and in the process she may discover that some categories she uses (perhaps ones based on racial stereotypes, for example) are improper or immoral, and then try to revise her conceptualization of these issues in respect of the equal dignity of all. (We will discuss reflection and endorsement in the context of the self-constitution of character further below.) And even if social factors run deep into the process of cognition, as long as choice is not determined by any antecedent psychological causes (including those operating on cognition itself, itself a psychological process), there must always be an element of choice that is completely free, and that part is autonomous and atomistic in nature.

In conclusion, the Kantian individual can be very socially embedded in terms of her preferences, influences on her judgment, and her cognitive processes themselves, but at bottom her choices are still her own, which, as I will argue next, defines the nature of the individual that distinguishes her and persists over time. And since this individualism is based on autonomy and dignity, it demands respect and also implies normative or political individualism, as detailed in the next two chapters.

Identity and character

The preceding discussion of atomism and social embeddedness primarily dealt with the proper inclusion of external (social) factors in one's moral deliberation. But, as we know, autonomy also requires an agent to allow her own preferences and inclinations to influence her decision-making only after being endorsed by her judgment (in concert with the moral law). But mainstream economists typically identify the individual with her preferences, so denying her preferences when they conflict with duty would mean denying that which makes her who she is.

This conception of the individual defined by preferences, however, has been thoroughly criticized. In chapter 3 of *The Theory of the Individual in Economics*, Davis argues convincingly (and conclusively) that an individual cannot be identified by her preferences, for reasons drawn from two philosophical identity conditions, identification over time and individuation of persons at any one time. At the risk of oversimplifying Davis's detailed account, simply put, preferences change (contrary to economists' standard heuristic assumption), rendering identification over time using preferences impossible; and preferences are not necessarily unique to each person, making it impossible to use preferences to distinguish between individuals. So preferences are not stable enough to represent who we are over time, nor do they pick out individuals as unique. It follows that if and when a person makes choices without considering her preferences, or even against them, she should not feel she is denying part of herself. In fact, I would argue (as I do in the next section) that she is expressing her true self, the self that lies beneath her mere desires and preferences—in other words, her character (made up of her judgment and will).

But maybe we are setting up an economic straw man with all this talk of preferences; despite economists' methodological strategies, surely no one thinks that a person's favorite flavor of ice cream defines *who she is*.[11] Many people would be more likely to identify themselves with their positions on weighty social issues: abortion, torture, affirmative action, universal health care, the role of the state, and the like. Certainly opinions on such issues, which are more likely to manifest themselves in principles than in "enlightened" preferences, say much more about who a person is than ordinary commodity preferences do. But these opinions, if they are well-informed and reflective, are based on values that derive from one's judgment, and the determination to act on those values—or even simply to express them in front of an unsympathetic audience—reflect one's strength of will. For both reasons, opinions do show more of who a person is, but only because they are so closely related to her judgment and will, which is to say, her character.

But others reject such an internalist view of the individual altogether, and look outward, rather than inward, to identify the individual. They may identify her by her social roles and ties: she is a daughter, sister, wife, partner, mother, aunt, grandmother; she is an employer, employee, partner (in a professional sense), associate, intern; she is a friend, confidante, acquaintance, rival, or enemy. In other words, it is claimed, individuals are not identified by who they are inside, but by where they fit in society's web: identity through social embeddedness.[12] After all, when we meet a new person, typically the first things we ask about her are what she does for a living, if she is married, and if she has children. Suppose we find out that our new acquaintance is a divorced lawyer with a son; certainly there is likely more than one divorced lawyer with a son in our community, perhaps even in our social circle. But if we determine her "neighborhood" in the social web in enough detail, it is possible we could identify her uniquely in terms of her social roles and relationships.

This idea certainly has its appeal, but also its problems, one common and one unique. First, one's placement in the social structure can change over time, often abruptly, such as when changing jobs, getting married or divorced, falling into a new set of friends, and so on. Of course, the importance of this shortcoming may be lessened if we consider that our various social links rarely change at once, making possible a "family resemblance" of our social states over time (the same could be said about preferences themselves). But in the extreme, if these factors did change simultaneously—upon entering the witness relocation program, for instance, an extreme case that completely refines our social status—we would not think of ourselves, deep down, as different people. So social links seem to have the same instability problems as preferences, but nonetheless even as our positions in society change, we remain who we are.

Second, social links are not primary; they are based both on circumstances that are out of our control and choices that are in our control. Those choices in turn will be based on a combination of preferences and values, which the autonomous agent will first filter through her judgment, and will therefore be an expression of her character. A married doctor with two kids who belongs to a local bird-watching club arrived at that social status through a combination of luck, desire, and effort. If we want to identify this person, it is more accurate to use what is primary—her judgment and character underlying the effort that brought her desire to fruition given her luck—than to use the consequences thereof. We can certainly use her social achievements (and failures) as proxies for her more essential attributes, but then we have to parse out the role played by good luck and circumstances (although perseverance in the face of bad luck or negative circumstances certainly demonstrates strength of character).

Please keep in mind that even if we end up rejecting the idea that our social relationships define us, we do not have to deny their influence on our decision-making, choices, and actions. As we saw above, Kantian autonomy does not imply this, any more than it forbids taking preferences into account—when appropriate. Just as a person should not lie to gain material advantage, she should not lie simply to please a friend. External and internal influences do and can influence our choices, but only to the extent that no duty is being violated by doing so. Furthermore, they must enter into our decision-making when doing so serves to fulfill a duty: if you mean to help a friend, you must know what sort of help she needs, and if the needs of two friends conflict, you are free to judge which you needs help more, or which friend is closer to you. As we saw in chapter 1, this represents the essential role that real-world, human information and context play in moral action, and speaks against one of the perpetual misunderstandings of Kant's ethics.

So, rather than identifying individuals with their preferences or their social roles and ties, I maintain that we should identify a person with her character. The understanding of character developed here can solve the problems of temporal continuity and individuation in a more constructive and intuitive way than preferences or social roles can. While one's memories, feelings, or preferences may be transitory, or may be shared among several persons, each agent's character—her judgment and will as reflected in her agency—is necessarily her own (as discussed above). Each agent has her own sense of the moral law as derived from her own reason and based on her own experiences, and as a result she will resolve moral dilemmas and conflicts of obligations differently from anyone else. Furthermore, her judgment may change with experience (as described in Chapter 1), and her will may strengthen and weaken over time (as described in Chapter 2), but these changes are usually neither sudden nor drastic, and they maintain enough consistency in character to identify her over time. And if a person's character were to change abruptly—for example, following severe physical or psychological trauma—it is both common and appropriate to say the person is no longer the person who was before.

But if every person, individually and independently, realizes the moral law within her—the categorical imperative, as Kant described—in her judgment, would that not make all persons identical rather than individuated and distinct? Harry Frankfurt forcefully makes this objection, which is worth quoting at length:

> The autonomous will can only be one that incorporates what Kant calls a "pure" will. It must conform, in other words, to the requirements of a will that is indifferent to all personal interests—that is entirely devoid of all empirical motives, preferences, and desires. Now this *pure will* is a very peculiar and unlikely place in which to locate an indispensable condition of individual autonomy. After all, its purity consists precisely in the fact that it is wholly untouched by any of the contingent personal features that make people distinctive and that characterize their specific identities. . . . The pure will has no individuality whatsoever. It is identical in everyone, and its volitions are everywhere exactly the same. In other words, the pure will is thoroughly *impersonal*.[13]

True, the basic contours of the moral law will be the same—the respect demanded for humanity, the general duties outlined by the categorical imperative, and so on—but the nuances and subtleties will be very different. While the same formal structure of the categorical imperative would (ideally) be realized by every rational person, each person will nonetheless implement it according to her own judgment based on her own experiences and perspective, and will execute those decisions to a degree based on her own will, combining to form her own character, which makes her unique.

We can draw an analogy to judicial decision-making, borrowing (as we did in Chapter 1) from the jurisprudence of Ronald Dworkin. Ideally, every judge in the United States follows the same Constitution, the same statutory law, and the same precedents, but nonetheless each judge may come to a different conclusion as to the "right answer" in any given case due to her own unique interpretation of the legal and political system.[14] Over time, her decisions build up a judicial record, and observant legal scholars can certainly differentiate between one judge's jurisprudence and that of another. And while any one judge's jurisprudential approach may shift or evolve over time, such shifts are rarely abrupt enough to lead one to say "is this really the same judge?" And if it were, that question would certainly be justified; we would say she is acting out of character, though the judge herself may disagree, based on our differing conceptions of her judicial character. Furthermore, her justification of her decision may offer new insight into her jurisprudence—or even her moral character, if her answer is regarded as insincere.

Now think of a person you know well—well enough for you to claim to know her character, how she thinks, and the decisions she is likely to make (and carry out). When such a person surprises you with a decision or action you did not expect, you may say "that's not like her" or "that's not the Maria we know."[15] Or, when confronting her, you may say "you've changed" or "it's like I don't know you at all," or, most pointedly, "it's like you're a *different person*." And this is not because her preferences, memories, or feelings have changed; all of that would be understandable, or, at the most, temporarily puzzling ("I didn't think you liked jazz"). Rather, it is because the essential elements of her character, her judgment and will—her very *self*—seem different.[16] For these reasons I argue that it is a person's character, her judgment and her will, that identifies her, distinguishing her from other persons as well as consistently picking her out over time (regardless of gradual change).

On the surface, this idea is similar, though not directly based on, Kant's own conception of disposition or character, which he termed *Gesinnung*.[17] As Henry Allison writes,

> Kant makes it clear that he recognizes that the choices of rational agents . . . must be conceived in relation to an underlying set of intentions, beliefs, interests, and so on, which collectively constitute that agent's disposition or character. Otherwise these choices and maxims could be neither imputed nor explained; they would have to be regarded as completely arbitrary expressions of a "liberty of indifference," without any "sufficient reason." . . . In addition, by enabling us to regard a person's specific acts and decisions as expressions of an underlying set of intentions or pattern of willing, which can itself be the object of a moral evaluation, it provides a means for thinking about the moral life of a person as a whole.[18]

Though my conception of character is not specifically drawn from *Gesinnung*, a much more subtle and nuanced concept with intricate links to related ideas in Kant's moral psychology, they are certainly of the same spirit, both representing the myriad of background influences and experiences that inform one's choice and contributing to a process of self-constitution, a concept to which we now turn.

Practical identity and self-constitution

When discussing identity, philosophers often distinguish between two senses of the concept: personal identity and practical identity. *Personal identity*, discussed above, is a matter of metaphysics: how is a person to be individuated from other persons, as well as identified over time as the same person? *Practical identity*, on the other hand, is a matter of action, morality, and responsibility, and arises from the common-sense realization that, regardless of metaphysical debates over the reality or illusion of the self, when a person acts she feels that it is *she* who is acting. Practical identity represents the standpoint, the idea of her self, from which she acts. As Christine Korsgaard, one of the foremost writers on personal identity, writes, "from the practical point of view our relationship to our actions and choices is essentially *authorial*: from it, we view them as *our own*. . . . We think of living our lives, and even of having our experiences, as something that we *do*."[19] This perspective demands that we see ourselves as actors in the world, inserting ourselves in the causal chain of events or initiating new ones—again, regardless of metaphysical debates over the nature of the self. Furthermore, we have to treat persons as actors in the world if we are going to ascribe moral status to their actions, as well as responsibility for them.

Korsgaard considers practical identity to be a different approach to discussing personal identity, and one that can answer both the individuation and continuity issues.[20] For instance, debates regarding personal identity usually focus on mental states of the person, such as memories in the version common attributed to John Locke. But this framework regards the person as a passive receptacle of these feelings or experiences, rather than as an active agent in the world. For instance, in response to Derek Parfit's contention that personal identity and self-perceptions are "nothing more than connections and continuity between events in the life of a person," philosopher Stephen Darwall argues that

persons have the capacity themselves to affect just what those continuities and connections are. . . . The capacity to choose our ends, and rationally to criticize and assess even many of our desires, means that our future intentions and desires do not simply befall us; rather, they are to some degree in our own hands. If this is true, there is a sense in which we cannot simply consist in connections and continuities, because we are ourselves capable of affecting these.[21]

In response to Parfit's normative claim that the illusion of selfhood renders unimportant the distinction of persons, Darwall argues (consistent with the discussion above), "Though there is a sense in which a person may have changed so much that we may wonder whether, for certain purposes, we should regard him as the same person, this is not the sense which underlies the moral distinction of persons. What underlies that idea is that we are distinct *choosers*, distinct centers of rational decision making."[22] And as he writes elsewhere, "the rational person is not constituted by whatever ends or preferences he happens to have at any given moment. Rationality consists, at least partly, in our capacity to make our ends and preferences the object of our rational consideration and to revise them in accordance with reasons we find compelling"—reasons which, in the case of the Kantian-economic model, are embodied in the moral law.[23]

In *Self-Constitution*, Korsgaard builds on this conception of practical identity, arguing not only that agency informs the general concept of practical identity, but also, more specifically, that persons are self-constituted through their actions, which both reflect, and contribute to, who they are:

> The task of self-constitution involves finding some roles and fulfilling them with integrity and dedication. It also involves integrating those roles into a single identity, into a coherent life. People are more or less successful at constituting their identities as unified agents, and a good action is one that does this well. It is one that both *achieves* and *springs* from the integrity of the person who performs it.[24]

In the Kantian-economic model, character works in much the same way, as the agent's judgment and will are both expressed and shaped by the choices she makes. Each decision she makes is a product of her judgment and will: the consequences of that decision (as well as her reflections upon it) inform her future judgment, and her strength or weakness of will in executing that decision affects her resolve in future decisions. In this way, the agent's character continually evolves as she moves through—and *acts in*—the world.[25]

Korsgaard nicely contrasts this self-constituting agent with static conceptions, which take the agent's essential properties to be fixed and immutable, and also posit a one-way, determinate relationship between her character and her actions.[26] But she argues that the idea "to be a person is to be constantly engaged in making yourself into that person," and therefore your character, your identity, is never settled; it is constantly in a state of change, which is usually smooth and gradual, but is occasionally abrupt in response to life-changing events.[27] As Joel Feinberg writes, "self-creation in the authentic person must be self-*re*-creation, rationally accommodating new experiences and old policies to make greater coherence and flexibility."[28] Importantly, Feinberg emphasizes the gradual, never-finished nature of self-determination, starting from the rudimentary character of the child, who cannot begin forming her character from scratch, but must instead be "implanted" with some principles from the start. Gerald Dworkin raises the same point regarding early agency: "to the extent that the self uses canons of reason, principles of induction, judgments of probability, etc., these also have either been acquired from others or . . . are innate. We can no more choose *ab initio* than we can jump out of our skins."[29] But as we approach maturity, we can and should reflect on those early influences, as much as possible, and ensure that we agree with them in light of our increasingly developed autonomous character (as described above in response to the Hodgson quote).

It is in this way that an agent is self-constituting: every person is a product of not only her experiences but also her choices, and each new choice either confirms who we are or changes it. Furthermore, the very process of deliberation, of considering all of the agent's preferences, social roles, responsibilities and obligations, and choosing an action, unifies her identity.[30] Korsgaard contrasts what she calls the Combat Model of the soul, in which reason and passion are (often) contrasting forces battling over control of the agent's choices and actions, and the Constitution Model, in which the agent herself stands above—but not separate from—her reason, passions, and all of the other incentives that may influence her choices, and *she* decides which force will be her will.[31] Drawing from Plato's description of the just state in the *Republic*, Korsgaard argues that an agent constitutes her self from the various aspects of her identity, and in the end "she identifies with her constitution," which if drawn up well will unify her as an agent who can act efficaciously and autonomously in the world.[32] As she notes, we commonly use language such as "pull yourself together" and "make up your mind" to describe conflicted choice situations, and in this case such idioms are rather accurate.[33] In the final paragraph of *Self-Constitution*, she expresses this idea nicely: "in the course of this process, of falling apart and pulling yourself back together, you create something new, you constitute something new: yourself."[34]

But at the same time, this language should not be taken too literally. Consider the arguments that the self is not unified, but that instead persons are composed of multiple selves, either at one time or over time, which battle or bargain with each other (or with the central, active part of the person) to control choice and action.[35] Phenomenologically speaking, though we may speak of various selves within our minds and fighting each other, each of us cannot help but feel that she is deliberating, choosing, and acting as one person. We are certainly not shunting off those tasks on someone else; if we are, then unity of agency is hardly our most serious problem. Some may claim that even though choice is eventually issued by one overarching self, it is the result of the struggle between various lesser selves. But while we may struggle with competing urges, drives, preferences, ends, goals, dreams, duties, and obligations, there seems no reason to name these various things "selves," for to do so is to grant those selves some of the status we ascribe to persons, such as dignity, autonomy, and agency, and therefore normative status that would demand respect. But is it realistic (if even useful) to suppose that these various selves have agency? I think Jon Elster sums it up best when he writes that

barring pathological cases . . . we ought not to take the notion of "several selves" very literally. In general, we are dealing with exactly *one* person—neither more nor less. That person may have some cognitive coordination problems, and some motivational conflicts, but it is *his* job to sort them out. They do not sort themselves out in an inner arena where several homunculi struggle to get the upper hand.[36]

Reflexivity

To be sure, social roles, links, and responsibilities also enter into this deliberative self-constituting process, and as with other experiences and choices, the agent is not a passive subject of her social identities.[37] As Korsgaard writes,

you are a human being, a woman or a man, an adherent of a certain religion, a member of an ethnic group, a member of a certain profession, someone's lover or friend, and so on. And all of these identities give rise to reasons and obligations.

Your reasons express your identity, your nature; your obligations spring from what that identity forbids.[38]

But before these identities can become a part of an agent's practical identity, her sense of self (or character) from which she acts, she must take an active role in endorsing these roles by choosing what groups to join, what people to associate with, and what social responsibilities to assume. Even the aspects of your social identity you are born into—being a child of your parents, a member of your community, a citizen of your nation—must be endorsed by you before they become part *of* you and reasons on which you can act autonomously. However the social identities come about, they "remain contingent in this sense: whether you treat them as a source of reasons and obligations is up to you. If you continue to endorse the reasons the identity presents to you, and observe the obligations it imposes on you, then it's you."[39] So like preferences, social identities, along with their constituent roles and responsibilities, are subject to the endorsement of an agent's judgment based on the moral law; as important as those features are to the agent's life, they are nonetheless secondary to her character.

The necessity of endorsement implies that the agent is reflective, in particular regarding her incentives for action; as Korsgaard writes, self-consciousness "transforms incentives into what Kant calls *inclinations*," which can be motivating in a way that mere incentives cannot.[40] The agent uses her faculty of judgment to assess her desires and then transform desiring into *having* a desire, thereby taking possession of it and deciding whether to indulge it; or as Korsgaard paraphrases Plato, "having an appetite for something and giving that appetite the nod are not the same thing."[41] Amartya Sen has also discussed the reflective nature of the person, which he calls *self-scrutiny*: "A person is not only an entity that can enjoy one's own consumption, experience and appreciate one's welfare, and have one's goals, but also an entity that can examine one's values and objectives and choose in the light of those values and objectives."[42] For the perfectly autonomous agent, this process of reflection will be decisive; her judgment will be sound and her will unwavering. The imperfect agent, however, will fail occasionally in this reflective process, either judging incentives or preferences incorrectly (relative to the moral law), or judging well but lacking the willpower to follow through on its recommendations.[43]

This also relates to John Davis's argument that individuals may be socially embedded, or defined by their place in the social web, but still be individual by virtue of being self-reflective: "by describing how individuals actively form self-conceptions—*precisely because of social influences operating upon them*—it succeeds in introducing agency into the conception of the individual as socially embedded in a nonarbitrary manner."[44] Indeed, in later work Davis has referenced Korsgaard's concept of the "reflective structure of consciousness" (though disavowing the explicitly Kantian aspects of her analysis), linking it to earlier discussions of metapreferences.[45] He acknowledges that social factors are open to endorsement, because while "social factors influence how individuals form self-concepts," reflexivity "implies that individuals can detach themselves in some degree from the determining effects of social factors influencing them,"[46] "rather than simply serving as passive repositories of those influences."[47]

Perhaps the only point of disagreement here regards to what degree they can do this, because the ability for "complete" endorsement is implied by autonomy, reaffirming the atomistic choice faculty of the individual. Indeed, Davis writes that "individuals may also fail actively to form self-conceptions (or have their self-conceptions determined for them by society."[48] Philosopher Marina Oshana, too, is doubtful:

Who persons are, how they define themselves, and the content of their motivations, values, and commitments are essentially fashioned by connections to other people, to cultural norms, rituals, tradition, and enterprises. We cannot refigure these phenomena at will. Indeed, given their enormous centrality to our lives, they are phenomena that might even elude our scrutiny, our attempts to direct a critical lens upon them and render them self-made.[49]

But if the Kantian agent failed in either of these ways, it would be her choice to do so, and in this way it still affirms the primacy of the individual's character. As Herman explains, a person forms herself to some extent by choosing how—and for whose sake—to fulfill positive duties such as beneficence: "part of what I do in satisfying imperfect duties is shape the relationships that make claims on me, and in so doing, shape myself."[50] True, the Kantian standard sets a high bar, but if autonomy (in the form of authenticity and self-realization) is to be understood as a normative goal (as suggested in Chapter 1), then realistic skepticism may be warranted, but defeatism is not.

This criticism also extends to Davis's endorsement of collective agency as a possible conception of social embeddedness.[51] *Collective* or *plural agency* is a philosophical framework for understanding the coordinated behavior of more than one agent. Philosopher Margaret Gilbert gives a simple example of two persons taking a walk: each person is walking, of course, but more importantly, *they* are walking *together*, as opposed to two strangers who just happen to be walking side-by-side.[52] Views on plural agency fall into three camps: the most extreme (and least held) maintains the existence of a "group mind" that issues intentions that are by their nature collective.[53] Others, in the "holistic" camp, deny the existence of a group mind, but nonetheless maintain that collective intentions are not reducible to the individual intentions of the participants in the shared action.[54] Yet others, sometimes referred to as "individualistic or atomistic," maintain that all intentions are individual, even if they concern collective action and are shared among others in the group; Raimo Tuomela, from whose account on plural agency John Davis draws, is among this group.[55] While affirming that "only individuals form intentions," Davis argues that "alongside those intentions expressed from a first-person singular point of view, individuals also express shared or collective intentions from a first-person plural point of view"; in other words, "I-intentions" co-exist with "we-intentions."[56] But Davis affirms that "a we-intention is an individual attribution of an intention to the members of a group to which the individual belongs, based on that individual both having that we-intention and also believing that it is held by other individuals in the same group."[57] Besides Gilbert's stroll, other common examples that illustrate this point are the players on the sport team working together towards victory, or the members of an orchestra playing a symphony, neither of which make sense if each individual in the group does not believe that the other members share the same intention.[58]

If we accept Kantian autonomy and the atomistic process of choice it implies, it is clear we cannot accept any sort of "group mind" hypothesis where choice is made at a supraindividual or collective level. As we have argued, autonomy implies that one's choices are her own, her unique contribution to the causal chain of events in the world; even if she lets another person unduly influence her actions, she alone chooses to let him do this. But as long as choice remains hers, there is no reason to deny that, in agreement with Tuomela and Davis, agents can self-consciously act in concert with other agents in groups or collectives. In Korsgaard's terms, the agent would have to endorse the shared intention and thereby make it a reason or an obligation for her. That collective intentions create obligations for the constituent individuals is a key theme for Tuomela, and another point of agreement with the conception I present herein. I can take a walk together with a friend, but despite the contention of the holists, I am choosing to take a walk with her, with the understanding that she has chosen to take a walk with me, and that both she and I understand each other's intentions (similar to the assumption of common knowledge in game theory). In that sense and *that sense alone* we together are taking a walk, but a Kantian view denies that there is a distinct and separate "we" making this choice and acting according to it. Tuomela prefers to refer to this coordination of intentions as *reciprocal* rather than shared, which supports my argument (reinforced below) that even individuals with atomistic choice processes can be socially oriented in various ways, such as according to reciprocity (which can be considered, after all, the normative force behind the universalization formula of the categorical imperative).

To summarize, the Kantian-economic approach maintains that agents are essentially individual, but at the same time they can be—and, ethically speaking, *must* be—social in orientation. I hope to have reassured those with concerns about sociality or community that individualism need not be threatening. In fact, if we treat persons as individuals imbued with autonomy and dignity, social harmony takes on much more meaning *because* it will be the result of free, individual choices, rather than coercively enforced order.

Social in Orientation

Having argued that the Kantian agent is essentially individualistic by virtue of her autonomy, we now turn to her social orientation. As I said in the first part of this chapter, her choices are hers and hers alone, and (ideally) are made in accordance with the moral law to the exclusion of undue internal and external influences. But despite this metaphysical and practical agency-based isolation, the moral law itself demands that she take social factors into account—especially the needs and desires of others. Autonomy is not simply the inner freedom that comes with the capacity for free choice; it is just as importantly a responsibility towards others, and it is this aspect of autonomy that lends Kantian ethics, and the Kantian individual, a fundamental social nature.

To be sure, Kant is not the first name people associate with sociality; as we have seen, his ethics are commonly regarded as cold, unfeeling, and better suited for transactions between strangers than friends or family, so any resulting sociality would likely be regarded by most as very "arms-length." As Louden writes (and then refutes),

Kant is often portrayed as an extreme moral individualist, one who holds that each moral agent is an end in itself, a discrete individual owed respect for its autonomy, an autonomy that is safeguarded by inviolable rights. Such an individualism, it is alleged, views person as atomistic, and cannot readily accommodate larger social units such as the family which transcend mere atomism.[59]

As with many misconceptions, this one nonetheless contains a kernel of truth. In fact, Kant spoke at length about friendship, family, and love; if he did not emphasize such close relationships when discussing moral duty, it was because, as with the pursuit of self-interest, we do not normally regard imperatives as necessary to generate kindness and affection among friends and family.

But the impression that Kant's is an ethics for strangers, while meant as a derisive indictment, is instead an insightful complement, for it implies that, to a significant degree, we owe the same kind of consideration, respect, and "love" to strangers as we naturally do towards our family and friends. As Sullivan writes:

Earlier Western philosophers had thought of morality as originating within the personal and private relationships of the family and extending outward from there to the public order. Kant, by contrast, situates morality primarily within human public life, which he defines in a formal and impersonal way.[60]

But nonetheless, we are perfectly free to pay more attention (and devote more resources) to those closer to us (in denial of yet another common misconception concerning Kant; more on this below).

In this part of this chapter, I argue that Kantian ethics, especially as embodied in the Kantian conception of the economic individual, is not only consistent with sociality of the highest degree, but it actively supports this sociality, and that it does so through the essential concepts of dignity and respect. And what's more, I think it does this in the context of the minimal government of Kant's political philosophy, so that the individual can flourish and prosper with minimal interference (and support) from the state, due to a mutual respect and support from her fellow persons. (This will lead us into the policy discussion of the last two chapters of the book.)

Perfect and imperfect duties again

Let us start from what we know (from Chapter 1): perfect and imperfect duties. Recall that perfect duties are usually negative and strict, allowing no latitude in execution (unless the duty is overruled completely by another), while imperfect duties are usually positive and wide, demanding no particular action but rather the sincere adoption of ends (and action in accordance with them when feasible). For the purposes of this chapter, I think we can safely overgeneralize and say that perfect duties are duties of noninterference (do not steal, do not injure), while imperfect duties are duties of beneficence (do help others).

Put this way, there is obvious similarity with Isaiah Berlin's distinction between negative liberty, which involves rights to noninterference, and positive liberty, which involves rights to assistance.[61] While perfect duties certainly imply rights to noninterference, imperfect duties do not imply any correlative rights, because they do not demand any particular action that could support such rights, and therefore do not generate a right to assistance in the sense of an enforceable claim. As Kant wrote, "no one is wronged if duties of love are neglected; but a failure in the duty of respect infringes upon one's lawful claim."[62] However, in a society of Kantian individuals, we will see that a person who is in need may expect assistance, if we understand expectation in the positive sense of prediction, rather than the normative sense of a demand or claim. But she *can* demand noninterference, especially if the perfect right that guarantees it is also a juridical right (one enforceable by the state).

Of course, this is a familiar idea from classical liberalism, and certainly noninterference is a minimal conception of sociality. After all, a hermit practices noninterference, but would hardly be considered a paragon of sociality; he does no harm, which is good, but neither does he help anyone, which is not. Nonetheless, we should not overlook the importance of noninterference; without a strong sense of, and respect for, personal boundaries, persons will be too concerned with protecting themselves, their loved ones, and their property to have much time or energy to devote to what we consider the more social virtues. (This is the same sense in which a wealthy country can better afford to invest in environmental safe-guards; if a nation's people are starving and disease-ridden, they will not have much will to evaluate and adjust their environmental impact.) Only when our personal boundaries are secure against hostile transgressors do we feel comfortable enough to relax them, especially to strangers. So we can say that noninterference—or perfect duties—are a necessary though clearly insufficient condition for a flourishing society.

Recall how perfect duties are usually derived: either from the consistency-in-conception test generated by the Formula of Autonomy or from the negative part of the Formula of Respect. That perfect duties demand respect is obvious; the prohibitions on murder, theft, assault, and lying all result from not treating humanity merely as means while not at the same time as an end—in other words, respect for the autonomy and dignity of fellow persons. But it does not demand anything more than respect; the hermit, after all, is nothing if not respectful. That perfect duties result from the consistency-in-conception test—an eminently logical and cold moral standard—is also very telling, for a person following only perfect duty is satisfying the minimal social requirements. A society built on that foundation may persist, but we would not expect it to prosper and flourish; more on this point below when we discuss the Kingdom of Ends (and a philosopher named Adam Smith).[63]

As with perfect duty, there are two standard sources of imperfect duties, both of which take a more humanistic point of view. The more direct derivation is from the positive half of the Formula of Respect—treat people always as ends—which impels us to take the well-being and happiness of our fellow persons into account as we travel through life. But the conception-in-the-will test also generates imperfect duties, by supplementing the logical test of internal consistency with the doctrine of ends-in-themselves—specifically, other persons (and the agent herself). Remember that Kant himself regarded the true domain of ethics to be imperfect duty; any minimally decent person knows not to steal or assault others, but he may need help remembering to keep others' well-being in mind.[64] Both of these formulae emphasize that acknowledging the dignity of persons requires not just that they be respected in a negative fashion, but that they be considered ends-in-themselves and treated in a positive fashion as well, included as an end among other ends in personal decision-making (as in the model developed in Chapter 1). Kant explicitly linked beneficence with a broader sense of sociality: "the maxim of common interest, of beneficence toward those in need, is a universal duty of human beings, just because they are to be considered fellowmen, that is, rational beings with needs, united by nature in one dwelling place so that they can help one another."[65]

Kant was also rather poetic on the necessity of both of these attitudes, respect and love: "by analogy with the physical world, attraction and repulsion bind together rational beings (on earth). The principle of mutual love admonishes them constantly to come closer to one another; that of the respect they owe one another, to keep themselves at a distance from one another."[66] Later in the same passage, Kant emphasizes the opposite nature of the two duties: "a duty of free respect toward others is, strictly speaking, only a negative one (of not exalting oneself above others) and is thus analogous to the duty of right not to encroach upon what belongs to anyone. . . . The duty of love for one's neighbor can, accordingly, also be expressed as the duty to make others' ends my own (provided only that these are not immoral)."[67] As we will see in the next section, Kant also held both attitudes to be essential to achieving the kingdom of ends.

When discussing Kantian beneficence, there is a danger of letting utilitarianism in through the back door. After all, we are saying that each agent has a moral responsibility to take into account the well-being of other persons based on equality of dignity, and that is precisely how some would justify utilitarianism. But there are several crucial differences, the most important being that in the Kantian conception, no particular beneficent or helpful act is required—and certainly not the utility-maximizing act.[68] As we saw in the discussion of the prisoners' dilemma in Chapter 1, Kantian ethics is not perfectionist, being much more specific about what *not* to do than what *to* do. Accordingly, taking into account the well-being of others does not imply extreme self-sacrifice (as exemplified by Peter Singer), nor does it require calculative wizardry (as mocked by Thorstein Veblen, as we saw in the last chapter).[69] This aspect of Kantianism is much more in the spirit of virtue ethics, which (at least in its Aristotelian guise) would counsel practicing kindness, benevolence, and charity in moderation, not through extreme self-sacrifice (nor through any particular act).

In addition, the Kantian idea of beneficence is much more nuanced than the standard utilitarian version, if only because respect for dignity remains paramount. Kant was very emphatic about the spirit in which help was to be given:

We shall acknowledge that we are under obligation to help someone poor; but since the favor we do implies that his well-being depends on our generosity, and this humbles him, it is our duty to behave as if our help is either merely what is due him or but a slight service of love, and to spare him humiliation and maintain his respect for himself.[70]

This is a natural impulse; it is common, in response to expressions of gratitude, to say "no problem," "it was nothing," or "anyone would have done the same." These express not only modesty on the benefactor's part, but are gestures that help preserve the self-respect of the recipient. What's more, Kant is clear that when one practices beneficence, it must always be geared towards the other person's own view of his well-being, not the benefactor's external judgment of it: "I cannot do good to anyone in accordance with *my* concepts of happiness (except to young children and the insane), thinking to benefit him by forcing a gift upon him; rather, I can benefit him only in accordance with *his* concepts of happiness."[71]

So Kantian beneficence is less specifically demanding, and more subtle regarding how it is practiced, than utilitarianism, but does it go too far in the other direction? Is this understanding of beneficence too permissive? Only if you need a moral philosophy to tell you exactly what to do, when to do it, how to do it, and to what extent to do it.[72] Setting aside the wonderful irony of contemplating the possibility that Kantian ethics may be too permissive, this perception reflects the often neglected but very important role that judgment plays in actual real-world decision-making. Recall that the categorical imperative is purely formal, helping us derive general guidelines for moral action, as well as reminding us why they are important (the equal dignity of all persons). Imperfect duties, if they are to be followed wholeheartedly—as they must—cannot be merely paid lip service, for the attitudes they prescribe must be sincere. The duty to keep others' well-being in mind is not something to be taken lightly; even if one cannot provide aid or assistance to others at any particular time, one must always be mindful of the circumstances her fellow human beings are in.[73] That, I think, is more than enough moral burden for most, who may prefer to write a check and feel comfortable putting the plight of others out of their minds for a while. Understood this way, the duty of beneficence, and the attention and care it demands we pay to each other, ties all persons—family, friends, neighbors, and strangers alike—together as one people, inextricably linked by the moral law in what Kant termed the kingdom of ends.

The kingdom of ends (and a man named Smith)

In Chapter 1, we mentioned the broad, teleological nature of Kant's moral theory as reflected in the third formula of the categorical imperative, the Formula of Legislation for a Moral Community (also known as the Formula of the Kingdom of Ends): "every rational being must so act as if he were through his maxim always a legislating member in the universal kingdom of ends."[74] While this formula is not meant to guide moral decision-making or the formation of maxims as such, the kingdom of ends does represent the final goal of moral endeavor, a utopian state of the world in which all persons can pursue their own ends in cooperation with each other:

For all rational beings stand under the law that each of them should treat himself and all others never merely as means but always at the same time as an end in himself. Hereby arises a systematic union of rational beings through common objective laws, i.e., a kingdom that may be called a kingdom of ends (certainly only an ideal), inasmuch as these laws have in view the very relation of such beings to one another as ends and means.[75]

It is worth emphasizing that Kant regarded the kingdom of ends as "certainly only an ideal," an analogy, of course, to the Kingdom of God envisioned by Christians. But as with all ideals, it points us in the direction of progress, improving society through mutual respect and beneficence.[76]

In detailing the kingdom of ends, he also shows how the basic concept of duty is based on relationships between persons of equal dignity (as well as how the final formula of the categorical imperative incorporates the first two):

The practical necessity of acting according to this principle, i.e., duty, does not rest at all on feelings, impulses, and inclinations, but only on the relation of rational beings to one another, a relation in which the will of a rational being must always be regarded at the same time as legislative, because otherwise he could not be thought of as an end in himself. Reason, therefore, relates every maxim of the will as legislating universal laws to every other will and also to every action toward oneself; it does so not on account of any other practical motive or future advantage but rather from the idea of the dignity of a rational being who obeys no law except what he at the same time enacts himself.[77]

This relates back to the sociality inherent in the Formula of Autonomy; the reason we must test our maxims for universalizability is based on equal respect for, and reciprocity toward, all rational (human) beings, which also corresponds to the Formula of Respect in both its negative and positive aspects.[78]

Just as he was realistic about human weakness and frailties (Chapter 2), Kant was just as realistic about persons' "*unsocial sociability*, i.e., their tendency to enter into society, combined, however, with a thoroughgoing resistance that constantly threatens to sunder this society."[79] While we have a natural propensity to live in society with others, he argues, we also have a desire to have things our own way, which we recognize others may resist (as we resist the same in others). But this self-centered aspect, while "unworthy of being loved," also fuels a competitive, ambitious drive in us, without which "all of humanity's excellent natural capacities would have lain eternally dormant."[80] Despite this practical advantage, our unstable coexistence is also threatened by the "ethical state of nature . . . in which the good principle, which resides in each human being, is incessantly attacked by the evil which is found in him and in every other as well."[81] In a Hobbesian spirit, humankind's "unsocial sociability" necessitates both a public law, arising from the state, and a moral law, arising from the wills of individual rational agents, both of which lead to the ideal of the kingdom of ends.

Corresponding to these two needs, achieving the kingdom of ends involves two stages, a moral civil community and an ethical community.[82] In Kant's terms, an ideal civil community is achieved when people follow their perfect duties, chiefly the juridical duties enforceable by the state, such as the duties (codified in laws) prohibiting murder, assault, and theft. At this stage, persons do not follow these duties for the sake of duty, as is the Kantian ideal, but rather follow them merely out of self-interest, that is, to avoid punishment.[83] However, an ethical society is characterized by citizens following both their perfect and imperfect duties, as well as doing so for the sake of duty, for imperfect duties cannot be enforced at all, and many perfect duties are impractical for the state to enforce (such as the duty not to lie, especially in noncommercial contexts).

While the moral civil community is a crucial step towards the kingdom of ends, it is merely an intermediary step; as we mentioned above, a world in which persons only fulfill their perfect duties towards each other may operate on some minimal level, but it would hardly be a world in which persons flourished and maximally furthered their ends. Recall that, according to Kant's consistency-in-conception test, a world in which no persons observed their imperfect duties (such as beneficence) could exist without internal contradiction, but it could not be willed rationally by any person because it would not be consistent with the recognition of persons as ends-in-themselves. Indeed, Kant referred to persons inhabiting such a society, however orderly it appears to be, as existing in an "ethical state of nature," in which they obey laws out of fear of punishment, not out of respect for the law (or the duties underlying it).[84] Only a truly ethical community—a world in which people observed both perfect and imperfect duties, treating each other (positively) as ends to be furthered and not simply avoiding (negatively) using others as means, both out of respect for the moral law—will allow all persons to pursue their ends in cooperation with each other.[85]

Perhaps a parallel to the thought of Adam Smith would give some perspective on the kingdom of ends and help show its applicability to sociality. A world in which agents follow only Kant's perfect (or negative) duties, such as duties not to harm others, would be much like the impersonal marketplace described in Smith's *Wealth of Nations*. This minimally ethical environment would certainly serve its purpose in facilitating trade, but certainly not as a model for a complete society in which people can not only survive but also prosper and flourish. Such a world needs *more*, which in Kantian terms would be a world in which agents also followed imperfect duties, his kingdom of ends; it would also resemble the world of Smith's *Theory of Moral Sentiments*, one in which persons exercise their capacity for sympathy, or fellow-feeling, resulting in benevolent sentiments.

In the twenty-first century, of course, Smith is mainly regarded as the father of modern economics (even if most modern economists treat him like the crazy uncle who lives in the attic), while Kant had very little of significance to say regarding markets or commerce. But it should not be a surprise that, as eighteenth-century moral philosophers, Adam Smith and Immanuel Kant were strongly linked, intellectually and historically.[86] Kant was exposed to both *Wealth of Nations* and *Theory of Moral Sentiments*, and evidence of their influence (especially the latter) can be seen throughout his work. Both scholars strongly emphasize impartiality as a core element of their moral systems, they were both strongly influenced by Stoic thought, and they shared a concern for human dignity and freedom from tyranny. However, while their substantive ethical thought was very similar, they differed in their positions on the basis of morality; Kant disagreed with Smith's (and Hume's) sentimentalism, preferring to ground his moral system in the respect for dignity and autonomy that issues from reason alone, regardless of feeling or inclination (see Chapter 1). More specifically, Kant held that beneficence should come from respect for the moral law rather than natural inclination, while Smith wrote that it arises out of sympathy, the capacity to imagine oneself in the circumstances of another. To Smith, it is this sympathy of persons towards each other that generates sentiments of benevolence: "it is, that to feel much for others and little for ourselves, that to restrain our selfish, and to indulge our benevolent affections, constitutes the perfection of human nature; and can alone produce among mankind that harmony of sentiments and passions in which consists their whole grace and propriety."[87] Setting aside details of moral psychology, however, both Smith and Kant recognized the need for other-regarding motivations and actions to create a complete social order, representing the best we can do, as opposed to the least we can live with.

With regard to Smith, there has been an enormous amount of work on the (apparent) contrast between his emphasis on benevolence (arising from the capacity for sympathy) in *Theory of Moral Sentiments* and the emphasis on self-interest or self-love in *Wealth of Nations*. It seems that the issue of consistency, which comprised the original "Adam Smith problem," has been resolved in the positive, and what remains is the "'new' Adam Smith problem concerning the precise nature of their relationship."[88] As I read him, in focusing on self-interest in *Wealth of Nations*, such as in the famous butcher-brewer-baker passage, Smith was outlining the *minimal* requirements for the operation of markets *only*—in particular, impersonal market exchanges amongst strangers or mere acquaintances, rather than close friends or family relations. Rather than recommending that market participants be motivated solely by self-interest, or endorsing such attitudes, Smith was arguing that *even if* they are so motivated, markets can operate smoothly; Samuel Fleischacker writes

that human beings can pursue even their individual interests *together*, that even society without benevolence need not be a hostile society, that economic exchange, even among entirely self-interested people, is not a zero-sum game. The emphasis is on the "even" in each case.[89]

Smith was not making a moral or prudential argument for self-love or egoism, nor was he arguing that self-interest was sufficient for a flourishing society outside of the market realm. He was merely making a case that a market *can* operate based on the participants' pursuit of their own self-interest, not that it *should* operate on such a basis.[90]

But at the same time, he did recognize that the majority of economic transactions in a developed commercial society would be between persons with little personal connection, for whom each need have no special concern.[91] Furthermore, he did say that often, benevolent actions will interfere with the proper operation of markets, but this is one extreme, the opposite of pure self-interest, and does not argue against motivations marginally deviating from self-interest. He was also making what we think of now as a Hayekian efficiency-of-information argument, that each person knows his or her own interest better than anyone else does, and is therefore better placed to pursue that interest, as opposed to the more distant—and therefore less informed—actions of policymakers.[92]

In *Theory of Moral Sentiments*, on the other hand, Smith was describing (and prescribing) appropriate conduct in a broader context, social interaction in general, outside the narrow confines of anonymous market exchange. The capacity for sympathy or fellow-feeling becomes essential to generate benevolence (and beneficence) towards others, which Smith deems necessary for a truly flourishing society. This is not to deny the obvious importance of some degree of self-love, of course, but rather tempers it with the sentiments arising from persons' sympathy for others' circumstances, especially those close to us, to whom general benevolence becomes more specific.[93] In market circumstances, sympathy does not play as significant a role, not only because of the relative lack of personal connection between buyer and seller, but also because participants can rest assured that all involved are tending to their own affairs to the best of their abilities, and do not need assistance or aid unless they ask for it (recalling the passage quoted from Kant above regarding respectful beneficence). But in more general social contexts, seeing someone in need naturally generates, through our capacity for sympathy, sentiments of benevolence, which manifest themselves in good deeds.

Smith's description of self-interest as the minimal precondition for the operation of the market resembles Kant's limited endorsement of a civil society based on state enforcement of perfect duty alone. In such a world, persons would respect each other merely in a negative fashion: they would not cheat, would not steal, would not harm each other, and so forth. This behavior, of course, is what we expect—at the minimum— from market participants, as they pursue their own self-interest within the broad constraints of justice: as Smith writes, "every man, as long as he does not violate the laws of justice, is left perfectly free to pursue his own interest his own way."[94] In the terms of the Formula of Respect, in such situations, persons do use each other as means to their own ends, but not merely so, for they also treat others as ends-in-themselves by following basic rules or duties of respect. I do use the baker to get my bread and feed my family, but I do not steal the bread from him, nor do I cheat him out of it. Voluntary transactions, absent coercion or deceit, satisfy the negative standard of treating people as means while also as ends (as will be emphasized in Chapter 5).

But this neglects the positive aspect of the Formula of Respect, which generates imperfect duties through the requirement to treat others as ends (not just abstain from using them merely as means). When considering a world of only negative duties, Kant was clear (and somewhat moving):

Would it not be better for the well-being of the world generally if human morality were limited to duties of right, fulfilled with the utmost conscientiousness, and benevolence were considered morally indifferent? It is not so easy to see what effect this would have on human happiness. But at least a great moral adornment, benevolence would then be missing from the world. This is, accordingly, required by itself, in order to present the world as a beautiful moral whole in its full perfection, even if no account is taken of advantages (of happiness).[95]

Likewise, as Jonathan Wight notes, "Smith would be appalled by a world that holds wealth above human connections, a world of markets unsupported by a social undergarment of moral fabric."[96] Both Smith and Kant envisioned a society where love for oneself and for one's neighbors coexist, supported to some extent by positive law, but primarily by morality (whatever its ultimate nature).

Generally, Smith and Kant would agree that the impersonal arena of the market is not an appropriate framework or mechanism for ensuring a flourishing society as a whole. Nonetheless, it is appropriate for organizing economic activity, especially transactions between anonymous strangers. As we saw above, the market does not represent the ideal kingdom of ends, which needs agents to observe both perfect and imperfect duties and take each others' ends as their own. But we are not required to take literally everybody's ends into account (as in utilitarianism); this requirement is flexible in terms of whom to favor or not, and how much. Even though I may not care at all for the well-being of my local baker, even if I think him a scoundrel and a cad, I must still treat him with the respect he is due as an autonomous person, and this is the essence of morality within the market: mutual respect if not mutual beneficence. Indeed, beneficence between strangers may even be inappropriate, given each person's lack of knowledge about the other, but what strangers can (and should) give each other is respect. So the market represents a kingdom of ends which is limited but nonetheless complete within its scope—ensuring the maximal freedom *from interference* consistent with the same freedom for all. It is the institutionalization of choice within the confines of justice, which is necessary in the context of interaction between strangers, where it may not be between friends.[97] (We will have more to say about the market and choice in the next two chapters.)

Relations and reciprocity

As we just discussed, the market represents a minimal level of ethical behavior, in which perfect duties are followed but imperfect duties little apply. This framework may be acceptable among strangers, but is definitely not appropriate when dealing with family or friends, or even neighbors or co-workers. Beneficence for strangers is simply a more moderate version of beneficence (or care) for friends and family. Since beneficence should always be respectful of the other person's dignity and autonomy, and we know much less about strangers and casual acquaintances than we do about close friends and family, the degree to which we can and should be beneficent, as well as the kind of kindness we can practice, is naturally more limited in such cases. In addition, an excessive degree or type of beneficence between strangers would generate a proportionate amount of gratitude in response, and Kant felt that excessive gratitude was demeaning (as we described above).

As we discussed, Kant's ethics are often criticized as being an "ethics between strangers," which would seem to imply that he dismissed friendship, which is patently untrue; indeed, Allen Wood argues that "one would have to go back to Aristotle to find a major philosopher for whom friendship is as important to ethics as it is for Kant."[98] However, Kant certainly endorsed the biblical injunction to "love thy neighbor," although he understood this "love" as a general benevolence, a well-wishing that could be extended to everyone: "when I say that I take an interest in this human being's well-being only out of my love for all human beings, the interest I take is as slight as an interest can be. I am only not indifferent with regard to him."[99] But then he considers that "one human being is closer to me than another, and in benevolence I am closest to myself. How does this fit in with the precept 'love your *neighbor* (your fellowman) as yourself'?"[100] The answer lies in the difference between mere benevolence, or well-wishing, and beneficence, or such feelings put into practice or action, "for in wishing I can be *equally* benevolent to everyone, whereas in acting I can, without violating the universality of my maxim, vary the degree greatly in accordance with the different objects of my love (one of whom concerns me more closely than another)."[101] Recall that the duty of beneficence is literally the duty not to be indifferent to others, which leaves a great deal of latitude to give more consideration and aid to those closest to you (including yourself), as long as you keep distant strangers in mind as well.

Korsgaard casts this topic in terms of reciprocity and responsibility, stressing that

to hold someone responsible is to regard her as a *person*—that is to say, as a free and equal person, capable of acting both rationally and morally. It is therefore to regard her as someone with whom you can enter the kind of relation that is possible only among free and rational people: a relation of reciprocity.[102]

In this understanding, reciprocity, and the responsibility implied thereby, is an expression of each person's recognition of equal dignity in others. Because of this dignity, we respect other persons, both in terms of living up to our commitments to them, as well as expecting them to live up to their commitments to us.[103] To do any less would be to treat them as less than rational, or as children. But reciprocity of respect in a negative sense is not enough (outside the market arena), for respecting the dignity of other persons also implies treating them as ends-in-themselves, and taking their ends as our own (to some extent). As Korsgaard continues, "to join with others as citizens in the Kingdom of Ends is to extend to our inner attitudes and personal choices the kind of reciprocity that characterizes our outer actions in the political state."[104] And finally, relations between strangers and between friends must both embrace reciprocity, but to a different degree; again, our duties of beneficence need not be exercised to the same extent with strangers as with family and friends, though all must embody a certain level of mutual respect due to each person's dignity. But, of course, reciprocity between friends goes much deeper, involving the sharing of intimate thoughts, feelings, and concern that is not necessary, not even appropriate, between strangers.[105]

The reciprocity that figures so strongly in Kantian ethics is a conscious attitude that each person rationally and morally takes toward others. But in recent years, many social scientists have written more naturalistically on the origins of reciprocal behavior, as well as its importance in maintaining social order. The simplest versions of this go back to Hume, who based reciprocal action on long-term self-interest:

I learn to do a service to another, without bearing him any real kindness; because I foresee, that he will return my service, in expectation of another of the same kind, and in order to maintain the same correspondence of good offices with me or with others. And accordingly, after I have serv'd him, and he is in possession of the advantage arising from my action, he is induc'd to perform his part, as foreseeing the consequences of his refusal.[106]

But modern evolutionary thinkers, including Herbert Gintis, write of *strong reciprocity*, in which a person is "predisposed to cooperate with others and punish non-cooperators, even when this behavior cannot be justified in terms of self-interest, extended kinship, or reciprocal altruism."[107] Gintis argues convincingly that this disposition evolved to promote group survival, and provides ample experimental and anecdotal evidence for its continued existence and influence over decision-making.

There is no reason to suppose, however, that this evolved reciprocity is incompatible with the Kantian version (recognizing that they are not identical in origin or implication). As I indicated above, Kantian reciprocity is a conscious attitude, while Gintis's version is an unconscious disposition. Kant values such inborn drives or feelings insofar as they help the agent adhere to dutiful action in the face of weakness, but would not regard action performed on their basis to be truly moral without a conscious realization of the rationale for doing so. This is not Gintis's concern, though; his goal is to explain the "high level of sociality [among human groups] despite a low level of relatedness among group members."[108] Nonetheless, agents who are naturally inclined to behave reciprocally in Gintis's sense may (or, for the sake of autonomy, *should*) eventually reflect upon this disposition and justify it normatively to themselves. (Or perhaps some of them will dismiss it as foolish sentimentalism, in which case they will long battle their basic drives, the difficulty of which those who have tried to lose weight or stop procrastinating know all too well.) Amartya Sen reconciles the two sources of behavior well, after lauding the advances made in evolutionary explanations of norms and values:

But, once evolutionary survival is taken into account, must the burden of selection fall *entirely* on that process (with conscious selection reduced to simple endorsement of natural selection)? Why can't the two means of selection be both actively at work? Since human beings are reflective creatures who take their values and critical powers seriously, the role of conscious and scrutinized selection will not be obliterated merely because evolutionary selection is also going on. Critical reflection does not give immunity from evolutionary selection, but nor does evolutionary selection convert reflective beings into thoughtless automatons.[109]

So while evolved reciprocity can explain some degree, perhaps a large degree, of observed sociality, it stops short of recognizing the reflective capacities (also the result of evolution) that were emphasized in the first half of this chapter. If agents consciously endorse their instinctive dispositions toward reciprocity, it may lose whatever conditional nature it has, and become a more solid foundation for a prosperous, flourishing society.

We started this chapter by consolidating judgment and will from the first two chapters into a conception of character, which identifies the Kantian-economic individual. But while she is essentially individual by virtue of her autonomy, she is socially oriented by virtue of the moral law which she sets to herself through exercising her autonomy. The chapter ended with a discussion of the same Kantian-economic agent's sociality, how autonomous agents interact in an atmosphere of mutual respect and concern, including the limited but essential role played by the market in preserving autonomy and dignity (within the bounds of justice). In the final two chapters of this book, we turn to matters of policy, or how the actions of the state are delimited by the respect owed persons because of their dignity. In Kantian ethics, the state has the same moral responsibilities that individuals do, because a person must be treated with respect by anyone. We will see that this realization has serious implications for the theory and practice of consequentialist welfare economics.

CHAPTER 4

Dignity, Efficiency, and the Economic Approach to Law

Up to this point in the book, we have focused on the individual: her autonomy and the dignity that derives from it, her duties towards herself and others, and how such a person fits into society. In other words, any interactions have been between individuals, and any discussions of duty dealt with obligations individuals have toward each other. In this chapter and the next, we turn to the state's interactions with the individual, issues of policy, examined through the lens of Kantian dignity and autonomy. We will see that a Kantian orientation poses just as many challenges for economic policymaking as it did for economic modeling of decision-making—perhaps more.

Luckily for us, Kant's moral and political philosophies are very closely related; as Roger Sullivan writes, "the two so mirror each other both in vocabulary and in structure that it can be argued that Kant's ethics is as much a political theory as a moral theory."[1] For instance, there is little difference between the obligations of the state towards individuals and the obligations of individuals toward each other. This is because all of these obligations derive from the same principle, the equal dignity of all persons: the state must respect the dignity of persons no less than persons themselves must. Accordingly, the state follows a variant of the categorical imperative known as the Universal Principle of Right: "any action is *right* if it can coexist with everyone's freedom in accordance with a universal law, or if on its maxim the freedom of choice of each can coexist with everyone's freedom in accordance with a universal law."[2] This bears obvious similarity to the formulae of Autonomy and of Universal Law (not to mention the Formula of the Kingdom of Ends) in its emphasis of universalization, which is ultimately based on the reciprocal respect owed all rational persons due to their dignity (also alluded to above).[3]

In Kant's political philosophy, the state exists only to protect the (outer) freedom of individuals from coercion by others, in order to allow each person the ability to express her autonomy maximally, while at the same time consistently with all other persons doing the same. This is the sole justification for state coercion, and, appropriately for Kant, it is not a consequentialist justification; it does not rely on an argument that state action will lead to greater welfare or happiness, or even that it leads to a greater degree of freedom for the citizenry, but rather that it is an essential constitutive aspect of that freedom: "the consistent exercise of the right to freedom by a plurality of persons cannot be conceived apart from a public legal order."[4] The state exists to protect persons from each other, enforcing select perfect duties against violence and interference, so that each may enjoy the freedom to pursue her ends. Recall from the last chapter that a civil society in which all persons follow (at least) their perfect duties toward each other is the first step towards the "kingdom of ends," and the development and existence of civil society includes this necessary exercise of state power.

There would seem to be a contradiction here, for Kant famously opposes coercion as an affront to dignity (as we saw in Chapter 1). How then, if he holds the state to the same ethical standard as persons (at least in terms of action), does he justify state coercion?

Resistance that counteracts the hindering of an effect promotes this effect and is consistent with it. Now whatever is wrong is a hindrance to freedom in accordance with universal laws. But coercion is a hindrance or resistance to freedom. Therefore, if a certain use of freedom is itself a hindrance to freedom in accordance with universal laws (i.e., wrong), coercion that is opposed to this (as a *hindering of a hindrance to freedom*) is consistent with freedom in accordance with universal laws, that is, it is right. Hence there is connected with right by the principle of contradiction an authorization to coerce someone who infringes upon it.[5]

Basically, coercion by individuals is wrong, so anything that limits that wrong is right. As Hans Reiss writes, "to restrict freedom in this manner does not entail interfering with the freedom of an individual, but merely establishes the condition of his external freedom."[6] State coercion is interference only with wrongful exercise of freedom, and therefore it is not only permissible, but required to ensure the maximal (rightful) freedom for all.

On the other hand, the state is forbidden from enforcing positive rights, such as claims to assistance or welfare, because to do so would involve illegitimately coercing others to satisfy them (that is, without justification based on right or duty). This too is consistent with Kant's ethics, as individuals have no claim on each other regarding assistance; the wide duty to provide aid cannot generate correlative (positive) rights to such aid. As Wolfgang Kersting writes, Kant's concept of equality based on dignity "lacks all economic implications and social commitments; it cannot be used to justify the welfare state and to legitimize welfare state programmes of redistribution."[7] Kant himself put it most directly and forcefully when he wrote:

A government that was established on the principle of regarding the welfare of the people in the same way that a father regards his children's welfare, i.e., a *paternal government*—where the subjects, like *immature* children unable to distinguish between what is truly useful or harmful to them . . . such a government is the worst *despotism* we can think of (a constitution that subverts all the freedom of the subjects, who would have no freedom whatsoever).[8]

Accordingly, the state is limited to enforcing what Kant called *juridical duties*, a subset of perfect duties constraining the exercise of outer freedom, such as duties prohibiting murder, assault, theft, and commercial fraud, which interfere with the due exercise of freedom on the part of others.[9]

Furthermore, even though persons should follow laws based on juridical duty out of respect for the moral law itself (as with all duties), the state cannot enforce persons' motivation for obeying the law; it can only enforce the external action performed according to (or in defiance of) the law. This also provides another reason why the state cannot enforce imperfect duties such as beneficence, which Kant sometimes called *ethical duties* (in contrast to juridical duties). Besides the fact (explained above) that they do not imply correlative rights, ethical duties are much more a matter of motivation, since imperfect duties require the sincere adoption of ends. If you do adopt such an end, you simply *will* act according to it when possible; if you perform the same act for another reason, then there is no sense in which you have followed imperfect duty at all. On the other hand, juridical duties can be performed out of naked self-interest if compliance is enforced by threat of official sanction.[10]

With this brief summary, I hope to have shown why Kant is widely considered one of the founders of classical liberalism (or economic libertarianism), insofar as he argues for a minimal, noninterventionist role for the state, much in the spirit of Robert Nozick's *Anarchy, State, and Utopia* or John Stuart Mill's *On Liberty*.[11] But his position does not rest on any cynicism about the efficacy of government, or on general opposition to a state *per se*; as we saw, Kant believes the state is a necessary component of the maximization of outer freedom among persons. But he does limit the legitimate use of state power to prohibiting this coercion, and therefore makes no room for positive, interventionist state action for the purpose of promoting any consequentialist measures of social well-being. Such measures, of course, are the domain of welfare economics and one of its primary applications, the economic approach to law, to which we now turn.

Welfare Economics and Consequentialism

Despite the various guises it has adopted over the years, welfare economics has always been essentially a consequentialist enterprise that seeks to maximize the sum of individual well-being.[12] Welfare economics assesses the effects on aggregate well-being of institutions, policies, or laws, with the ultimate aim of increasing or maximizing welfare by either manipulating existing arrangements or instituting new ones.[13] Such analysis is often expressed in terms of *efficiency*: changes that increase welfare are described as "more efficient," while ones that maximize welfare are simply called "efficient." (The various meanings of efficiency will be explored later in this chapter.)

From a Kantian point of view, the most immediate problem with welfare economics and efficiency analysis, as with any consequentialist decision procedure, is that whenever actions are taken that transfer resources from one party to another with no justification based on wrongdoing or desert, the party losing resources is treated simply as a means to the end of the party who gains them. Just as it is wrong for an individual to treat another (or herself) like this, because it violates the respect owed every person by virtue of her dignity, it is wrong for the state to do so as well (according to the Universal Principle of Right). Another way to put this objection is that welfare economics denies the existence of any rights which are not themselves derived from welfare (other than the implicit right of the state to do whatever it deems necessary to increase welfare), which gives the losing party no recourse against the offending policy. If maximizing welfare is the one and only goal of policy, then the acknowledgment of rights that threaten to reduce welfare would obviously be counterproductive.[14] But in order to have any true, independent meaning whatsoever, a right must stand against welfarist considerations in some nontrivial situations—in other words, sometimes the just recognition of a right will result in lower welfare.

To give two examples of the standard treatment of rights in welfare economics, we will look at externalities and antitrust policy.

Externalities and Pigouvian taxes

While voluntary, consensual transactions are generally assumed to be efficient, based on the assumption that individuals will only consent to deals that will benefit them and thereby increase their well-being, one qualification to this presumption of efficiency is the possibility of third-party effects or *externalities*.[15] Classic examples of negative externalities include pollution (in which the transaction between a factory and its customers imposes costs on the surrounding community) and traffic congestion (in which each additional driver adds to the travel time—and aggravation—of the drivers already on the road), while positive externalities include lawn care (in which a homeowner who takes care of her lawn increases the property value of surrounding homes). Economists typically analyze externalities in terms of the disparity between private and social effects of such activity: for instance, a person deciding whether to drive to the store will naturally take her own private costs and benefits into account, but usually not the costs her action imposes on other drivers. Therefore, she will make the decision which maximizes her personal utility, but it will not maximize social utility since it imposes additional costs on other drivers without providing an offsetting benefit to them. Likewise, the homeowner who takes fastidious care of her lawn chooses the level of care that maximizes her own utility, but it is socially inefficient because there are unrealized social benefits (to surrounding homeowners) from additional lawn care on her part.

The standard policy response suggested by externality analysis is to tax the activity that leads to negative externalities and subsidize activity that leads to positive externalities. (From now on, I will ignore positive externalities, as they are of comparatively negligible policy interest—and rightfully so, as I will explain below.) This approach has come to be known as Pigouvian taxation, after the primary exponent of the concept, Arthur Pigou, and the appropriateness of such intervention is virtually unquestioned by economists.[16] (Even Ronald Coase, who showed that under certain conditions Pigouvian taxes were unnecessary, did not necessarily regard them as improper.) Of course, externalities are defined in terms of their consequences, costs which are assumed to be numerically comparable and can therefore be optimized—not minimized or eliminated, but optimized or made efficient, since there are often also positive consequences of the behavior creating the negative externalities. For example, economists do not want to eliminate traffic altogether, since it clearly has positive benefits; rather, they want to manage it and maximize the utility of it by deterring the drivers (with tolls, for instance) who would lower others' utility by more than they would increase their own.

Students are often shocked when economics professors first explain to them that pollution cannot be eliminated without even higher costs in lost productivity, income, and general well-being. This demonstrates the tension between declaring something "bad" or "wrong" but then seeking to *manage* it rather than eliminate it. It is one thing to try to eliminate a "bad" or a "wrong" but fail because of lack of means; certainly as a society we do not want any crime, but it is not possible to eliminate all crimes without devoting all of society's resources to the task, or excessively infringing on essential civil liberties.[17] But we do not set out to optimize crime—recall the criticism leveled at 2004 presidential candidate John Kerry's statement about achieving a "manageable level of terrorism"— but yet economists do optimize pollution, traffic congestion, and so on. (Imagine the plight of the clever young economist who computes the optimal degree of torture!)

The problem is that if, like crimes, such externalities involve *wrongful* harms, involving a violation of rights defined by duties, we should not seek merely to optimize them—we should try to eliminate them. But Pigouvian taxes are not necessary to do this, because we already have an institution designed for determining compensation for harms: tort law, which determines the conditions under which a harmed party can shift her losses onto the party who harmed her. A person can sue her "injurer" in court, and if the injurer is found liable—which usually involves a finding of fault or wrongdoing—he will compensate his "victim" for her harm. Furthermore, Ronald Coase famously showed that if the parties can bargain, and if one party clearly holds the operative right in the situation (as determined by law, commonly), then the parties will bargain between them and find the efficient solution to their conflict, with or without the explicit involvement of the court.[18] (The parties can bargain between themselves rather than go to court, or use the court-determined damages as a starting point for negotiations.) Hereby, against the background of the law of torts, the harm from the externality is shifted to the party who is found liable. This also has the happy result of providing incentives to would-be injurers not to cause wrongful harms in the first place, providing the deterrence that Pigouvian taxes are meant to create, while also providing compensation for the harm (unlike Pigouvian taxes, unless explicit redistribution is included in the program).

Other advantages of the legal method of dealing with wrongful harms over the Pigouvian method are familiar. First and foremost, the informational demands on the authorities charged with designing the Pigouvian tax are insurmountable. Because the benefits and costs of all activities are subjective and knowable only to the persons involved, government agents cannot determine the efficient level of the externality-generating activity, much less the degree of inefficiency extant or the precise level of tax that would remedy it. Furthermore, the amount of power such a scheme would vest in the hands of a few officials charged with designing, implementing, and enforcing the Pigouvian tax would make them targets of special interests, introducing the strong possibility of political influence over the tax rates or the incidence thereof. Finally, the Pigouvian tax is a one-size-fits-all solution, whereas every case of harm is different and not all of the activity that falls under the tax actually leads to harm (much less wrongful harm).

But what about harm that is not wrongful—driving can hardly be considered wrongful to other drivers, for instance—and therefore does not fall under the aegis of tort law? If harm is not wrongful—if it does not violate a legally enforceable right of the harmed party—then it is of no concern to the state, whose only legitimate role (in the Kantian view) is to enforce juridical duties, and thereby protect any correlative rights. As a matter of common sense, most things we do affect others for better or for worse, in trivial or significant ways. But not all of those effects, even the negative ones, are wrongful; not all of them violate rights. Does a driver have a right—moral or legal—to get to her destination in a certain amount of time, a right that would be violated when an extra driver enters the road?[19] Of course not; drivers know that there are other drivers on the road, and the level of traffic varies, as does their travel time. But she *does* have the right—legal and moral—to not be hit by another car, and if she is hit, that is a matter for her and the other driver (or their insurance companies) to handle against the backdrop of the legal system. (This is also the reason that positive externalities are of no legitimate concern to the state, for no right is violated by not engaging in beneficial activity *enough*.)

In addition, activity which is not wrongful is often protected by a right itself. For example, it is often said that the First Amendment guarantee of free speech is more important in protecting speech we dislike than speech we like (and with which we would have no problem anyway). Offensive (but not obscene) speech—such as that of the racist on his soapbox, to use the common example—certainly harms, in a way, some (if not most) who hear it. However, not only do passersby not have a right against being offended, but the racist has a right to say what he chooses (to which, of course, passersby have the right to respond).[20] Recall that a right, in order to be meaningful, must trump welfarist considerations in at least some nontrivial cases; this is but one example, as are many of the guarantees in the Bill of Rights, such as freedoms of religion, association, and the press. In this sense, too, a driver has just as much right to use the public roads as any other driver (assuming she obeys the traffic laws and is not using her vehicle to commit a crime).

Pigouvian welfare economics focuses exclusively on benefits and harms without considering the rights or wrongs behind them, or the justice or injustice of the situation creating them. All effects are morally equivalent, which leads the internal dissonance inherent in the concept of optimizing a "bad." If the bad is not also wrong, it may be regrettable but is of no interest to the state; if the bad *is* wrong (but falls short of criminality), then it should be dealt with completely and conclusively, preferably by the parties involved, acting through the law of tort (implicitly or explicitly). The concept of externalities, however, by ignoring the issue of wrongness, treats all inefficient situations alike. The important thing about externalities is not the distinction between private and social utilities, but between rights and wrongs.

Market failures and antitrust

To the mainstream economist, perfect competition is the epitome of efficiency or welfare maximization when it comes to markets and commerce. If everything works perfectly (literally speaking), the marginal benefit of the last unit of a good produced will be equal to its marginal cost, so every unit worth its marginal production cost to consumers is produced—no more, no less. In other words, total surplus to consumers and producers—the version of welfare typically used in studies of industrial organization—is maximized by perfect competition. And most economists support free markets only insofar as they adhere to this idealized conception; in fact, many economists go so far as to define "free market" to mean a perfectly competitive industry, conflating the consequentialist ideal of efficiency with the deontological concept of outer freedom. Indeed, the term "market failure" has been coined to describe any deviation from perfect competition, including imperfect competition and monopoly (as well as externalities, public goods, and so forth).[21] But this attribution of "failure" is grossly unfair—the only failure here is a failure to live up to an impossible standard, to do that for which the market was never designed or intended, and which it can only do under fantastically unrealistic circumstances. So according to this view, market failure is everywhere, inevitable and unavoidable.

As with externalities, the typical economist recommends government action to solve the problem: if the market fails (which it inevitably will, almost by definition), than the government must act to fix it by manipulating the market, directly and indirectly, to create or simulate the conditions of perfect competition, and thereby bring about its efficient consequences. There are, of course, many practical problems with this, similar to those involved in Pigouvian taxation, such as the informational demands of such a program, the incentive problems inherent in a system with no feedback or discipline, and the resulting potential for fraud. These are well known, and economists argue endlessly about the efficacy of competition policy (as they do with regard to Pigouvian taxes). But for our present purposes, the question is not whether the government *can* do anything about so-called market failure, but whether the government *should* do anything about it. Is the government justified in using its coercive power to interfere with business operations in an attempt to increase some consequentialist measure of social welfare?

In cases of monopoly, price-fixing, cartels, mergers, and other "anticompetitive" behavior, the prescribed government action is antitrust. As far as most economists are concerned, if anticompetitive behavior constitutes evidence of the devil on earth, antitrust is the avenging angel. But in the real world, antitrust enforcement is far from perfect, as even its fiercest adherents admit. Although the inefficiency of monopoly or monopolization is easy to identify in general, it is notoriously difficult to correct in specific cases. In fact, behavior that is used to support antitrust allegations can just as well be interpreted to show competitive behavior (take predatory pricing, for example, which is evidenced by low prices that are normally encouraged by authorities). The antitrust laws are vague, some extraordinarily so, and when combined with the changing tide of politicized regulatory policy and Supreme Court decisions, they result in a chaotic environment for business owners, who are left with little idea what comprises legal activity and what does not. Finally, there are numerous problems with determining the efficient remedies for antitrust violations, including the possibility of second-best outcomes, efficiency-raising mergers, and other welfarist quandaries.

But while many economists acknowledge these practical difficulties, few of them have any reservations about the justification of antitrust; almost never do they question the right of the government to use its coercive power to punish firms for failing to maximize social welfare.[22] To most economists, the term "free market" describes a result of maximal efficiency, not an institution embodying secure property rights. In their view, antitrust is justified if it helps achieve that maximal efficiency; for example, Richard Posner, a staunch defender of antitrust law and economics, writes that "the issue in evaluating the antitrust significance of a particular business practice should be whether it is a means by which a rational profit maximizer can increase its profits *at the expense of efficiency*."[23] But in the Kantian (or, more broadly, classic liberal) view, antitrust is a violation of property rights with no rights-based justification—in other words, with no initial violation of property rights which antitrust action seeks to offset. Richard Epstein forcefully makes this point, emphasizing that most conceptions of property rights include the right of disposition, meaning that property owners have the right to transfer some or all of their property to another party under whatever terms the parties agree to.[24] The owner can give the property away, loan it to someone, or offer it for sale at whatever price he chooses. If the potential buyer does not judge that price to be worthwhile, she does not have to buy it. Consumers have no right to be sold an item at the price they would like to pay, for invoking such a right would involve a coercive transfer from the property owner, violating his right of disposition (and using him simply as a means). Presumed "anticompetitive" behavior is similar to nonwrongful externalities in that, while such activity may not maximize welfare, the firms engaging in such behavior are not violating any rights of consumers or competitors.

Most antitrust prohibitions fall under two broad categories, mergers of assets and restrictions on terms of sale. Their prohibition is normally justified by citing the negative consequences thereof: higher prices, lower consumer surplus, or lower social welfare (less efficiency). But are any rights violated by these actions—or, in other words, would Kantian ethics prohibit charging high prices as a juridical duty, thereby providing justification for state action to prevent such behavior? Using the Formula of Autonomy, we could ask if there is any logical contradiction in all firms being able to raise their prices. This practice, if universalized, may certainly have negative consequences, obviously for consumers, and also positive ones, in particular for firms that do not choose to raise their prices and may gain competitive advantage. But there is nothing logically contradictory in such a scenario: in fact, most firms are able to raise their prices at will, even with no "justification" based on increased costs or increased demand. Rather, such price adjustments are usually regarded as an essential part of the market process, wherein firms experiment with raising and lowering prices to find the one that maximizes profit (under the conditions prevailing at that point in time). And such a world is obviously not unimaginably atrocious, so the test of contraction-in-the-will generated by the Formula of the Law of Nature fails to rule out raising prices as well; this would also apply to selective increases in price, such as price discrimination.

Of course, it is not the act of raising prices that is prohibited by antitrust, but rather behavior that may lead to greater ability to increase prices in the long run, such as mergers. Does the categorical imperative rule out asset mergers? Is there any logical contradiction in all firms being able to merge their assets with other firms when they wish? There is nothing in the concept of opportunistic merger that, when universalized, contradicts itself—the efficacy of merger does not rely on other firms' not being able to merge—so it is difficult to see how the categorical imperative would rule it out.[25] Again, we can apply the stronger test of contradiction-in-the-will: could a universal right to merge be willed by a rational agent, or does it result in such a horrific state of affairs that no one could will it to be without sacrificing some ends-in-themselves? Even though some people, such as consumers, may not like a world in which firms could merge whenever desirable, there would seem to be nothing in the idea that is impossible for a rational agent to conceive of or will.

Other prohibited behaviors that are understood to lead to higher future prices include predatory pricing, exclusive dealings, tying, and bundling. These actions can also be seen to put competitors to a disadvantage, another negative consequence, but is there a justification grounded in rights or duties for forbidding these activities? All of these practices are, generally speaking, restrictions on the terms of trade, in which the seller places or changes the limits on the terms he is willing to accept before finalizing a transaction.[26] Would universalizing possible restrictions on terms of trade be contradictory in any way? As with raising prices (also a restriction on trade), other restrictions may shift the benefits of transactions from one party to another, but they do not contradict their very use (or fail to promote ends-in-themselves), so it is difficult to see how to construe a duty not to restrict terms of trade based on the universalization formulae of the categorical imperative.

So we found no basis in the universalization formulae of the categorical imperative for any duty not to merge assets or restrict terms of trade (including price), and therefore no correlative juridical rights that can be enforced through the state by consumers or competitors. This is supported by the observation that, like externalities, not all mergers or restrictions on trade are prohibited by the state, but rather only those that are seen to be particularly detrimental to consumer surplus, social welfare, or efficiency. If there were rights or duties involved, these activities would be unambiguously wrong, and the state (or the harmed private parties) would have a *per se* justification for pursuing all such cases, as with wrongful harms (discussed above). As things stand, however, the only criticism that can laid upon mergers and restrictions is that they have possibly negative consequences, but if these effects result from nonwrongful activities (those that violate no duties or right), then the state has no business punishing firms for them.

We can also approach this question from other directions, such as "don't consumers have rights to low prices, or other firm owners to their livelihood?" If such rights do exist, then they would have to follow from duties imposed on sellers, forcing them to charge low prices or refrain from certain restrictions on terms of trade such as predatory pricing, and we saw above that no duties exist. (In fact, these would be somewhat contradictory duties, one prohibiting prices too high, the other prohibiting prices too low!) We saw above that Kant did not endorse rights based on imperfect duties such as beneficence, for to claim a right to a certain level of well-being would imply that others have a perfect duty to provide it, which in turn would treat the providers merely as a means to an end.

The astute reader will remember that, in Chapter 1, I discounted the importance of the universalization tests, so the emphasis given them in this example may seem excessive (perhaps even opportunistically hypocritical). So let us turn instead to the Formula of Respect, on the basis of which some may ask, "don't firms who merge and restrict terms of trade use their consumers or competitors as means to their own profit-making while not treating them also as ends?" If this were so, then all business owners would be guilty of this sin, including Adam Smith's tradesmen who sell their wares not for the good of their customers, but to improve the well-being of their own families. But remember that the second formula states that persons cannot use others *simply* as means, without at the same time treating them as ends. As discussed in chapters 1 and 3, we use other people all the time: we use grocers to obtain food, mechanics to keep our automobiles running—and cabbies when they are not. But we do so while treating these persons with respect, chiefly through honestly eliciting voluntary provision of their services. Only deceit and fraud, specific instances of the general phenomenon of lying and therefore violations of perfect duty, would represent (along with outright coercion) violations of the Formula of Respect in the commercial realm. As long as the seller behaves honestly and openly, and the buyer is free to accept or reject the terms of trade as offered, then the seller is not using the buyer merely as a means, but is at the same time respecting the buyer by being truthful and honorable in his business.[27] So no duties prohibiting mergers or restrictions on terms of trade can be derived from this formula of the categorical imperative either, unless we throw away the baby with the bathwater and condemn all commercial activity.

To summarize, if we accept that there is no duty on the part of firms to avoid mergers and restrictions on terms of trade—or that consumers have no right to low prices, or competitors to a particular standard of livelihood or success—then there is no basis for state enforcement of laws prohibiting "anti-competitive" behavior. Since antitrust law and enforcement can be justified only by consequentialist logic, any punishment of such violations would be counter to the limited role that Kant granted the state.[28] Firms found guilty of antitrust violations have not violated any duty-based rights of consumers or competitors, but merely have acted in a way that failed to maximize social welfare (in the state's estimation), which may be suboptimal but is not wrongful.

Law, Economics, and Efficiency

What we have discussed above regarding the ethics of efficiency has serious implications for the field of *law and economics*, which can be regarded as a *reductio ad absurdum* of welfare economics. Otherwise known as the *economic approach to law*, law and economics is by many measures the most successful instance of economic imperialism, the application of economic principles to fields of study traditionally considered outside of its domain.[29] Law and economics is now seen as a valid approach to the study of law, with economists sitting on the faculty of most law schools, and law-and-economics scholarship published by the top-ranked law reviews (and many dedicated law and economics journals). Addressing the appeal of economics to law professors, George Fletcher (a prominent legal scholar himself) writes:

> American law professors have been receptive to economic analysis . . . because the culture of American law has long had strong ties to utilitarian thought. The devotee of [law and economics] writes in a long line of theorists who think that all legal institutions should serve the interests of society . . . . Yet we have traced a remarkable transformation. The discussion begins with Pareto's principles of efficiency, grounded in the values of secure property rights, individual choice, and the necessity of voluntary transactions. In light of Kaldor's modest amendment . . . we end up with a theory of legal intervention that permits the periodic redefinition of property rights for the sake of a collective vision of efficiency. A theory of individual supremacy ends up as a philosophy of group supremacy. This is a remarkable metamorphosis. Any theory that can successfully obfuscate the difference between individual sovereignty in the market and the dominance of group interests in coercive decision making will surely gain a large number of followers.[30]

In the spirit of Fletcher's comments, I argue that approaching the law with welfare economics, with its sole focus on efficiency to the exclusion of independent considerations of rights or justice, conflicts directly and forcefully with the essential nature of law, which trades in terms such as fault, blame, guilt, wrongdoing, and responsibility—all of which a Kantian approach can easily accommodate with its grounding in dignity, right, and justice, as we saw in the preceding discussion of externalities and antitrust.

Of course, legal economists have been able to account for all of the concepts mentioned above by collapsing them to welfare or efficiency. As leading law and economics scholar Richard Posner once wrote,

> a second meaning of "justice," and the most common I would argue, is simply "efficiency." When we describe as "unjust" convicting a person without a trial, taking property without just compensation, or failing to require a negligent automobile driver to answer in damages to the victim of his carelessness, we can be interpreted as meaning simply that the conduct or practice in question *wastes resources*.[31]

But most people do not understand terms like justice, guilt, or blame based on utilitarian considerations; for instance, we do not reserve our judgment regarding a criminal defendant's guilt or innocence until we calculate the relative impact of each on social welfare. We would prefer to think that when someone is found guilty, that is the best assessment of the truth of the accusations regarding his wrongdoing (and perhaps even an accurate reflection of his character). This conception lies behind legal excuses such as insanity, which serves no utilitarian end but absolves someone of legal responsibility based on a lack of moral responsibility. Furthermore, once someone is found guilty, we demand that he be punished primarily because he deserves it, not because of some expected benefit to the rest of society based on deterrence or other consequentialist considerations, and we recoil at the thought of lessening his due penalty to further some other end (such as in the practice of plea bargaining, discussed below). The same principle would apply, perhaps a bit less dramatically, to determinations of liability in accident cases or breaches of contract; such disputes should be settled according to rights and justice, not calculations of efficiency and welfare.

By excluding these normative considerations, law and economics has taken utilitarianism to the extreme, justifying the criminal status of theft as due merely to the resulting misallocation of resources; allocating rights based on considerations of cost; justifying coercive takings and transfers on the basis of hypothetical compensation and consent; holding criminal sanctions to represent mere prices to potential lawbreakers; or manipulating convictions and punishments merely to deter rather than to punish. These positions often surprise those not schooled in the economic approach to law, due to the fact that many of our intuitions about the law are not based in brute utilitarianism. Therefore, I will argue that due to its emphasis on duty, rights, and human dignity, Kantian ethics is much more consistent with traditional thinking about the law than utilitarianism is.[32]

Specifically, the "economics" in law and economics is neoclassical, in both its positive and normative forms. In descriptive terms, it adopts the model of the utility-maximizing economic agent, his choices completely determined by his preferences and constraints, which we discussed in Chapter 1 (and continued below). In prescriptive terms, it adheres to the consequentialist standard of efficiency, operationalized as either Kaldor-Hicks efficiency (discussed below) or Pareto improvement and optimality (discussed in the next chapter). But as we know, a Kantian would take issue with these foundational concepts, both of which reflect a basic ignorance of, or negligence to consider, the essential dignity of the persons legal economists purport to model.

The most important (and legitimate) role that economists have to play in legal analysis is to recommend how scarce resources are to be allocated to achieve the purpose of the legal system. It is not by accident that economists claim that this purpose is to promote efficiency, and neither is it an accident that lawyers were attracted to it so quickly, as Fletcher explained in the passage quoted above. Elsewhere, Fletcher attributes economics' success in tort law (the most developed field within law and economics) to the "scientific image" granted by the formal, multistep process of the cost-minimization model, which thereby "basks in the respectability of precision and rationality . . . . Yet associating rationality with multistaged argumentation may be but a spectacular lawyerly fallacy—akin to the social scientists' fallacy of misplaced concreteness (thinking that numbers make a claim more accurate)."[33] But the purpose of the legal system is not necessarily to promote efficiency, or any utilitarian goal for that matter. For instance, many legal scholars argue that the purpose of the tort system is to ensure corrective justice, which holds that victims of wrongful harm are entitled to compensation from their injurers as a matter of right.[34] A tort system based on corrective justice may lead to lower accident costs, but that is not its primary purpose, goal, or motivation. Likewise, some argue that the criminal justice system should not be oriented toward efficient deterrence of future crimes, as the economic model of crime recommends, but rather toward the punishment of guilty persons, a stance generally known as *retributivism* (to be discussed more later in this chapter). Again, a retributivist criminal justice system will naturally lead to some degree of deterrence as well, but that would not be its primary goal. Finally, the purpose of the court system, rather than arriving at efficient outcomes, can be to arrive at truth and justice, even though cases may still be decided efficiently. Justice, right, truth—these are all immeasurable and not quantifiable, but are nonetheless core concepts of a liberal society, and they challenge the analytically straightforward but normatively unsatisfying goal of efficiency that dominates neoclassical law and economics.

Fairness versus welfare

As an illustration of the devotion of prominent law-and-economics scholars to consequentialism, consider Louis Kaplow and Steven Shavell's 2002 book, *Fairness Versus Welfare*, the most extensive defense of law-and-economics methodology since Richard Posner's *The Economics of Justice* several decades prior. In their book, Kaplow and Shavell make the claim that legal decision-making should be performed solely to maximize social welfare, with no independent regard given to factors such as fairness, justice, or rights. Certainly, for those partial to the prevailing method in law and economics, this book would seem to reinforce their beliefs and practices. However, the authors provide nothing to convince the skeptic of the truth of their position, and their argument ends up being completely tautological with little original contribution. To be sure, most of *Fairness Versus Welfare* consists of impeccable law-and-economics analysis, comparing and contrasting the effects of various rules based on standard tools and methods in the discipline. But where the authors fall short is in their attempt to justify the exclusive use of welfare economics and its attendant consequentialist logic to use economics to study the law.

The book consists of three parts. In Part One ("Framework"), the authors give an overview of their argument that "the welfare-based normative approach should be exclusively employed in evaluating legal rules. That is, legal rules should be selected entirely with respect to their effects on the well-being of individuals in society" (3–4).[35] They discuss both their definition of well-being (preference-satisfaction) as well as the various "notions of fairness" against which they argue throughout the book. The authors use the term "fairness" to lump together all alternatives to welfarism, including justice, rights, equality, equity, as well as fairness as commonly understood. This usage leads to claims of "conflicting notions of fairness" (471), whereas most advocates would likely choose one or another; naturally, inconsistent conceptions of fairness are bound to conflict.[36]

Part Two ("Analysis") comprises the bulk of the book, in which the authors apply a common analytical approach to four areas of legal studies: torts, contracts, legal procedure, and law enforcement. In each area, the consequences of the welfare economics approach are contrasted with those of the fairness approach, and not surprisingly, the welfarist approach always leads to the best consequences—measured in terms of welfare. To conclude each chapter, the "appeal" of concepts of fairness is assessed and then dismissed in favor of welfarism. Part Three ("Extensions") concludes the book with a more detailed look at the conflict between welfare and fairness. One of the chapters in Part Three examines the appeal of fairness to different groups of people (ordinary individuals, government decision-makers, and legal academics, to whom the most attention is given). Another chapter provides the authors' responses to anticipated criticisms of the welfare economics approach; the same chapter also includes their extended treatment of "tastes for fairness," which I discuss below.

The central argument of *Fairness Versus Welfare* consists of two parts, one positive and one normative: deviation from a pure welfare-maximization rule *will* result in less-than-maximal welfare, and as a result legal principles *should* be decided on the sole basis of welfare-maximization. The first part of this statement is essentially a tautology, which the authors acknowledge at several points throughout the book (7, 58), but they claim that the point is still important to demonstrate formally since the welfare loss from such deviations is not "well appreciated" (8). The second part cannot be derived directly from the first, and holds strength only for persons predisposed to the standard economic way of thinking, or consequentialist ethics in general. As the authors admit several times (61, for instance), they cannot prove the superiority of one value system over another, and in fact, they do not try: "we suppose, however, that most of us do believe that individuals' well-being matters, and we suspect that the fact that any notion of fairness may involve making everyone worse off will be seen as troubling" (468–9). They do provide arguments against alternative approaches to policymaking based on fairness, justice, or rights, some of them quite interesting, but based ultimately on a welfare criterion, for which the authors never provide a positive argument. So we are back to the tautology that only welfare-maximization maximizes welfare, and if the latter is desired, the former is recommended.

Furthermore, the authors treat alternatives to welfarism with derision. After considering the arguments for fairness, the authors "discover very little basis for the use of notions of fairness as independent evaluative principles" (8), but since their evaluation is conducted in terms of welfarism, a negative response is all but guaranteed. "The point that giving weight to fairness in the choice of legal rules may harm all persons *should be deeply troubling* to analysts who suggest that notions of fairness ought to serve as independent evaluative principles" (8, emphasis mine). The authors seem to deny that one can honestly and sincerely hold to principles other than welfarism, and they further imply that once such a person realizes the welfare cost of fairness, he will surely change his mind. They continue: "some writing on notions of fairness takes the principles to be self-evident and thus not needing any explicit justification" (8; see also 59). But the authors never provide explicit justification for their own welfarist views, taking them to be self-evident, and they use them to refute all other views, as if they are on firmer ground just because the authors say so. (On page 436, for instance, they claim that well-being has "moral force," without any supporting argument.)

According to the authors, advocates of fairness "must provide the reasons why a society should willingly make its members—possibly all of them—worse off in order to advance a particular conception of fairness" (10). If fairness, justice, or right is the primary concern to some scholars, that *is* their reason, just as maximizing well-being is the authors' reason for their conclusions. For instance, they claim, quite correctly, that "theories of corrective justice also fail to indicate the value of providing corrective justice relative to that of meeting other possible objectives" (97). But this misses the point: corrective justice *is* the value, rather than having instrumental value in terms of some other, "higher" measure. The authors would contend that corrective justice must be evaluated in terms of its effect on welfare, but others would say that they are both alternative values, or perhaps rather that wealth-maximization must be assessed in terms of its effects on corrective justice.

Kaplow and Shavell write that the "policy-oriented legal academic literature that uses notions of fairness as criteria for assessing legal rules rarely confronts or even acknowledges the existence of the conflict between giving weight to notions of fairness and advancing individual's well-being" (58). But there is no reason why the authors of this literature should acknowledge this conflict if they do not give weight to notions of well-being in the first place. After all, Kaplow and Shavell, like most law-and-economics practitioners, do not acknowledge the cost of their recommendations in terms of justice, fairness, or rights, because they consider well-being to be the sole consideration. They note that some legal and moral philosophers *"appear* to hold an absolute view wherein considerations of fairness trump any concern for individuals' well-being" (106n51). But the authors hold just as absolute a view in favor of well-being over considerations of fairness.[37]

Kaplow and Shavell do try to include nonwelfarist moral factors in their analysis, though at the level of individual preferences rather than policy-making processes. They claim throughout the book that they take preferences to be general enough to incorporate tastes for fairness, such as preferences over the pattern of outcomes rather than the personal value of the outcomes themselves (403). One may prefer to live in a world of greater equality, even if that means less wealth for the average person. One may prefer to live in a world where innocent persons were not punished for crimes they did not commit, even if that means that more guilty persons are acquitted, possibly implying lower welfare. One may prefer to live in a world where rights are respected to such an extent that welfare is lower. The authors admit such positions as preferences, as economists often do, but as I argued in Chapter 1, they are more appropriately modeled as duty, principle, or constraint, which the authors do not consider.

But even when they are treated as preferences, Kaplow and Shavell do not take such tastes seriously, either neglecting to include them in their examples or claiming that they cannot be as strong as ordinary tastes for goods and services (433). This rhetorical strategy is understandable, of course: if they include tastes for fairness, all of their conclusions could be reversed if those tastes are made strong enough, as they acknowledge (141–2), dismissing it as an empirical issue (but not one important enough to contemplate).[38] But if they do not include them, they are arbitrarily restricting the range of preferences that their analysis takes into account. This restriction makes their main thesis all the more tautological: welfare-maximization maximizes welfare, especially if welfare is not based significantly on any nonwelfarist preferences. They ultimately dismiss the importance of tastes for fairness, claiming that were such persons made aware of the welfare costs of these tastes, they would "change their minds" (433), since principled tastes are obviously no match for welfarist ones.[39]

To be sure, Kaplow and Shavell's central thesis has been roundly criticized, more so by "traditional" legal scholars than legal economists.[40] Most law-and-economics practitioners have been reluctant to embrace openly the extreme welfarism of *Fairness Versus Welfare*, but nonetheless there has not been much change in their methodology. Seeing that, we now turn to the most popular evaluative tool used in law and economics, Kaldor-Hicks efficiency.

Kaldor-Hicks efficiency

The Kaldor-Hicks efficiency test endorses a change in policy or law if and only if the gains to those who benefit from the change, measured in dollars, exceed the losses to those who are harmed, ensuring a net benefit overall. There are well-known difficulties with this concept, not central to my argument, but worth mentioning all the same. First, Kaldor-Hicks efficiency compares benefits and losses in monetary terms, which grants the illusion of metrical ease, comparability, and stability, but these calculations are based on willingness-to-pay, a hypothetical measure with no verifiability. Second, even if the willingness-to-pay figures are taken to be accurate, this process is biased against persons with fewer discretionary resources. Those with more resources will be able to pledge higher amounts in support of their preferences regarding the proposal, lessening the ability of the poor to influence policy outcomes; to make matters worse, diminishing marginal utility of income also shifts the balance of power away from the poor, and may contribute to the approval of changes that, in nonmonetary terms, result in net harm rather than net benefit. For instance, assume Group A pledges $5 million to support a project and Group B pledges $4 million to block it. But if Group B is largely made up of lower-income persons, then it is very possible that Group B's lower pledge represents more of a sacrifice to its members than Group A's nominally larger pledge. In monetary terms, the project results in $1 million of net benefit, but in terms of well-being and relative sacrifice, it may be a net loss. As Coleman writes, this system is "normatively prejudiced in a particularly insidious way: namely, it turns out that what is efficient depends on what people are willing to pay, [which] in turn depends on what they are capable of paying. In short, the greater one's wealth, the more likely one is to increase it."[41]

Compared to the stricter standard of Pareto improvement or superiority, which approves of only those changes that make at least one party better off without making any parties worse off, Kaldor-Hicks efficiency is seen as more practical, because it can evaluate proposals that carry both benefits and harms. But economists realize that there are ethical difficulties with intentionally harming some persons to benefit others, so they justify Kaldor-Hicks analysis by recourse to *hypothetical compensation*: if Group A benefits more than Group B loses, then Group A can (hypothetically) compensate Group B for their total losses, leaving them in the same position they were before the change, while Group A is guaranteed positive residual benefit (since their original gain was larger than the loss). If Group B is in fact compensated, and that compensation makes Group B truly as well off (or marginally better) compared to before the change, then the change would be a Pareto improvement (since Group B benefits and Group A is not harmed, at least in financial terms; more on this in the next chapter). For this reason, changes approved by Kaldor-Hicks efficiency are often called "potential Pareto improvements," based on the theoretical possibility (or potentiality) of compensation.[42]

There are numerous ethical difficulties with this picture, particularly from a Kantian point of view. First, hypothetical compensation does not make those harmed by the change any better off; it will buy nothing more than a hypothetical cup of coffee. Advocates will claim either that the responsibility for compensation lies with politicians, not economists, or that the transaction costs of arranging for compensation prohibit its use. Neither argument holds up to scrutiny, because if the need for compensation is taken seriously, the necessary arrangements should be included in any proposed change in policy or law that by design will impose undeserved harm on persons. If economists want to generate actual Pareto improvements, they will personally see to it that compensation is arranged, and will not shift the burden to politicians. The excuse of high transaction costs is equally invalid, though all too often used to justify injustices in the name of efficiency; there is no principled reason that the costs of compensation should be neglected in the process of policy design.

If compensating those harmed by the proposal is too costly, that should cast doubt on the wisdom of the policy itself, not the practice of compensation. Finally, hypothetical compensation can be seen as a strategic ploy to hitch Kaldor-Hicks efficiency to Pareto improvement's wagon, since the latter standard has practically been elevated to sainthood by neoclassical economists. However, Pareto efficiency is more objectionable than it may seem, depending on its precise relationship to consent, an integral aspect of respect for the dignity of persons, which is the topic of the next chapter in this book.

The most basic ethical problem here is that Kaldor-Hicks efficiency, with its reliance on hypothetical compensation, is a clear violation of the Formula of Respect, because it treats the party who loses resources merely as a means to the end of the party who gains them. Indeed, even were the compensation to occur, but without the explicit consent on the part of the harmed party, the practice would still be objectionable, since the compensation is imposed on, rather than freely accepted by, the harmed party. The absence of compensation serves to compound this offense to dignity; as Anthony Kronman recognizes, in the case of hypothetical compensation,

someone committed to the Kantian idea of individual autonomy would rightly feel that his moral principle had been violated, and it would not make any difference, from his point of view, that compensation could potentially be made even though it was not. *For a Kantian, the Kaldor-Hicks test has no significance.*[43]

As we noted above, a common argument for hypothetical compensation is that the transaction costs of compensation are too high. In such cases, law-and-economics advocates recommend that the authorities should "mimic the market" and order the transaction that the parties involved "would have" made in the absence of transaction costs.[44] Aside from the informational problems involved with knowing what the parties "would have done" in a different state of the world, there is no rationale for justifying coercive transfers based on high transaction costs unless efficiency is valued more highly than rights. Posner's answer to this objection is to suggest that in fact compensation does exist, in the form of *ex ante* compensation.[45] He offers the example of a man who buys a lottery ticket and then loses the drawing; according to Posner, he has "consented" to the loss due to his knowledge of such a possibility before purchasing the ticket. More generally, if making policy decisions according to the Kaldor-Hicks standard minimizes transaction costs and increases total wealth, the average person is thereby compensated *ex ante* for any losses she may incur *ex post*. In other words, since total gains always exceed total losses from Kaldor-Hicks efficient actions, a person can expect to experience a net gain over her lifetime, and would therefore (by assumption) consent to any losses incurred at times.

Coleman is very critical of this view of consent.[46] He offers the counterexample of someone deciding whether to buy a relatively expensive house in a safe neighborhood or a relatively inexpensive house in an unsafe neighborhood. If one chooses the cheaper house, one has consented to the increased risk, but that does not imply that if the house is burgled, that the homeowner consented to that as well. Posner responded to Coleman's criticism by claiming to use a broader sense of the word "consent," implying simply that the man who bought the lottery ticket cannot complain or claim unfair treatment if he loses.[47] But this broad conception of consent is not strong enough to justify the use of efficiency to judge social affairs and impose policy based on it; in the end, Posner admits that "wealth maximization as an ethical norm gives weight both to utility, though less heavily than utilitarianism does, and to consent, though perhaps less heavily than Kant himself would have done,"[48] though he earlier claimed to base his idea of consent in Kantian ethics.[49]

Coase and the instrumental nature of rights

Related to Kaldor-Hicks efficiency, another implication of the utilitarian nature of law and economics (and welfare economics as well) is the instrumental and contingent nature of rights. As far as advocates are concerned, the rights of individuals are secure only insofar as no one else values them more; in this framework, rights are treated as merely a means to maximize efficiency, rather than as claims against it. As the argument goes, if possible, rights will eventually be sold to the parties that value them most, so judges, legislatures, or regulatory agencies should reach that eventual outcome more quickly (with lower transaction costs). Of course, we can anticipate two problems with this, one practical and the other ethical: it is impossible for anyone besides the parties involved to have all of the information necessary to make accurate decisions as to who values the right more, and even if this information were available and known, individuals should not be forced to relinquish their deserved rights, even in the name of efficiency.[50] As we know, dignity mandates that persons be accorded respect, one aspect of which takes the form of rights or claims against others. These are not simply legal rights, to be granted or retracted at the will of the state, but moral rights, guaranteed to each person by virtue of his or her dignity, which exist whether or not they are formally recognized by the state.

Ronald Dworkin has taken the lead in emphasizing the negligence of intrinsic rights in law and economics. One of the central tenets of his legal philosophy is that, at least in some nontrivial cases, rights should "trump" considerations of welfare.[51] But as maintained in law and economics, rights are secondary to efficiency, implying that dignity of some is sacrificed for the "well-being" of all, and "the institution of rights, and particular allocations of rights, are justified only insofar as they promote social wealth more effectively than other institutions or allocations."[52] For instance, Posner claims (in rather Orwellian fashion) that economics does recognize absolute rights: "the economist recommends the creation of such rights . . . when the cost of voluntary transactions is low . . . . But when transaction costs are prohibitive, the recognition of absolute rights is inefficient."[53] Dworkin also points out that law and economics scholars— Posner, specifically—apply this reasoning not only to "less important rights, like the right to an injunction in nuisance or to damages in negligence," but also to "determining the most fundamental human rights of citizens, including their right to life and to control their own labor rather than be slaves to others,"[54] not to mention a woman's "right to determine her sexual partners"—that is, to be free from rape.[55] But derived in this way, rights have no independent justification; as Dworkin argues, Posner uses wealth maximization to justify the rights that wealth maximization justifies, a tautology that has nothing to do with the intrinsic moral value of rights or persons (and recalls Kaplow and Shavell's "arguments" for welfarist policymaking).[56] Posner acknowledges, however, that this is not a concept of rights that rights theorists would agree with, and I presume he would (correctly) include Kantians in that group.

The concept of instrumental rights can be further illustrated by reviewing one of the foundational concepts of law and economics: the Coase Theorem. Derived from Ronald Coase's landmark paper "The Problem of Social Cost," the most common version of the Coase Theorem states that if rights are fully and clearly assigned, and transaction costs are zero (or sufficiently low), then the parties involved will reach the efficient solution to any legal dispute between them, regardless of the initial assignment of rights. Taken in isolation from later developments, the Coase Theorem is simple, elegant, and brilliant. Suppose Alice is playing music in her apartment too loudly for her neighbor Brad, who likes to spend quiet evenings reading Kant.[57] There are two options: Alice can turn down the music, which she would do for no less than $25, or Brad can wear earplugs, which he would do for no less than $30. We will assume that Alice and Brad can costlessly come to an agreement, and that one of them has an unambiguous and undisputed right to determine the volume of Alice's music (determined by the lease, previous legal judgments, or even social mores). If Brad has the right to quiet, then Alice will turn her music down, at a subjective cost of $25, because the alternative, paying Brad $30 to wear earplugs, is costlier. If Alice has the right to play her music as loud as she pleases, then Brad can wear earplugs, at a subjective cost of $30 to him, but he would rather pay Alice between $25 and $30 to turn down her music (and our assumptions ensure that she will accept this offer). So no matter who has the controlling right, the result will be that Alice lowers the volume of her music, which is the more efficient (least cost) option out of the two suggested.[58]

That much is uncontroversial from an ethical point of view. This basic application of the Coase Theorem relies on voluntary transactions that reflect each party's subjective valuation of the available options, against the background of the tort system (as explained above in the discussion of externalities). Furthermore, it results in unqualified Pareto improvements, since actual consent is required from both parties, so we can safely assume that it is in both parties' interests (however broadly interpreted) to accept the transaction. The ethical problems begin when law and economics scholars ponder what to do when the necessary conditions for the Coase Theorem are *not* met: if transaction costs are too high for the parties to bargain on their own, or if rights are not clearly assigned at the outset (which implies high transaction costs of a more general kind). In either case, the parties will take their dispute to court, and a judge will decide what the result will be if the right-holding party is clear, or who will be granted the right if it is not.

The question is *how* the judge should arrive at this decision. According to law and economics, we saw above that the judge should "mimic the market" and try to determine what agreement the parties would arrive at if they could bargain with low transaction costs. This is an incredible amount of information for a judge to handle, and involves the same problems of estimation of costs and benefits discussed earlier in the context of Kaldor-Hicks efficiency (which is, after all, the criterion the judge would be using). If rights are clearly assigned, then the judge "only" has to determine the most efficient solution, and order the party without the right to pay for it. There are several dangers implicit in this: the more specific, economic danger is the possibility of an incorrect solution from the judge that ends up in an inefficient solution, though it is possible the parties can negotiate around this (if transaction costs fall sufficiently to allow it). This is known as the *irrelevance-of-law* aspect of the Coase Theorem: in the end, if parties can bargain, the judicial or legislative assignment of rights does not affect the realization of the efficient solution (only who pays for it). The more general ethical danger is one we have seen before (and will see again, especially in the next chapter): the imposition of a coerced solution, which is based on a third party's impressions of the interests of the parties involved and justified by high transaction costs, but does not respect the dignity of either party.

What if rights are not clearly assigned? In that case, according to law and economics, the judge determines the efficient solution (somehow), and then vests the right in whichever party values it the most (according to the judge's estimates); the reasoning is that this party would purchase the right anyway (in the absence of transaction costs), and the use of judicial fiat saves the transaction costs of negotiating over it. (And if the judge's determination is incorrect, then the right will be sold anyway.) Note that the assignment of the right is not based on any moral claim based on desert or justice, but rather on relative estimated valuations, with all the attendant problems discussed previously. Reasonable persons can argue over whether it is Alice or Brad who has the right to control the volume of Alice's music, but few people—outside law and economics—would claim that this right should be assigned according to who would pay more for it. According to the figures I gave above, a legal economist would argue that Brad should be granted the right, since it is worth $30 to him and only $25 to Alice. (And even this assumes that their incomes are equal, so diminishing marginal utility of income is less of a concern.) Of course, we could tweak the numbers a bit and— *voilà*—the right would go to Alice. Whatever criteria they may use to determine who has the right in this situation, few people, outside of utilitarians and legal economists, would make that decision with a calculator.[59]

In such cases, we see again that, to legal economists, rights are regarded as instrumental to welfare, and are assigned by a legal authority (subject to later bargaining) to ensure the lowest-cost (or highest-value) outcome. But Kantians consider rights very differently, holding that they are based on duties, not on a evaluation of consequences. Posner objects to this view, writing that adherence to a Kantian system "requires an arbitrary initial assignment of rights."[60] But rights are not "arbitrarily assigned" in Kant's view, but instead are determined by duties; for instance, a duty not to steal implies a correlative right not to be stolen from.[61] In his original paper, Coase used the example of a farmer's crops which are harmed by straying cattle belonging to a neighboring rancher. He then showed that if transaction costs are low, and either party is assigned the right to control the use of the land, the farmer and the rancher will bargain over the use, and the party that values it the most will purchase or retain that right. In the absence of these conditions, he argued that the law should award the right to the party who would have purchased it in an ideal bargaining context. But in a Kantian interpretation, the rancher violated his duty to respect the property of the farmer by failing to restrain his cattle from grazing on the farmer's land. The farmer is free to sell his right to the rancher, but that right is clearly his to begin with, and should not be assigned to the rancher if he is not willing to pay for it, merely because it is worth more to him.

Yet another aspect of the neglect of meaningful rights within the efficiency framework is the treatment of causation, stemming primarily from Coase's work, but also seen in that of Calabresi.[62] The common application of the Coase Theorem depends on *reciprocal causation*, wherein neither party in a conflict is judged worthy of blame or fault; the only concern is determining the overall efficient solution. As Coase wrote, "the question is commonly thought of as one in which A inflicts harm on B and what has to be decided is: how should we restrain A? But this is wrong. We are dealing with a problem of a reciprocal nature. *To avoid the harm to B would be to inflict harm on A*."[63] To use Coase's example, enforcing the farmer's right to protect his crops inflicts harm on the rancher by preventing him from violating that right, and society should be morally indifferent between these two instances of harm, leaving only the relative costs of each harm to determine the efficient solution.

While agreeing with Coase's economic analysis, Richard Epstein criticizes his reliance on reciprocal causation, explaining that while Coase holds to it in theory, his numerous examples are given in terms of unidirectional harm: "Coase describes each situation by the use of sentences that differentiate between the role of the *subject* of each of these propositions and the role of the *object*."[64] The harm only becomes reciprocal when the harmed party seeks compensation: "it would be a grave mistake to say that *before* the invocation of judicial remedies the grounds of dispute disclosed reciprocal harm . . . . The notion of causal reciprocity should not be confused with the notion of redress for harm caused."[65] Talbot Page makes a similar point, writing that the notion of reciprocal harm confuses "a physical harm with the effects of a remedy."[66]

In response to Epstein, Posner claims that "most torts arise out of a conflict between two morally innocent activities, such as railroad transportation and farming. What ethical principle compels society to put a crimp in the latter because of the proximity of the former?"[67] The answer is rights: such actions are not "morally innocent" if they violate someone's right (implied by duty). As Richard Wright notes, "the structure and content of the modes of rectification for infringement [of rights] will be implicit in the rights themselves."[68] Also, Posner "is perplexed *why* a society should decide to allocate accident costs in accordance with Epstein's admittedly plausible notions of causation. What social or ethical end is advanced?"[69] Again, the answer (though perhaps not Epstein's answer) seems clear: respect for the dignity of persons and, in a broader teleological sense, the harmony of individual ends envisioned in the kingdom of ends. Finally, predating Kaplow and Shavell's criticism of "fairness" advocates, Posner says that "the general impression that Epstein creates in the mind of this reader is that, while he will not admit explicit considerations of cost in his analysis, he is hopeful that his noneconomic approach will not do serious economic damage."[70] Whether or not that was in fact Epstein's hope, it does reflect our present Kantian outlook: consideration of the consequences of actions is less important than the duties or rights that are respected or violated in producing them.

Page compares Coase's normative framework with that of Pigou, finding that the difference between the two is that Coase relies on efficiency without a notion of responsibility, which explains his position on reciprocal causation.[71] Pigou, on the other hand, had a similar appreciation for efficiency, but he combined it with responsibility, so that one party is understood truly to harm the other (even if, as we explained above, the harm is not wrongful). Responsibility alone, however, does not determine the extent, or even the existence, of compensation, and this is where Pigou introduces the concept of efficiency. When examined in this light, Coase simply removed, or claimed irrelevant for his purposes, the sense of responsibility inherent in Pigou's system, and it is this omission which Kantians would find troublesome (without endorsing Pigou's amoral conception of harm). On the other hand, Coleman offers the suggestion that Coase was not denying nonreciprocal causation, but merely holding that the assignment of blame or fault is irrelevant to determining and obtaining the efficient solution.[72] In our example, even if the farmer is thought to have the moral right in Coase's example, the efficient solution will be reached whether that right is recognized or not. But however much Coase truly believed in the normative implications of nonreciprocal causation, the field of law and economics has continued with his stated position, and any noninstrumental rights are rarely recognized.

Examples of the instrumental approach to rights can be found in all areas of law and economics, especially in private law (tort, contract, and property). For instance, a central concern of the economic approach to tort law is the minimization of costs involved with accidents (and their prevention) through the choice of optimal liability rules.[73] The purpose of tort law is common understood to be to determine under what circumstances a victim of harm has the right to demand compensation from her injurer—in other words, under what conditions the injurer is liable for the victim's harm. The two basic rules of liability are strict liability and negligence: under *strict liability*, the injurer is always responsible for harms caused, regardless of any precautions taken, and under *negligence*, the injurer is responsible for harm caused only if she failed to take the "due standard of care" (defined by economists as the efficient level of precaution). There are many arguments for either strict liability or negligence based on justice and rights, to be sure, such as the arguments from corrective justice cited above, but the economic approach considers the issue one of efficiency: the efficient rule is the one that minimizes accident costs, understood as the sum of harm to the victims, costs of precaution, and costs of the legal system. As a result, the rights of victims to compensation are held hostage to utilitarian calculations rather than evaluated according to principled arguments based on rights and justice.

Another example comes from the economics of contract law, in which a central issue is "efficient breach," in which it is considered efficient for one party to break the terms of a contract unilaterally.[74] As with torts, the economic approach to this problem is to determine the proper remedies (damages) so that the party who desires to breach will do so only when it is efficient overall, bringing private incentives in line with public interests. (Efficient liability rules in tort law can be couched in the same language.) Payment of *expectation damages*, which compensate the harmed party for any expected losses resulting from nonperformance, is the efficient rule in simple cases, since it forces the breaching party to internalize the costs imposed on the other party, but it denies the other party any right to enforce performance by the breaching party. Under the alternative remedy of *specific performance*, the non-breaching party has the right to enforce the contract as written, and can sell that right to the party who wants to breach if an agreement can be reached (assuming the conditions necessary for the Coase Theorem hold). Specific performance preserves the right of both parties to maintain the contract both agreed to, and thereby appeals to a rights-based approach to the law, but whether legal economists would endorse it depends ultimately on efficiency, not rights; a right to specific performance is only of value to the economist if it leads to efficient outcomes.[75]

Property law is the most straightforward application of the Coase Theorem, and is therefore directly subject to all the scholarly criticisms discussed above. But issues of property rights and efficiency became an issue of much public debate after the 2005 Supreme Court decision in *Kelo v. New London* regarding *eminent domain*, the legal doctrine under which the government may appropriate (with compensation) the real property of a private owner for public use.[76] Traditionally, eminent domain was invoked only for public use projects such as highways, airports, schools, and hospitals. But more recently, as in the *Kelo* case, it has frequently been used to appropriate property for the benefit of private developers, at the expense of residents and business owners who refused to bargain with them. Local governments had incentive to facilitate such deals due to the increased tax base and revenues that would come with the upscale residences and commercial areas.

In a 5–4 decision, the Supreme Court held that such takings for public benefit (such as increasing tax revenues) did count as public use. In her dissent, Justice Sandra Day O'Connor emphasized that this decision would hit the poorest members of society the hardest:

Any property may now be taken for the benefit of another private party, but the fallout from this decision will not be random. The beneficiaries are likely to be those citizens with disproportionate influence and power in the political process, including large corporations and development firms. As for the victims, the government now has license to transfer property from those with fewer resources to those with more.[77]

This is an direct implication of the criticisms of Kaldor-Hicks made earlier in this chapter, now codified as legal precedent by the highest court in the United States. Setting aside consent issues for the next chapter, the more general point is that such manipulation of property rights to maximize some measure of social welfare fails to respect the dignity of the original landowners who, for whatever reason (financial or not), did not accept the private developers' offer for their land, as should have been their legal right (and is still their moral right).

Crime and punishment

The one area of the law in which the utilitarian, economic approach is perhaps the most inadequate is criminal law.[78] In the economic approach to criminal law (or the "economics of crime" for short), the sole purpose of enforcement and punishment is the efficient deterrence of future crime, not the punishment of wrongdoers, the pursuit of justice, or the expression of community outrage. Words like "guilt," "blame," and "wrongdoing" are not used in the literature on economics of crime—in fact, writers in the field have to bend backwards to explain why crimes are undesirable at all and thereby merit societal resources devoted to their prevention. For instance, to law-and-economics scholars, the criminal status of theft is not due to the fact that a property right is violated—property rights are only supported insofar as they lead to efficient outcomes, so they cannot justify anything *a priori*. After all, if Jim values Kathy's car more than she does, then Jim's theft of the car will result in a more efficient outcome according to Kaldor-Hicks efficiency. (Of course, Jim may not value the car more than Kathy does, but given the wealth of thieves relative to those from whom they frequently steal, diminishing marginal utility of income suggests that the case described above may be common, if not the norm.)

But law and economics scholars *know* in their hearts that theft is wrong, and it would be a embarrassment if they could not explain why. The simplest law and economics explanation is that theft leads to an inefficient private allocation of resources devoted to preventing it, primarily in the form of security expenditures, but also in abstaining from utility-increasing purchases out of fear of losing them to theft.[79] The absurdities abound: first, in this "ideal" efficient state of affairs with no private or public measures taken to combat theft, theft would of course prosper, which would inevitably lead to tremendous public outcry. (After all, it is doubtful that the common citizen, not schooled in neoclassical economics, would embrace the efficiency of having her property stolen.) Second, this analysis implies that it is the security measures taken by private citizens, rather than theft itself, that are the source of the inefficiency, and therefore it is *their* behavior that should be criminalized and punished. Finally, if private expenditures taken against theft are inefficient, what explains the public expenditures toward the same end, such as the costs of police officers, prosecutors, and judges that deal with suspected thieves? (One answer may be the public outcry mentioned earlier, but then we must ask what justifies the public outcry—people should realize theft is efficient!)

A more general and reasonable economic explanation of the category of crime, due to law professor and economist Alvin Klevorick, is based upon the types of transactions endorsed by society. He writes that society establishes a "transaction structure [which] sets out the terms or conditions under which particular transactions or exchanges are to take place under different circumstances."[80] Criminal activity is understood in this analysis as crossing the boundaries of the transaction structure instituted by society, and therefore it is in society's interests to devote public resources to preventing it.[81] While this theory is preferable to the simplistic one presented above, we still need to know what end is served by the chosen transaction structure; if the answer is efficiency (as Posner would say), then as with all utilitarian arguments, the result is wholly contingent on the particular calculation used to arrive at it. To his credit, Klevorick realizes this, arguing more generally that, even given his suggested economic definition of crime, we still need a political theory of rights to support it.[82]

It does not take a specifically Kantian perspective to recognize that the transaction structure theory, while elegant, misses the boat. Responding not only to the transaction structure idea but to all economic theorizing about crime, Coleman writes that

such a theory has no place for the moral sentiments and virtues appropriate to matters of crime and punishment: guilt, shame, remorse, forgiveness, and mercy, to name a few. A purely economic theory of crime can only impoverish rather than enrich our understanding of the nature of crime.[83]

Another prominent legal scholar, Herbert Morris, subtly indicts the law and economics approach, which "subordinates principle to the realization of social goals, a mode of thinking that focuses, not upon exculpation of the innocent and conviction of the guilty, that is, upon justice, but upon keeping social disruption at an acceptable level."[84] Unfortunately, such criticism too rarely comes from economists, but most often comes from legal scholars and moral philosophers (many of whom criticize the efficiency norm in the economics of private law as well).

Another unique aspect of crime as opposed to the private law is the institution of punishment. In the economic analysis of criminal law, the standard justification for punishment is deterrence, whereby preventing future crime increases expected social welfare or utility. Additional purposes for punishment mentioned in the literature include rehabilitation or incapacitation (chiefly in the case of imprisonment), but these too are often justified by utilitarian considerations, each increasing social welfare by lowering the incidence of future crime.[85] The most prominent alternative to deterrence is *retributivism*, which holds that punishment is deserved on the basis of wrongdoing and is therefore morally obligatory based on considerations of justice.[86] As usually understood, retributivism is not a utilitarian notion, as "the horse has already left the barn," so to speak; the crime has been committed, the harm has been done, and except in the case of purely monetary crimes, the wrong cannot effectively be remedied. From a utilitarian point of view, policy must look to the future and serve to deter future crimes, not devote resources to dealing with past ones, unless that serves the cause of deterrence (and thereby utility).[87]

Despite their nearly exclusive focus on deterrence, legal economists have discussed retributivism to some extent; however, as expected, most are dismissive, disparaging, or even mocking. Posner characterizes it as "widely viewed as immoral and irrational, or at least as primitive and non-rational."[88] He does endorse its "social function" in "primitive and early societies," in which it may temper the desire for private acts of vengeance, but dismisses its usefulness in modern societies, in which the function of law enforcement is assumed by the state. He concludes (without explicitly considering arguments from justice) that "retributive theories of punishment appear to belong to particular historical circumstances rather than to have a timeless claim to be regarded as just."[89] In *Fairness Versus Welfare*, Kaplow and Shavell apply their welfarist analysis to retributivism, showing that any penalties not determined purely on the basis of efficient deterrence will fail to deter efficiently, before dismissing retributivist thinking as based simply on intuitions, "a philosophized version of tastes for retribution," largely because "the degree of alignment between their theory . . . and tastes for retribution seems too close to be due merely to chance."[90]

However, this condescending and derogatory attitude toward retributivism is not universal among law and economics scholars. For instance, Donald Wittman provides the most fair and elaborate consideration of retributivism within the law and economics tradition, in which he models justice as a function of punishment and the number of criminals and innocent persons punished.[91] He assumes that justice is maximized at the punishment which is (exogenously) judged to "fit" a given crime and declines (linearly) as punishment rises or falls from this level. He uses this model to analyze the relative injustice resulting from deviations from the just punishment, from failing to punish all criminals and from punishing the innocent, and he also constructs a social utility function that would generate a societal preference for retributivist punishment. While most retributivists (and deontologists in general) would be uncomfortable with the idea of even a vague "measure" of justice, Wittman's approach, if extended modestly, would enable analysis of the necessary trade-offs involved with retributivist punishment in a world of scarcity.[92]

Along with G.W.F. Hegel, Kant is traditionally regarded as one of the seminal retributivists, arguing that retributive punishment alone fulfills the requirements of justice based on duties and rights.[93] Affirming the dignity of even convicted criminals, he writes that such persons must be punished according to right before any consideration can be given to social welfare:

> Punishment . . . can never be inflicted merely as a means to promote some other good for the criminal himself or for civil society. It must always be inflicted upon him only *because he has committed a crime*. For a human being can never be treated merely as a means to the purposes of another . . . [The criminal] must previously have been found *punishable* before any thought can be given to drawing from his punishment something of use for himself or his fellow citizens.[94]

Any deterrent effect of just punishment is certainly to be appreciated, but this is not the justification of the form, content, or amount of the penalty. If punishment is meant solely to deter, then the guilty party is being used solely as a means to the ends of the rest of society; in fact, as Murphy writes, "those of a Kantian persuasion [must] object just as strenuously to the punishment of the guilty on utilitarian grounds as to the punishment of the innocent."[95] As always, equal dignity and reciprocity are the paramount considerations in Kantian ethics, even in regard to punishment; for instance, Kant wrote that while a criminal cannot *will* (in his own interests) to be punished, he did freely choose to perform a punishable action. It follows that since he wills that others should be punished for similar acts, and that the laws that he would apply to all others must apply to him as well, he cannot (rationally) claim that his punishment is unjust.[96]

As emphasized by scholars such as Braithwaite and Pettit, retributivism cannot be a theory of punishment alone, but must address the broader criminal justice system as well.[97] For example, a common practice that would be objectionable to retributivists is plea bargaining, in which an accused party receives a smaller penalty either by admitting guilt in terms of a lesser crime, thereby saving both sides the cost and risk of a trial, or by providing information to the authorities to help capture or convict a more "important" criminal. While this practice may serve a clear utilitarian goal, it is hard to see how the deserved sentence of one wrongdoer can be traded off for the easier conviction of another, no matter how important the latter may be to the authorities, without sacrificing justice (to some extent); as Kant wrote (in one of his most eloquent moments), "woe to him who crawls through the windings of eudaemonism in order to discover something that releases the criminal from punishment or even reduces its amount by the advantage it promises."[98] Along similar lines, Kenneth Kipnis writes that "in its coercion of criminal defendants, in its abandonment of desert as the measure of punishment, and in its relaxation of the standards for conviction, plea bargaining falls short of the justice we expect of our legal system,"[99] and Herbert Morris sees plea bargaining as one symptom of the declining role of guilt in society and the courts.[100] The only consideration that may justify plea bargaining, as with other acts of prosecutorial discretion, is the scarcity of resources available for the criminal justice system, forcing authorities to make hard choices regarding the allocation of those resources, choices that necessarily affect which criminal defendants to prosecute with greater effort and which with less (if at all).[101] This is the most important and appropriate role for economics in the study of legal punishment (or, more broadly, criminal justice, or even policy in general), but success in allocating resources within the legal system depends critically on more elaborate and inclusive models of individual decision-making, to which we now turn.

Legal behavior and individual choice

Combining John Austin's sanction theory of law, which defines law as commands issued by a sovereign and backed by threats,[102] with Oliver Wendell Holmes's belief that to understand law, "you must look at it as a bad man, who cares only for the material consequences which such knowledge enables him to predict,"[103] it is understandable that law and economics would adopt the standard economic model of self-interested, utility-maximizing agents who respond to legal incentives as they would to prices.[104] In this view, potential criminals choose between legal and illegal activity with no apparent concern for the law besides the threat of punishment that it poses. Damages in private law (tort, contract, and property) are understood to work similarly, providing incentives for self-interested agents to take efficient actions by forcing them to internalize the costs of their actions (without necessarily realizing or caring that their actions may be wrong in a moral sense).

From the early part of this book, we recognize the dangers of such a limited conception of decision-making for understanding economic choice in general, and we see these problems exemplified by the use made of these models in law and economics.[105] As social economist Mark Lutz writes, criticizing this aspect of law and economics, "a law as such will have no effect on personal conduct but only the probability of punishment making illegal behavior more costly. . . . In other words, obedience to the law is wholly contingent upon calculations of self-interest."[106] Concepts such as duty and obligation play just as important—if not *more* important—a role in determining persons' reactions to changes in the law as they do in other choice situations, and their inclusion would therefore have a tremendous influence on both predictive and normative results in law and economics.

Analogues for this issue can be found in legal philosophy, particularly in H.L.A. Hart's distinction between obligation and being obliged. The typical economic agent, like Holmes's "bad man," would only feel *obliged* to obey the law for fear of punishment, while the Kantian (or otherwise moral) agent would feel a deeper, moral *obligation* due to her recognition of a duty to obey the law.[107] This distinction is parallel to another one Hart poses between *internal* and *external* points of view; the latter is characterized by detachment from the legal system, in which rules and punishment enter decision-making merely as data, while the former places the individual within the legal system, from which she considers the law to be binding on her in a normative sense, regardless of the existence of a threat of sanction.[108] Of course, this issue does not simply apply to crime; much more work needs to be done incorporating an explicit moral sense into the choice models used in all aspects of law and economics.[109] For instance, how would optimal liability rules change if potential injurers were ethically motivated to take precaution against harm? Or how would optimal remedies change in contract disputes if parties to a contract maintained some degree of ethical commitment?

The perfectly autonomous Kantian agent from Chapter 1, you might imagine, would have no need for sanctions at all, as inclination would have no effect on her decision-making. However, in the context of crime, Thomas Hill argues that punishment may actually be seen as a moral motivation in a Kantian sense.[110] While Hill acknowledges that simply trying to avoid monetary sanction or imprisonment is an empirical motive with no moral worth, a deeper fear of punishment, an aversion to the justified approbation of one's fellow citizens, may be moral insomuch as it is a result of one's moral judgment. If punishment is just, and we recognize the moral imperative in the law, then the impulse to avoid punishment can be seen as one and the same with the recognition of and motivation from duty: "what we call 'fear of punishment' can, at its best, be a specific form of respect for the moral law and so a worthy motive."[111] However, even if we accept punishment (or damages in private law) as a moral motive, it ultimately relies an internal point of view regarding the law, which as we have seen is not found in the economic approach to the law.

Also at issue is the deterministic nature of choice in economic modeling (Chapter 2), which is integral to both positive and normative law and economics. In positive analysis, it allows theorists to suppose a direct and precise causal link between legal and policy changes and behavioral responses, which in turn provides a firm basis for optimal policy design. The analogy to price effects is obvious: if grocers raise the price of bananas by a certain percentage, market research can predict the size of the resulting drop in purchases of bananas according to the estimated elasticity of demand for them. But when a legal sanction is changed, the process is more complicated (ignoring practical issues such as how this knowledge is spread). Not only does the moral aspect of the agent's judgment interfere with the predicted result (as described above), but so does the agent's strength of will in obeying the law (or consciously disobeying it for the sake of principle, even in the face of sanctions).[112] The imperfectly moral (heteronomous) agent will sometimes fail to obey the law purely for its own sake, and punishment will play an important role in preventing her from behaving illegally, to the extent or degree that she allows inclination to affect her maxims. Integrating character—judgment and will—into models of legal behavior has untold promise, but legal economists have to enlarge their conception of individual choice first.

In this chapter, we discussed how the use of efficiency as the sole evaluative criterion for policy fails to respect the dignity of persons, by imposing harm on them for the purpose of benefiting others, with no regard to the elements of right, desert, or justice inherent in the situation. The next chapter will extend this theme of dignity and respect thereof to more subtle but no less important offenses, those in which persons are denied the opportunity to give or refuse consent to policies that affect them, through consideration of two examples: the Pareto improvement standard and normative behavioral law and economics.

CHAPTER 5

Consent, Pareto, and Behavioral Law and Economics

In the last chapter, I explained that a Kantian would reject the base consequentialism of Kaldor-Hicks efficiency, and therefore much of welfare economics and normative law and economics which are built upon it. The basic reasoning is that coerced takings from one party to benefit another violate the respect owed persons possessed of dignity and autonomy; even if compensation were arranged, the lack of consent to the transfer—which can be considered the more intrinsically offensive aspect of the situation—would still remain. Pareto improvement or superiority would seem to overcome this, because it rules out changes in which any person is made worse off, usually as estimated by an outside party based on material and financial impact. But this is not the same thing as consent, because agents may be concerned with more than their financial well-being when considering a policy proposal. (For instance, we may expect a pacifist to reject a proposal to sell arms to rogue states in order to finance tax cuts which may significantly raise her wealth.) But actual consent, unlike estimates of value made by third parties, can be based on more than just material well-being or even other-regarding preferences; consent or refusal thereof may be based on a principle, value, or other desire-independent reason. As in the case of Kaldor-Hicks efficient proposals, law and economics scholars will claim that transaction costs prohibit them from obtaining actual consent from the parties affected by the policy, but if the policy endangers basic rights of the parties involved, transaction costs do not justify coercive policies based on Pareto calculations.

This chapter focuses on the important role that consent plays in ensuring that persons are paid the respect owed them by virtue of their dignity. We begin the chapter by discussing Pareto superiority, during which we will review and elaborate on Kant's position on coercion and deceit, and also by asking *whose* consent is necessary in a given situation. Then we will turn to the relatively new and popular field of behavioral economics, in particular behavioral law and economics. By incorporating insights from experimental psychology and economics, behavioral economists claim to account for anomalies in rational decision-making, such as inaccurate risk assessment, endowment effects, and weakness of will. In terms of positive science, behavioral economics is certainly headed in the right direction, but despite the advances they have made in detailing the thought processes behind decision-making—and the problems with them—behavioral economists still model rational choice as a deterministic process by which preferences, constraints, and beliefs determine the decision made.[1]

However, it is in its normative guise that behavioral economics poses a danger to dignity, especially when combined with a utilitarian, policy-oriented field like law and economics. Behavioral economists are not satisfied merely to describe the anomalies in everyday choice situations, or even to recommend ways for individuals to correct for them. They go one step further—a *big* step further—and conclude that it is the responsibility of the government to "help" individuals overcome the problems in their decision-making processes. Doing so leads to regulatory and legislative proposals to create strategically designed manipulations of choice options and sets—"nudges," to use the term introduced into popular discourse by Richard Thaler and Cass Sunstein's bestselling book—which, in the view of adherents, will help the individual achieve her own goals and desires better than she could have done on her own (given her dysfunctional choice processes). While they have termed this style of government intervention "libertarian paternalism," it is paternalism nonetheless (and its libertarianism is questionable)—and as such, it is inherently manipulative and coercive, and therefore an affront to dignity as maintained by a Kantian framework.

Pareto Improvement

One of the most persistent problems in economics is that of social choice. How should a governing body—be it a national legislature or a local zoning committee—make decisions that will affect a number of persons, some positively and others negatively? More precisely, along what lines should such a decision be made—economic welfare, personal well-being, justice, or some other criterion? Can individual preferences be aggregated, in a way that respects common intuitions of liberalism and democracy, in order to arrive at a social welfare function? Kenneth Arrow's famous Impossibility Theorem, and the huge literature it spawned, casts doubt on this, but to many, a combination of well-being and justice or fairness would be ideal, were it feasible. Despite Kaplow and Shavell's protestations to the contrary (as we saw in the last chapter), any pursuit of collective ends must be tempered by considering only just and fair means, which may potentially limit the extent to which the economist's ends—utility, wealth, well-being—can be maximized.

However, true to the utilitarian roots of economics, its models of social decision-making consider only the consequences of various options, with little thought given to the implications of such choices or choice procedures on justice, human dignity, or essential rights. For instance, consider the two primary evaluative standards of Kaldor-Hicks efficiency and Pareto improvement. As we saw in the last chapter, Kaldor-Hicks efficiency demands only that the net change from a proposed policy is positive, but by sanctioning harm to some persons in order to generate benefits to others, with no concern given to rights or desert of any of the persons involved, such policies use some persons merely as a means to help others. The Pareto principle would seem to avoid these problems, since it mandates that no one be harmed by a policy under consideration, and therefore it is presumed that all persons, whether affected or not, would "rationally" consent to the policy, further assuring policymakers that total welfare is increased.

In fact, the Pareto criterion is almost universally regarded as unquestionable, especially in the mainstream economics literature. For instance, in 2001, Kaplow and Shavell published a six-page article (previewing the core of their book) in the *Journal of Political Economy*, a top-ranked mainstream economics journal, with a title presumably meant to be self-evidently conclusive: "Any Non-Welfarist Method of Policy Assessment Violates the Pareto Principle."[2] And this attitude is not exclusive to economists—for instance, philosopher James Griffin writes that "it is hard to see how one could resist such a principle."[3] But legal philosopher Jules Coleman, a frequent critic of the use of both Kaldor-Hicks and Pareto to ground normative economic analysis of law, derisively calls the concept of Pareto improvement "everyone's golden boy."[4] Historian of economic thought Mark Blaug devotes a page in his treatise on economic methodology to claims regarding "the dictatorship of Paretian welfare economics" in regard to modern liberals and classic liberals alike.[5] Perhaps the most well-known challenge to Pareto superiority is Amartya Sen's 1970 article "The Impossibility of a Paretian Liberal," the title of which plays on the inherent faith that most scholars place in both concepts. Sen's article spawned a huge literature—most of which, as he noted later, sought to modify the definition of liberalism Sen relied upon, rather than question the Pareto principle itself.[6]

In this section, I will argue that there are significant ethical concerns with Pareto improvement, most of which center—ironically—on the very concept of consent which is usually understood to be its ethical grounding.[7] In practice (as well as in most theoretical treatments), actual consent is rarely attained or even pursued when policies are evaluated according to the Pareto improvement standard. Rather, consent is merely inferred, with no guarantee of actual endorsement on the part of affected persons. Furthermore, this inferred consent is most often based on preferences, which is problematic for several reasons. Aside from the informational problems involved in ascertaining a person's preferences, there are many reasons why one's preferences are not identical to one's well-being, as is normally assumed. But even if preferences do represent a person's true well-being, her actual consent would not necessarily be given based on her well-being or preferences alone. Rather, she may be motivated by concerns for justice, fairness, or any other factor that overrides her preferences—whether self- or other-interested—when making choices. The existence of such desire-independent reasons such as duty or commitment implies that preferences do not drive choices or behavior exclusively, and makes it impossible to infer an agent's consent from her preferences alone.

There are two important aspects of consent that have been largely neglected in the economics literature. The first is epistemic: actual consent is the best way to ensure that the agent's wishes are being respected and her interests furthered, regardless of their basis: well-being, justice, fairness, or some other criterion.[8] The more fundamental point is ethical: in Kantian terms, a true consent requirement is necessary to guarantee respect for the inherent dignity of persons.[9] While a person can never be robbed of her dignity, since it is intrinsic to her, other persons or parties can fail to respect that dignity, most clearly by manipulating her by means of coercion or deception, as is made clear in the Formula of Respect. By failing to acquire true consent from affected parties, the implementation of the Pareto improvement standard can be considered as an instance of coercion, and therefore as a failure to respect the dignity of persons, despite the common perception to the contrary.

Well-being, preferences, and choice

Most commonly, a Pareto improvement is defined as a change that makes at least one person *better off* and no person *worse off*.[10] It does not take a philosopher to recognize that the italicized terms in that statement are vague at best; for instance, the meaning of "better off" depends on a chosen theory of the good, of which there are many.[11] Regardless of the theory of the good adopted, the concept of Pareto superiority (like Kaldor-Hicks efficiency) is essentially consequentialist, based on the outcomes or results of a policy: "better off" and "worse off" imply comparisons between the states of the world with and without, or before and after, the change under consideration. But unlike Kaldor-Hicks, Pareto does not simply add positive and negative changes and assess the net result; Pareto is constrained by not allowing negative changes at all, rendering it a constrained variant of utilitarianism (assuming "better off" refers to changes in utility or well-being) within the confines of "no harm."

Economists (and some philosophers) would typically define being "better off" as having a higher level of preference-satisfaction or "utility." Therefore, they often define a Pareto improvement in terms of preferences: a policy is a Pareto improvement if at least one person prefers the state of the world after the change, and no one prefers the state of the world before the change.[12] But do a person's preferences necessarily represent her well-being, and can an increase in preference-satisfaction or utility be equated with an increase in well-being? Trivially, the answer is yes, if we define well-being as preference-satisfaction, as welfare economists normally do. But few scholars outside of mainstream economics believe that well-being is completely described by the content of preferences (or the social welfare function normally derived from them).[13]

For instance, there are clearly cases in which a person's preferences do not promote her well-being, such as self-destructive preferences. Heroin addicts have strong preferences for the drug, and it may even bring them some kind of utility in the immediate, hedonistic sense, but it stretches credulity to state that it increases their well-being in any meaningful sense.[14] Of course, there are also other-regarding preferences, such as those for performing altruistic acts, working for racial equality, or simply caring for the interests of a friend, relative, or lover. Other-regarding preferences may be malicious as well, such as vindictive or spiteful preferences which are satisfied only upon the recognition (or causation) of pain in others (whether classes of persons or specific individuals). Persons also have preferences over events that have little if any direct effect on them; Jennifer may prefer that Mars be colonized someday, but that certainly would have little effect on her well-being, especially if it happens long after her death. Again, satisfying such preferences may please an agent happy (assuming she is alive), but do they truly increase her well-being, or make her "better off"? If Jim enjoys seeing his best friend, or perhaps a member of a racial minority, get a well-deserved promotion, in what sense does either make Jim better off? Again, by definition it does if well-being is defined as preference-satisfaction, but any broader measure of well-being casts this link into doubt.[15]

Other-regarding preferences can wreak havoc with attempts to link preferences (to the extent they are revealed by choice) to well-being. Benevolent other-regarding preferences, based on altruism, care, or love, pose less of a problem than negative ones. For instance, if a policy is proposed that benefits 10 percent of the population without harming the other 90 percent (in material terms), then altruistic preferences on the part of the otherwise unaffected 90 percent would not affect the Pareto superiority of the policy.[16] In fact, if we define "better off" in terms of preference-

satisfaction, then all persons in this situation are made better off—the rising tide lifts all ships, psychologically if not materially. However, negative
other-regarding preferences can be a problem, and not just theoretically.
Consider the policy above, but now assume that the 90 percent who did
not receive the financial benefit have preferences based on envy or resent-
ment of others' good fortune. Even though no one is made worse off in
absolute material terms, those who did not benefit materially are worse
off in terms of their envious preferences, and the policy would fail to be a
Pareto improvement if all preferences are taken into account.[17]

These problems are fairly well-known and uncontroversial among
decision theorists and philosophers, among whom preferences are commonly understood to be based on desires, and who recognize that our
transitory desires do not necessarily correspond to our true, more stable
sense of well-being (as opposed to the more narrowly or formally defined
welfare or utility of economists). Most philosophers who do ground well-
being in preferences are forced to make an agent's preferences "rational" in
order to represent the preferences that the agents would have under conditions of full knowledge and lucid rationality.[18] But the resulting "cleansed"
preferences are artificially constructed and external to the agent herself,
representing what the agent *would* prefer *if* she reflected on them under
certain *ideal* conditions—all according to the judgment of those con-
ducting the cleansing. Presumably, Pareto improvement is supposed to
be about *choice*, even if that choice is inferred rather than observed. If a
policy under consideration would make some persons better off and no
persons worse off (by whatever measure we choose), then it is presumed
that all persons would consent to, or choose to endorse, said policy. But
if we are making those judgments based on idealized preferences, not the
actual preferences on the basis on which agents make choices, then these
judgments do not predict those agents' choices, but only what an ideal
agent (with ideal preferences) would choose.[19]

As we saw in the early chapters of this book, many economists and
philosophers have elaborated on the simple structure of preferences assumed by most decision theorists, suggesting second-order preferences
or metapreferences, which are often overwhelmed by our immediate,
first-order preferences. But these alternative systems of preferences would
render impossible the equivalence of preferences and well-being: which

preferences would we use in calculating well-being? A smoker who wants to quit nonetheless truly enjoys smoking—we may say he is better off because he is doing what makes him happy, or worse off because his "true" (second-order) desire is unsatisfied. Or perhaps we could judge his well-being based on some function of both levels of preference, which divorces the concept even more from actual choice.

Where does this leave us? If preferences do not represent a person's true well-being, then we must find another measure of well-being upon which to base decisions. Some would point to objective measures of well-being, such as wealth, primary goods, or capabilities, and others would stick closer to utilitarianism's hedonic roots, endorsing measurements of happiness or fulfillment not based simply on preferences or desires.[20] Pareto improvements would then have to make at least one person better off and no one worse off according to the chosen criterion. But this still does not address the issue of consent; unless we have some independent reason to believe that the agent's choice or consent would be based on the analyst's chosen criterion, economists will not be able to use consent as a nonconsequentialist justification of Pareto superiority.

At bottom, the problem here is a familiar one from the early pages of this book: that actual choice (or here, granting of consent) is not necessarily based on preferences, material interests, or well-being, as economists—and, indeed, most philosophers—assume. As Coleman recognizes, we need to emphasize "the importance of the distinction between what a person prefers and what that person is prepared to consent to."[21] We saw that choice can be influenced by desire-independent reasons, factors in decision-making that are not ranked with other options in the structure of preferences, but instead can overrule preferences altogether. They often take the form of principles (whether noble or vicious), such as fairness, justice, equality, retribution, love for humankind, or racial hatred. (One basis for such principles is duty, of course, but this concept is much broader than "just" Kant or the Kantian-economic model of choice developed earlier in this book.) Recall the example from Chapter 1 of the woman who has a strong preference to see her fiancé, but will not push an elderly man away from a taxicab in order to satisfy it. To say that she has a preference for not harming the elderly is akin to forcing a square peg into a round hole: her strongest preference may very well be to get that cab, but she knows that this does not justify pushing the man down, and this principle overrides even her strongest preference. No matter how badly she wants that cab, she will not harm the man (wrongfully) to get it; we would like to think that she would not even consider it. There is no ranking between the cab and the elderly man that can be changed by relative price changes or income effects; there is no increase in urgency sufficient to make her choose to hurt the elderly man. Simply put, the woman observes a principle of not harming others for her own gain, and this transcends his preferences (self-interested or not).

People ignore their preferences, or sacrifice their well-being, for principles every day. Activists devote their lives and personal resources to fighting for causes that affect them only marginally. Citizens vote for candidates or policies that they believe are better for the entire community even if personally they will suffer higher taxes or lower benefits. The policy example above can be restated in terms of desire-independent reasons if the 90 percent who are unaffected financially by the proposal rejected it in terms of principle; perhaps they felt that the other 10 percent did not deserve the benefit for some reason (good or bad). Furthermore, it is easy to imagine that a proposal that taxed the 90 percent to finance the benefit to the 10 percent could be unanimously approved despite the financial harm to the majority—for instance, if the unfortunate 10 percent were victims of a natural disaster. Even though the 90 percent will be made financially worse off, and they may have no altruistic preferences toward the 10 percent, they may feel a duty or obligation to help, and thereby consent to the proposal even though it denies their preferences or well-being. If the Pareto standard is meant to respect agents' choices, then anything that influences choice, including preferences *and* principles, must be taken into account.[22]

So far, we have focused on the epistemic point regarding consent, arguing that the only way to ascertain an agent's true well-being, broadly considered to incorporate her preferences, principles, and other influences on her choices, is to secure her consent. Now we turn to the normative point, that consent is also the only way to ensure respect for the dignity of persons.

Consent, dignity, and coercion

In the last chapter, we discussed how the Kaldor-Hicks test denies individuals their basic dignity: absent compensation (at the very least),

172 Consent, Pareto, and Behavioral Law and Economics

some persons are used simply as a means to furthering the ends of others. We also mentioned that the superior ethical status ascribed to Pareto improvement is often extended to Kaldor-Hicks as well based on the possibility of compensation, terming such changes "potential Pareto improvements" since the winners can potentially compensate the losers and make both parties no worse off than before. But as long as the compensation is merely hypothetical, so is the respect for dignity shown by the policy; as Coleman writes, "that [Kaldor-Hicks efficient changes] are potentially Pareto superior has as much bearing on how they should be treated as the fact that I am potentially President of the United States has on how I should be treated now."[23] The implication inherent in the phrase "potential Pareto improvement" is that the absence of compensation is the only ethical problem with Kaldor-Hicks, and without this complication, policymakers could be comfortable with the resulting Pareto improvement. I am arguing that consent is the primary issue here, not compensation, but first let us ask: why cannot compensation be sufficient to ensure respect for dignity, even in the absence of consent?

Suppose that compensation were arranged (at sufficiently low cost), and a Pareto improvement (in material terms) is thereby generated. In practical terms, of course, this is very unlikely. Aside from the costs of arranging for the compensation, simply calculating the proper compensation accurately would be incredibly difficult (if not impossible). For compensation to make the harmed parties "whole," presumably ensuring their implied consent (setting aside for the moment the reservations expressed in the last section), their subjective valuations would have to be taken into account, and the possibility that some persons would be impossible to compensate completely is all too real (due to incommensurability of sentimental value and financial value, for example). More moderately, there may easily be cases where a person's subjective valuation is significantly higher than the best third-party (or market) estimates, even without assuming strategic, opportunistically inflated claims.

There is still the possibility that a person may reject compensation based on a principle rather than her preferences, regardless of the apparent sufficiency of the financial remuneration alone. For example, a person may object to the government's offer of $1 million for a house with a market value of $250,000 because she promised her father, long since passed, that she would never sell the house he built with his own hands and in which he and his wife raised their children. It is not that she does not want or need the money, nor it is that she values the house itself more than what the government is offering. She may *need* the money, she may *want* to sell the house to get it, but she simply feels she *cannot*. This is not a matter of preference, unless we want to mangle the term beyond all usefulness; this is a desire-independent reason overwhelming her preferences, guiding her to do what she feels is right rather than what she feels is good.

For these reasons, compensation does not imply consent; or, in Ronald Dworkin's words, "the fact of self-interest in no way constitutes an actual consent."[24] Only actual consent guarantees that the person finds the offer of compensation sufficient according to whatever standards she holds dear, even if it is *less* than full monetary compensation (implying another reason for the agent to accept it). Compensation without consent not only throws the adequacy of the compensation into question but ignores the essential problem with Pareto improvement (and Kaldor-Hicks efficiency), which is the lack of respect for the dignity of persons. As Walsh writes,

the Pareto principle embodies the idea that the only information relevant to judging social states is information as to what individual preferences happen to be. . . . The present dispute is thus yet another case of the conflict between ordinal utilitarianism (or preference utilitarianism) and moral philosophies which can give due recognition to rights, goals, agency, responsibilities, and duties.[25]

The consequentialist nature of the Pareto standard narrows its focus to the outcomes, the final levels of well-being resulting from a change, but not on the process by which that well-being is obtained (a standard deontological consideration), which may constitute an essential component of an agent's judgment and consent.[26]

Those (such as Posner) who attempt to link Pareto to consent maintain that inferred consent, based on outcomes, is sufficient to ensure respect (see the last chapter), but they neglect to consider that the very absence of true consent negates that inference. To some, the inability to provide or deny consent is the deal-breaker, regardless of any material payoff; as Coleman explains, while some people may be able to place a finite dollar value on their right to consent, such that they can be potentially compensated in full for both their financial harm and the injury to their dignity, it is very possible that others will place infinite or incommensurable value on their consent, and no amount of money or material wealth will make up for lack of consent over matters that affect them.[27] Furthermore, if we impute a commensurable value to consent or autonomy and include it in our preference ranking, it becomes yet another component of our interests as normally understood, and cannot have any independent, deontological status; in other words, consent would no longer be important enough to justify Pareto judgments as adherents wish it to. As Coleman puts it:

> If autonomy or consent is reducible to utility or preference satisfaction, it is impossible to defend policies that maximize preference satisfaction on autonomy grounds. Such a move simply bases the pursuit of utility on the pursuit of utility. Yet it was the desire to defend Paretianism on nonefficiency grounds that motivated the argument in the first place.[28]

But we have yet to answer the core question: why does a Pareto improvement (or compensated Kaldor-Hicks change), without securing actual consent, necessarily violate the dignity of the persons involved? I argue that a transaction imposed without the consent of an affected person is coerced upon that person, and coercion is one of cardinal methods (along with deceit) by which a person can be used simply as a means while not at the same time as an end, violating the respect owed her by virtue of her dignity. If a person does not have a chance to freely give or deny consent to a policy that affects her, she is being coerced into accepting the policy without being able to influence it through providing her consent. Coercion by definition does not include the coerced as an independent actor in the situation; it treats her as a tool, a thing, a means to the controlling person's end.[29]

I hope the reader will forgive me for repeating (from Chapter 1) this passage from Kant's discussion of making false promises in the context of the Formula of Respect:

> [T]he man whom I want to use for my own purposes by such a promise *cannot possibly concur with my way of acting toward him and hence cannot himself hold the end of this action.* This . . . becomes even clearer when instances of attacks on the freedom and property of others are considered. For then it becomes clear that a transgressor of the rights of men intends to make use of the persons of others merely as a means, without taking into consideration that, as rational beings, they should always be esteemed at the same time as ends, i.e., be esteemed only as beings *who must themselves be able to hold the very same action as an end.*[30]

For example, in order for Stan to respect the dignity of Ann, Ann must rationally be able to assent to Stan's ends, or to take Stan's ends as her own. This does not mean that she has to *want* to share in Stan's ends, or even agree with them—Stan's ends are not relevant here, and may be noble or base, selfish or altruistic. Rather the question is: *can* she, or is she *able* to, rationally will Stan's end? Can she make it her own (regardless of whether she would want to)? Or, as Korsgaard writes, "it must not be merely that your victim will not like the way you propose to act . . . but that something makes it impossible for her to assent to it . . . that something makes it impossible for her to hold the end of the very same action."[31]

As we saw earlier, deceit and coercion are the two primary acts that deny the "victim" the ability to assent to and hold the other person's end, because she is either unaware of it or is not given a chance to assent to it. If Stan lies to Ann to further his end, she is kept unaware of relevant details regarding Stan's end, and is therefore unable to knowingly share it. Coercion more clearly violates this principle, because she cannot rationally will that she be denied the outer freedom to express her autonomy. Both use the victim as a "tool" with no control over her role in the events in which she is involved; as Korsgaard writes,

The idea of deciding for yourself whether you will contribute to a given end can be represented as a decision whether to initiate that causal chain which constitutes your contribution. Any action which prevents or diverts you from making this initiating decision is one that treats you as a mediate rather than a first cause; hence as a mere means, a thing, a tool.[32]

In the same way, lack of consent represents coercion, for it denies the affected person any input—positive or negative—on a decision that affects her. She must accept the decision imposed upon her, and the subsequent changes to her life made by it, even though she had no say regarding it: "in any cooperative project . . . everyone who is to contribute must be in a position to *choose* to contribute to the end."[33] If Betty's local government claims the lot on which her business is located in order to build a park, paying her fair market value but without her consent, she is being used simply as a means, a tool, to further the ends of the municipality. Whether she agrees with those ends or not, she has had no chance to freely acquiesce to them; and if she had been asked—which very well may have happened—she presumably did not consent, and her property was confiscated regardless in an act of (legal) coercion. Ideally, as Anthony Kronman writes, "the Pareto principle assures that no one will ever be made the unwilling instrument of another's welfare . . . . [and] represents a moral ideal based on respect for the autonomy of individuals and acceptance of the idea that one should always treat others as ends in themselves and not merely as means."[34] But in the absence of actual consent, Pareto improvement fails to meet this standard of respect for the dignity of persons.

But whose consent?

Broadly, respect for the dignity of persons requires that individuals be given the chance to agree or disagree on proposals that affect them. But not every person's consent is necessarily relevant to a given proposal's approval, because not everyone's interests or rights are affected significantly enough by it. For instance, suppose the local government buys all the land in a certain area to construct a new park, and all of the displaced property owners freely consented to sell their homes for the price offered by the government. However, for some reason, other members of the community disapprove of the new park, and would not consent to the project if asked. Should this proclaimed dissent rule out the project as a Pareto improvement? The new park is making some people worse off in some sense, and on this basis those people would deny their consent if they were asked. Out of respect of the dignity of those persons, should the local government put a stop to the construction? We can use the previous example again as well: if a policy enhances the wealth of 10 percent, at no material cost to the 90 percent, should the latter group's possible disapproval (on the basis of principle, perhaps, or even simple envy) be considered when evaluating the policy?

In other words, should universal consent be necessary to justify a Pareto improvement? This is the problem at the heart of Sen's argument in "The Impossibility of a Paretian Liberal," in which he gave the example of the "prude" who preferred that no one read a racy book. The traditional liberal ideal of a "sphere of privacy" would deny that the prude's feelings or preferences should count in any way, assuming one's choice of reading material fits into that protected zone, but the Pareto principle does not distinguish between those whose preferences "matter" and those whose preferences do not. (And the Pareto standard itself can be of no help in determining whose preferences should count without leading to a circular justification, similar to the problems that wealth effects cause for Kaldor-Hicks efficiency.)

With reference to the Kantian ideal of respecting the dignity of persons, Onora O'Neill distinguishes between the treatment of persons with different relationships to the change under consideration:

> The morally significant aspect of treating others as persons may lie in making their consent or dissent *possible*, rather than in what they actually consent to . . . A requirement that we ensure that others have this possibility cuts deep whenever they will be much affected by what we propose. There is not much difficulty in ensuring that those who will in any case be no more than spectators have a genuine possibility of dissent. They need only be allowed to absent themselves or to express disagreement, distaste or the like. But those closely involved in or affected by a proposal have no genuine possibility of dissent unless they can avert or modify the action by withholding consent and collaboration. If those closely affected have the possibility of dissent, they will be able to require an initiator of action either to modify the action or to desist or to override the dissent. But an initiator who presses on in the face of actively expressed dissent undercuts any genuine possibility of refusing the proposal and chooses rather to enforce it on others.[35]

But that still leaves the question: what determines whether a person is actually affected by a change, or is instead a "mere spectator"?

This is closely related to another famous problem in political philosophy concerning whose and which preferences to count in utilitarian calculations. This question becomes practical in the following dilemmas: Must we count sexist or racist preferences in making social decisions? Are we compelled to satisfy expensive preferences in order to equalize preference-satisfaction among persons?[36] Since the Pareto principle can be considered an exercise in constrained preference-utilitarianism, this problem extends to it as well. An obvious answer seems to be that only an agent's preferences concerning her own interests should count; whether someone reads a racy book affects only the reader's own interests, not those of the prude. Yet the prude may very well argue that it does affect her interests—perhaps she suffers great discomfort, based on disgust, when she finds out that people are reading "that" book.[37] One person's well-being can certainly be affected, in a very real way, by other people's behavior, and such an effect may very well count among her interests, so this approach is problematic.[38]

One way out of this conundrum, inspired by Robert Nozick, rests with another implication of respecting dignity: respecting the rights which derive directly *from* that dignity, such as (but not limited to) the right to make decisions within one's sphere of privacy. The requirement of the government to obtain actual consent for policy proposals can be understood as respecting the right of persons to grant—or withhold—consent within that sphere.[39] Respect for the dignity of persons also denies other persons any right of consent concerning proposals which do not affect their own realms of privacy (such as the prude in Sen's example). More precisely, it denies the *state* any right to base social decisions on the consent of anyone whose personal sphere of privacy is not affected by the policy, even if those decisions are imposed by the majority of the populace (recalling John Stuart Mill's "tyranny of the majority" argument).[40] In Sen's example, the government should not base any policy decisions on the fact that the prude would deny her consent to anyone reading the book, because it does not affect her sphere of privacy—it is not a decision over which she (or the state) should have any power. This solution resembles Nozick's position that rights delimit the options available to policymakers; any social decision must be made within the parameters established by pre-existing rights.[41] Here we have formulated this principle in the language of dignity, which in the Kantian framework grounds any rights claims, such as (but not limited to) the right to give or deny consent to social decisions that intrude on one's sphere of privacy.

Of course, individuals certainly have a right to have opinions about matters affecting other persons, and may also try to persuade them regarding their choices. As Korsgaard writes:

> To treat others as ends in themselves is always to address and deal with them as rational beings. Every rational being gets to reason out, for herself, what she is to think, choose, or do. So if you need someone's contribution to your end, you must put the facts before her and ask for her contribution. If you think she is doing something wrong, you may try to convince her by argument but you may not resort to tricks or force.[42]

This would preclude using the coercive power of the state to impose one's opinions on other free persons, which would be failing to respect their dignity. In that case, it would be as if one person were acting through the state coercively to control the other person against her will, using the second person as a means to further the ends of the first (the prude, for instance). The burden is then on the first person to demonstrate why the proposal intrudes on her sphere of privacy (which would involve arguments over how narrow or broad that sphere is).

The Pareto principle is commonly regarded, by social scientists and philosophers, to be ethically unquestionable, if not trivially obvious. This section has challenged this presumption, pointing out some ethical difficulties with the concept, including, ironically, ones related to consent, which is the supposed ethical justification of the principle itself. Without actual consent, decisions "justified" by the Pareto criterion are inherently coercive, failing to respect the dignity of persons. In Kantian language, such policies use those who were not given the opportunity to consent simply as a means to further the ends of the policymaker (and those who did consent). Only the solicitation of actual consent, freely given, can ensure that the dignity and autonomy of persons are given adequate respect. At the same time, persons who are not affected by the policy must be denied any right of consent, for policy decisions based on their input would again violate the dignity of those who are truly affected by the policy and deserve the right of consent.

This leaves us with an important question: what does the Pareto standard give us above and beyond the consent requirement? If Pareto is simply consent reworded, then it seems redundant—especially if consent is assumed to be based on self-interest. If it bypasses actual consent, then consent cannot be used to justify it, and it is simply constrained utilitarianism with no deontological component derived from the right of those affected by the policy to veto a proposal, regardless of its apparent positive consequences (from an outsider's point of view). But that does not seem to be in the spirit of the Pareto principle, which should serve to protect individuals' rights to dissent to policies that adversely affect them for *whatever* reason they feel is important to them. It is *choice*, not well-being, that should be promoted by the Pareto standard. Persons may or may not make choices based on their well-being, but in either case we can safely assume that the choices they make are supported by personal, subjective, and possibly unknowable reasons which are theirs, and this will guarantee respect for their intrinsic dignity.

Behavioral Law and Economics

The same issues of consent, coercion, and dignity arise in recent work in *behavioral law and economics* (BLE), a field that resulted from the merger of law and economics (as discussed in the last chapter) and behavioral economics. While the term *behavioral economics* has been used for years to represent a generally pluralistic and empirically motivated approach to studying economic behavior, the "new" behavioral economics focuses on integrating psychological insights into economics, as exemplified by veterans such as Nobel laureate Daniel Kahneman and Amos Tversky, as well as relative newcomers such as Richard Thaler and Matthew Rabin.[43] Behavioral economics strives to examine how persons actually behave, versus how mainstream economic models predict they will (or should) act; in the words of Colin Camerer and George Loewenstein,

behavioral economics increases the explanatory power of economics by providing it with more realistic psychological foundations . . . [to] improve the field of economics on its own terms—generating theoretical insights, making better predictions of field phenomena, and suggesting better policy.[44]

Mainstream law and economics seeks to use economic theory to predict the effects of laws (its positive side) and to recommend reform to law based on this theory (its normative side); BLE, therefore, uses behavioral insights to improve our understanding of how persons react to laws and to recommend reforms based on this improved understanding.[45]

One of the more successful developments in behavioral economics is the description and exploration of various cognitive biases and dysfunctions, anomalies in the way that human agents weigh and choose between options that differ in some respect other than simple price, size, or quantity: immediate versus later rewards (or costs), resources either in or out of one's possession, and risks that differ in magnitude and are either regularly or rarely experienced, just to name a few. Not only do these biases cause actual choice to differ from the predictions of preference-satisfaction models, but perhaps more important, they often deviate from what persons report that would like to choose if they could correct for or otherwise avoid the biases (as evidenced by persistent efforts to lose weight, reduce spending, increase savings, stop procrastinating, and so forth).

Based on these findings of suboptimal choice, BLE advocates—most notably, Richard Thaler and Cass Sunstein, authors of the bestseller *Nudge* as well as much academic work on the topic[46]—have endorsed what they term "libertarian paternalism" (also called "light" or "soft" paternalism by other authors).[47] Mainstream economics has long endorsed utilitarian social policy and regulation in the name of optimizing third-party effects (or externalities) in the interest of the greater good (as seen in the last chapter), but this has usually been tempered by a qualified respect for individual choices in the name of "consumer sovereignty" which helped to restrain any paternalistic impulses. However, behavioral economics has questioned this respect based on evidence that agents exhibit systematic, cognitive biases that can prevent them from making the choices they say they would have liked to make. From this observation, behavioral economists conclude that paternalistic laws are justified, which is where behavioral *law* and economics comes in; BLE scholars use insights from behavioral economics not just to analyze the effects of laws on human behavior, but also to design laws to manipulate that behavior, ostensibly in persons' own interests.

This seems to preserve mainstream economists' respect for consumer sovereignty, in that ideally a person's own goals and ends are retained, because the behavioral law and economics expert claims merely to be helping the agent achieve her goals by correcting for her cognitive failures. Furthermore, the recommendations of BLE seem fairly benign: for example, rearranging the order and presentation of options to help people make the "best" choices (such as organizing a cafeteria to steer people toward healthy options), and setting default rules and options (with the possibility of opting out) to what people would "really" want (such as with automatic enrollment in 401(k) plans).[48] BLE advocates argue that their libertarian paternalism is less intrusive and more respectful of individual autonomy than old-fashioned paternalist measures such as banning or taxing disapproved behavior: as Sunstein and Thaler write, "Libertarian paternalism is a relatively weak and nonintrusive type of paternalism, because choices are not blocked or fenced off."[49] By subtly rearranging the choice environment, policymakers portend to "nudge" people to make the choices that they would make if they had complete information, perfect rationality, and flawless self-control.

But this thinking betrays a profound lack of respect for the dignity and autonomy of persons based on the Kantian tradition, by refusing to acknowledge their ability to determine their own true interests, interests that are unknowable to policymakers unless revealed through choice or consent, which is necessary to ensure that dignity is respected. As BLE advocates emphasize, preferences are imperfect reflections of true interests, but even the most stable, coherent, and "rational" preferences do not capture agents' complete and true interests, which may also include principles that override preferences. Because of this complexity, too often ignored by both behavioral and mainstream economists as well as economics-oriented legal scholars, the best way (understood prudentially and morally) to ascertain an agent's true interests is to obtain consent or observe choice over the decisions that affect her, as we discussed in the section on Pareto improvement above. While the agent's choices may not always be best from her own point of view, due to cognitive biases and dysfunctions, the policymaker has no way—or right—to judge this for himself. Neglecting persons' dignity is a crucial step in justifying paternalism and other legal manifestations of utilitarianism in social engineering.[50]

Implicitly, BLE considers a person as a thing to be manipulated, a machine that needs to be fixed, if only for its own good. In the case of cognitive bias or dysfunction, the processing mechanism (the brain) is not working properly, so the inputs must be "adjusted" to achieve the desired ends. The source of this problem lies in BLE's understanding of human behavior and action, which lacks an appreciation of Kantian autonomy; ironically, this renders BLE's conception of choice no more advanced or sophisticated in this regard than that of mainstream economists. To both, choice is wholly determined by a person's preferences and constraints (to which BLE would add her limited cognitive capacities). So, as we saw in Chapter 2, there is no true choice involved, in the sense that a person can never do anything but what is determined for her by factors over which she has no control. In this way, BLE does not advance the concept of human choice past the mainstream economics conception at all.

Of course, to go from observing cognitive biases to endorsing paternalistic laws takes both an epistemic and an ethical leap, neither of them unfamiliar to economists and legal scholars. The thinking starts with "I don't think people make choices in their best interests," and concludes with "I *can* and *should* help them make better choices to further those interests." But there are deep, interrelated problems with both the positive and the normative claims in the second statement. In this section, I will argue first that regulators do not, and indeed *can* not, have enough information to engage in these activities, and second, that there is no way for regulators to know that people are making suboptimal choices without verification from the agents themselves. Then I will turn back to Kant's concepts of autonomy and dignity to show that, similar to judgments of Pareto superiority, BLE's manipulation of choice is morally questionable because it fails to respect the dignity owed to rational persons. Finally, I will discuss the claimed "inevitability" of paternalism in circumstances of cognitive failures, and offer alternatives that respect the dignity of agents.

Well-being and judgment substitution

Typically, BLE advocates talk of well-being or welfare when discussing what is important to (or for) agents: "we argue for self-conscious efforts, by private and public institutions, to steer people's choices in directions that will improve the choosers' own welfare."[51] As we have seen, mainstream economists (including legal economists) normally take preference-satisfaction to be the appropriate measure of an agent's welfare. On a basic level, preference-satisfaction respects the heterogeneity of valuations across persons, and imposes no substantive constraints on preferences themselves, imposing only structural constraints such as transitivity. But, as discussed in the first half of this chapter, it is difficult to maintain that preferences completely describe well-being, given the widely recognized existence of other-regarding, self-harming, and other preferences that substantively contradict common-sense ideas of well-being.

To its credit, BLE does not hold preference-satisfaction to be equivalent to welfare, as it regards preferences—at least, the immediate, operational preferences upon which choices are made—as unstable, transitory, and manipulable.[52] However, if we rule out preference-satisfaction as a measure of personal well-being, regulators must find another, and two possibilities immediately come to mind, both of which the reader will recall from the Pareto discussion. The first is an objective measure of well-being, such as wealth, health, security, capabilities, or some combination thereof, that both defines and avoids the problem of self-destructive preferences. This makes measurement significantly easier, but we lose the subjectivity and respect for individual differences that preferences give us (even those we may judge to be imprudent, foolish, or reckless). The second is to use an idea of "rational" preferences, or what an agent *would* want *if* she were fully informed and not under the influence of any cognitive biases. The two theories of personal well-being can be collapsed into one if we assume—as is commonly done— that when of "sound mind," agents would make choices in their long-term well-being, comprising wealth, health, security, and so forth.[53]

But as we know, this is problematic, for it is impossible for the policy-maker to know what a person's informed or rational preferences or choices would be under ideal conditions. J. D. Trout writes that paternalistic intervention designed to counter the effect of cognitive biases "promotes the agent's autonomy by intervening when the agent's decision is not one that, if fully informed and cognitively unbiased, the agent would have made."[54] But Robert Sugden asks:

How, without making normative judgments, do we determine what counts as complete information, unlimited cognition, or complete willpower? Even if we can specify what it would mean to have these supernatural powers, how do we discover how some ordinary human being would act if he were somehow to acquire them? And what reason do we have to suppose that this behaviour would reveal coherent preferences?[55]

Whether we call them rational, informed, or real, these "preferences," and any measure of well-being derived from them, are artificially and arbitrarily constructed by someone other than the agent herself, and cannot be held to represent the agent's true interests (or predict her choices, as detailed earlier). Furthermore, any policymaker's judgment about what should comprise an agent's well-being necessarily involves the preferences of the policymaker himself. Dan Brock sums up the problem in his review of several views of paternalism:

paternalistic interference involves the claim of one person to know better what is good for another person than that other person him- or herself does. It involves the substitution by the paternalistic interferer of his or her conception of what is good for another for that other's own conception of his or her good. If this involves a claim to know the objectively correct conception of another's good— what ultimate values and aims define another competent individual's good, independent of whether that other accepts them—then it is ethically problematic.[56]

This problem is by no means unique to behavioral law and economics; besides the example of Pareto improvement above, in which policymakers' external judgments are substituted for actual consent in the evaluation of policies, we can find another case in contract law. *Unconscionability doctrine* allows judges to refuse to enforce contract terms as written if they deem the terms to be unfair to one party or the other. While the standard assumption is that the contracting parties would not have agreed to the contract had it not been in their best interests (at the time the contract was agreed upon), unconscionability doctrine allows the judges to substitute their own judgment of the parties' best interests for the parties' own interests as expressed when they consented to the contract terms. Disputing unconscionability doctrine does not require that we hold all decisions of contracting parties to be flawless, but absent information regarding the parties' true interests, judges have no basis on which to substitute their own judgments when invalidating contract terms based on consent in the absence of coercion or deceit; not surprisingly, therefore, unconscionability doctrine is widely held to be paternalistic.[57]

Bad choices

So I agree with BLE proponents when they say that preferences are not stable or coherent, nor are they are closely linked to well-being. But neither do preferences or well-being completely explain choice—as we know, principles and other desire-independent reasons also play an important role, and they may well steer choice in directions opposed by preferences or well-being. As a result, assuming all choice is made on the basis of preference or well-being is a gross misunderstanding of decision-making and of what agents' true interests actually are. I use the term *interests* here to refer to whatever matters to an agent and motivates her choices, whether that be preference, principle (or duty), or any other reason for choice. As such, interests are broader than economists' standard concepts of preferences, self-interest, or well-being, incorporating any influences on choice that she regards as important. For the purposes of this discussion, I make no assumptions about the "wisdom" of these interests, nor do I make any judgment regarding their morality or prudence. An agent's interests are simply what matters to her, or what she has the most compelling reasons to care about and devote her time, attention, and resources to attaining.

BLE proponents maintain that people often make bad choices, defined in terms of being the suboptimal means to further their interests:

> Drawing on some well-established findings in behavioral economics and cognitive psychology, we emphasize the possibility that in some cases individuals make inferior decisions in terms of their own welfare—decisions that they would change if they had complete information, unlimited cognitive abilities, and no lack of self-control.[58]

Of course, people do sometimes make bad choices—*but no one knows they are bad choices except the person making them.* This is because no one knows what an agent's true interests are other than that agent, so choices that are optimal from that agent's point of view, given her true interests, may appear puzzling (or "unfathomable") to an outsider who lacks access to information about the agent's ends.[59]

Understanding that an agent makes choices according to her interests, which cannot be narrowed down to simple preference or any objective sense of well-being, the "rationality" of choices becomes impossible for the outside observer to evaluate. A choice which seems counterproductive or "irrational" to an outside observer may not be based on biased or irrational preferences or cognitive processes, but rather on stable, coherent preferences that may seem "odd" to others, or on firmly held (and perhaps moral or noble) principles, and as such it may be perfectly sound from the agent's point of view, however much it may seem to contradict what the observer takes to be her well-being. For example, pundits often question the choices of voters who support candidates who are likely to raise their taxes or lower their government benefits. But economic policy is just one element of a candidate's platform—though they remain concerned with their material interests, voters may choose candidates for reasons they consider more important, such as their positions on war, abortion, religion, or any number of noneconomic issues that have more in common with principle than payoffs. The observer assumes the voters' only interest is economic, an assumption that has no normative justification, and is merely a judgment substitution (and a particularly naïve one at that).

Trout, an advocate of what he terms "bias-harnessing" measures, argues that "regulation can be permissible even when it runs counter to that person's spontaneous wishes, particularly when the regulation advances the agent's considered judgments or implicit long-term goals."[60] But this assumes too much knowledge on the part of the decision-makers; as Claire Hill asks, "what is a better guide than people's choices? Even if people may really want something else, what might that be, and on what grounds can we claim we have access to it that gives us a better claim on what they are going to do than what they otherwise would choose?"[61] The only way that policymakers can be certain about an agent's interests is, indirectly, to observe them through choice, or, directly, to obtain consent to policies that affect them. If the agent admits or reveals that, in her own judgment, she is making suboptimal choices, she is free to seek help from private or public sources. But a policymaker has no basis on which to assume or infer that her choices are suboptimal, and thereby impose "nudges" on her. As Gerald Dworkin writes,

> from the fact that in some particular case it would be rational for the agent to have his choice restricted, it does not follow that others may do this for him against his will. Whereas the question of what is in the best interests of the individual is relevant to deciding issues of when coercion is justified, it is by no means conclusive. A decent respect for the autonomy of individuals will lead us to be very wary of limiting choices even when it is in the rational self-interest of the individuals concerned.[62]

The paternalism in "libertarian paternalism" consists in substituting the policymakers' own ends for those of the agents being "nudged." While ostensibly respecting choice, BLE proponents are structuring the choice environment to manipulate these choices toward furthering what they believe (or want to believe) are the agent's true ends. For instance, with regard to decisions about smoking and drinking, Sunstein and Thaler boldly claim that "people's choices cannot reasonably be thought, in all domains, to be the best means of promoting their well-being."[63] However, they cannot know the agent's true ends (or interests) without observing them through choice or consent in the absence of manipulation of the options themselves; as Buchanan writes, "While the economist may be able to make certain presumptions about 'utility' on the basis of observed facts about behavior, he must remain fundamentally ignorant concerning the actual ranking of alternatives *until and unless* that ranking is revealed by the overt action of the individual in choosing."[64] Nonetheless, regulators impose their version of the agent's well-being through the manipulation of the choice environment, and their imposed values are then "confirmed" when the agent makes the "right" choice. Even Richard Posner—who, you will recall from the last chapter, recommends that judges "mimic the market" when deciding civil cases, in presumption of knowledge of persons' interests—writes that, under the influence of BLE, regulators would be "charged with determining the populace's authentic preferences, which sounds totalitarian to me."[65] As Mitchell writes, "the proper evaluative view of choice behavior from the libertarian perspective is not an objective consequentialist view, but rather one that examines only the quality of *individual consent.*"[66]

Consider the much-lauded automatic 401(k) enrollment and "Save More Tomorrow" programs: policymakers decide that agents should save more, and that they would really like to save more "if they only could." To this end, they manipulate the choice options for 401(k) plans (through the default choice, to be discussed below) such that agents "choose" such plans more often. Then the resultant higher participation rate is given as evidence that this is what the savers *really* wanted to do: "very few of the employees who join the plan drop out."[67] But all this tells us is that before the manipulation, employees were too lazy to enroll, and after, they are too lazy to drop out—not that enrolling is necessarily what employees *really* want to do. Sunstein and Thaler write,

if employers think (correctly, we believe) that most employees would prefer to join the 401(k) plan if they took the time to think about it . . . then by choosing automatic enrollment, they are acting paternalistically by our definition of the term . . . steer[ing] employees' choices in directions that will, in the view of employers, promote employees' welfare.[68]

But recall Ronald Dworkin's succinct wisdom quoted above: "the fact of self-interest in no way constitutes an actual consent,"[69] which implies that even if higher savings were important to employees, and truly in their self-interest (narrowly defined), they may have other reasons not to increase their savings, reasons that should be respected as important to them.[70]

Here is a hypothetical scenario (I hope): suppose the members of a local election board, charged with designing the ballot for an upcoming presidential election, "know" who the local voters should choose, based on what (the board thinks) is good for them, but they are afraid voters may choose the other candidate based on emotional appeals and negative advertising. So they use BLE principles to structure the ballot in such a way that more voters will "choose" the "right" candidate. They are still free to choose the "wrong" candidate, but the ballot was designed to lead the voters to the "right" conclusion—the candidate that represents their "true interests." I hope the reader will find this "nudge" less benign, and that this example illustrates the danger of BLE policies when taken beyond the realms of saving and diet.

There is no need to question the intentions of such policymakers or of the adherents to BLE and "libertarian paternalism." They may indeed be trying to help people better their lives, like the "therapists" of the title to Loewenstein and Haisley's recent paper.[71] But unlike actual therapists, BLE advocates are "helping" in a way that fails to respect agents' true interests, instead substituting their ideas of what is important for the agents' own. Despite their benevolence, their actions nonetheless use persons as means to ends that are not necessarily their own, and to which they may have active opposition, based on preferences or principles that conflict with the policymaker's definition of well-being. This is the most important objection to paternalism—that it substitutes judgment of others for a person's own—an aspect that is as present in libertarian paternalism as in the old-fashioned variety.[72]

The true libertarian choice is clear, and it is the one that respects the essential dignity of autonomous persons. As we know from earlier chapters, autonomous agents in the Kantian sense can determine their own ends and interests, independent of their inclinations, preferences, or personal well-being, in accordance with the moral law which they legislate for themselves according their individual judgment. No one else has access to those judgments, and no one else has access to the true interests that each agent chooses for herself. To substitute the policymaker's ends for the agent's own is to fail to recognize her autonomy and to respect her dignity as an autonomous agent.

As we saw in the first half of this chapter, the two seminal ways that one can fail to respect a person's dignity are through deceit and coercion, both of which treat the person simply as means to the violator's own ends. The person who is deceived or coerced cannot rationally assent to the true actions or the ends of the other person, because either she is not aware of them at all (in the case of deception) or she is not given the chance to assent to them (in the case of coercion). Remember that the agent need only be rationally *able* to hold the same end, not that they would actually *want* to. The agent can disagree with the ends of the other person, thinking them inappropriate, ridiculous, or offensive. The important thing is that she has the opportunity to consider them at all, which requires the absence of deceit or coercion. O'Neill states it well when she writes:

> To treat others as persons we must allow them the *possibility* either of consenting to or of dissenting from what is proposed. The initiator of action can ensure this possibility; but the consenting cannot be up to him or her. The morally significant aspect of treating others as persons may lie in making their consent or dissent *possible*, rather than in what they actually consent to or would hypothetically consent to if fully rational.[73]

In this sense, manipulation of choice sets or default options is paternalistically coercive in the sense that it uses the agent merely as a means. According to Gerald Dworkin, in instances of paternalism "there must be a usurpation of decision-making, either by preventing people from doing what they have decided or *interfering with the way in which they arrive at their decisions.*"[74] The person whose options are rearranged was not a participant in the manipulation, and was given no chance to assent or dissent to it. Her consent was not sought out; the presumption is that she would consent if asked, because it is being done in her best interests. But "inferred consent . . . is not actual consent that remains unexpressed. It is simply a judgment about what the agent would have agreed to under certain circumstances."[75] Since the agent had no chance to express her position on the "choice architecture," it fails to respect her dignity as an autonomous person, and uses her simply as a means.

The BLE advocate may reply that choice is manipulated *for* the agent, not just *to* her. In other words, she is treated as a means, but also at the same time as an end, because her well-being is the end being sought. But, to turn to Gerald Dworkin again,

> [t]he denial of autonomy is inconsistent with having others share the end of one's actions—for if they would share the end, it would not be necessary to usurp their decision-making powers. At one level, therefore, paternalism seems to treat others as means (with the important difference that it is a means to their ends, not ours).[76]

But we know that it is not the agent's interests that are being furthered, despite the benevolent intentions of the policymaker, but rather the policymaker's own judgment about what the agent's interests *should* be. The agent cannot share in the ends of the policymaker, not only because she has no chance to assent to them, but also because she is not aware of them—they are not hers, for only she has access to that private knowledge, and she reveals it only through choice or consent, neither of which are consulted in cases of choice manipulation.

The "inevitability" of paternalism

BLE proponents often defend libertarian paternalism by arguing that choices must be made *somehow*—options have to be arranged, defaults have to be determined—so how else should this be done but paternalistically? The parties responsible for presenting choice options must design them in some way, they argue, so why not design them for "good"? As Sunstein and Thaler argue,

The first misconception is that there are viable alternatives to paternalism. In many situations, some organization or agent must make a choice that will affect the behavior of some other people. There is, in those situations, no alternative to a kind of paternalism—at least in the form of an intervention that affects what people choose.[77]

They are correct, of course, that defaults and arrangement must be designed somehow, and there are many options available, but BLE advocates are drawn to the paternalistic option too quickly, due to their lack of respect for the dignity of autonomous (if imperfectly rational) agents.[78] As we have seen, the problem is with their conception of the "good": rather than respecting each agent's individual conception of the good as best revealed by her choices, it substitutes the policymaker's own judgment of what that good is.

The two most common policy examples in the BLE/libertarian paternalism literature are manipulation of the choice environment (such as in the cafeteria example) and the determination of default options (such as the automatic 401(k) enrollment). Concerning the arrangement and presentation of options, there is little doubt that these factors play a role in the resulting choices, but this does not justify taking advantage of this effect to further an end, even if that end is presumed to be in the interests of the chooser.[79] For instance, sometimes there is a natural ordering, such as alphabetical or numerical; a cafeteria can be ordered by the stages of a meal (soup, salad, entrees, dessert). Is there anything necessarily "better" about these orderings? They certainly do not serve a greater purpose or goal, but if the only "goal" that entails a respect for dignity is to allow for choice without manipulation, any ordering *other* than the paternalistic one will do (even a random ordering). At least the chooser will not suspect that the choice set was manipulated for him, unlike under paternalistic ordering, in which he cannot help but notice that the fruit is well-lit at eye level, while the cake is hidden in the dark where he cannot reach it. Being respected as an individual capable of choice is a goal, but one that is defeated by manipulation.[80]

Concerning default options, there are two separate but related issues here: setting the default for the first time a choice is made, and also when the choice can or must be renewed. Take the example of a new employee, who must decide on her retirement or health plan options upon starting at her new job, and who later faces this decision periodically (such as during open enrollment periods for health insurance). Despite the claims of BLE proponents, who argue that "because both plans alter choices, neither one can be said, more than the other, to count as a form of objectionable meddling,"[81] the choice of default rules is not neutral with regard to freedom and dignity in either of these cases. When an employee starts a new job, she has agreed to provide certain labor services in exchange for a package of payment and benefits. She has not signed over control of her life choices to her new employer (unless doing so is specified in her contract or in pre-employment negotiations), nor has she agreed to be nudged in the direction her employer finds prudent. It follows that, if dignity is to be respected, the default rule should be chosen as the least disruptive to individual plans and choice. She did not agree to be signed up for a 401(k) plan automatically, and if she does not make an active decision to enroll, she should not be enrolled. Perhaps she forgot, or she was negligent of the effects of such a plan on her future well-being—either may be true, but there is no way for any other party to be certain of this, and no justification to take any positive action based on a supposition to that effect. The default rule for periodic renewals of decisions should be set by the same principle. If the employee made an active choice to enroll or not to enroll in the 401(k) plan, then the rule should affirm (and thereby respect) this choice, and continue her chosen status until such time as she makes an active choice to change it.[82]

For the most obvious alternative to paternalistic manipulation, we need look no further than the market. Since markets are based on voluntary transactions, choice, and consent, they ensure respect for the dignity and autonomy of persons (as discussed in Chapter 3). Buyers and sellers in markets act for their own ends, and of course do use each other as means to those ends, but not *merely* as means—they also treat each other as ends by relying on voluntary exchange assured through mutual consent and thereby avoiding deceit and fraud. Buyers and sellers can easily assent to each others' ends, since their goals are clear and apparent: buyers want goods and services for the money they offer, and sellers want money for the goods and services they provide.

Robert Sugden provides a vigorous defense of the market as an alternative to "inevitable" libertarian paternalism (without claiming that it is superior in every case, which he regards as an empirical question, albeit an unaddressed one).[83] He argues that incoherent preferences do not automatically justify paternalism, but instead actually make the argument for markets stronger, based on their ability to harness and unleash creativity. Using the example of a cafeteria selling cakes, he admits that consumers' preferences over cakes may be vague and undefined before they see the offerings, but this provides an incentive for the cafeteria to experiment with different sizes, colors, and flavors—as well as presentations—to earn the consumer's money. If the consumer likes one of the cafeteria's cakes better than anything else she could spend her money on, she buys it. He writes:

> I want it to be the case that they try to offer me products that I want to buy. I want their cakes to look attractive, and to be presented in ways that stimulate my appetite. It is not that I am a paragon of informed desire, acting on complete information with unlimited cognitive abilities and no lack of willpower. It is just that I would rather have my willpower challenged by tempting cakes than license cafeteria managers to compromise on the attractiveness of their products so as to steer me towards the ones that they think best for me.[84]

Ultimately, the market leaves choices up to the buyer and the seller, ensuring that the dignity of both is respected. Obviously, the state does not share the profit-maximization goal assumed for private firms—nor should it—but the market does provide a powerful counterexample for the "inevitability" for paternalism.

If there is evidence that the way options are presented affects choice independent of the options themselves, respect for dignity would require that manipulation be avoided, not embraced. Policymakers only manipulate choice when they disapprove of the choices made, and we have seen that there is no logical or normative basis for doing that, absent the consent of the choosers themselves. In Kant's words (quoted in Chapter 3), "I cannot do good to anyone in accordance to *my* concepts of happiness (except to young children and the insane), thinking to benefit him by forcing a gift upon him; rather, I can benefit him only in accordance with *his* concepts of happiness."[85] In the minds of BLE advocates, their nudges may be gifts, but unless they are explicitly requested, they are wrongful, presumptive impositions.

Conclusion

Dignity. . . above all, dignity.
—Don Lockwood (Gene Kelly), *Singin' in the Rain* (1952)

Now that we've reached the end of the book, let's walk back through it to the beginning. As we saw in the last chapter, policymakers fail to respect the inherent dignity of persons by denying them input into policies that affect them, substituting external judgments for the person's own, and neglecting the epistemic and ethical nature of choice based on a person's true interests. They devalue the importance of free choice and the countless influences on it—most notably, principles and values, especially those that lead us to subsume concern for our narrow self-interest. But it is by means of this ability to craft our own standards and, through this process of self-constitution, our own identities, that human beings reveal their true potential. And, of course, because of this capacity for autonomy, we have incomparable and incalculable worth, value—dignity.

Why do economists seem to have no consideration for autonomy and dignity in their modeling of human decision-making? The explanation takes us back to the early part of this book: most economists cling to a mechanistic conception of the individual, in which her choices are wholly determined by preferences, expectations, and endowments of material resources and time. As such, there is no role for true agency or choice in economic models of decision-making—the person never *makes* a choice or decision, as her choice or decision is predetermined by the factors influencing it. If there is no true choice, the "agent" has no autonomy, and therefore no dignity, that demand respect in the way I have described herein. Mainstream economists see the decision-makers in their models as machines, and behavioral economists further see these machines as flawed due to various cognitive biases and failures, requiring repair or (at the very least) adjustment, explaining (though not justifying) their impulse to regulate behavior.

But this is wrong; not only that, it's depressing, reflecting a terribly limited view of human nature and potential. Perhaps, after reading this book, economists might start seeing the person as Kant did: capable of determining her own ends and interests in consideration of both preferences and principles, the latter based on the moral law that she sets to herself. A person is also able to make free choices according to the moral law, choices based on her judgment and will, which develop over time and through experience to form a unique character that distinguishes her from other persons, identifies her over time, and represents who she truly *is*. Seen like this, it should be obvious that human beings have unlimited potential, and that realizing that potential is the responsibility of each of us, but we each must choose to realize it, and realize it well. Rather than being a cold, finger-wagging, stifling ethic, Kantian morality affirms this potential, this responsibility, this choice—all based on our autonomy, which in turn grants us dignity. And the greatest offense to dignity, perhaps, is to waste it.

Please don't.

Notes

INTRODUCTION

1. As well as the fact that, at bottom, no science is value-free, of course.

2. For elephants, too; as the good Doctor wrote, "I meant what I said and I said what I meant, an elephant's faithful, one hundred per cent."

3. Etzioni, "Toward a Kantian Socio-Economics" and *Moral Dimension*.

4. Minkler, "Problem with Utility" (and later, *Integrity and Agreement*).

5. Such economists would do well to read Andrew Yuengert's *Boundaries of Technique* or Deirdre McCloskey's *How to Be Human*.

6. For standard critiques of utilitarianism, see Rawls, *Theory of Justice*, 22–7; Smart and Williams, *Utilitarianism: For and Against*; and Scheffler, *Consequentialism and Its Critics*.

7. See McCloskey, *Bourgeois Virtues* and "Adam Smith"; and van Staveren, *Values of Economics* and "Beyond Utilitarianism and Deontology."

8. See, for instance, Sherman, *Making a Necessity Out of Virtue*, and Engstrom and Whiting, *Aristotle, Kant, and the Stoics*.

9. *Groundwork*, 393. (All references to Kant in this book will cite the standard Akademie Edition pagination, which is included in all reputable editions of his work; see the Bibliography for the precise translations from which I quote.) On the precise nature of the relationship between Kant's "good will" and virtue ethics' character, see Louden, "Kant's Virtue Ethics," 476–9.

10. *Groundwork*, 421.

11. Ibid., 429.

12. Van Staveren, "Beyond Utilitarianism and Deontology," 28.

13. *Groundwork*, 438.

14. Herman, "Practice of Moral Judgment," 74–5.

15. *Groundwork*, 389.

16. Ibid., 410–1.

17. Hicks, *Value and Capital*, 18.

CHAPTER I

1. This paragraph hardly does justice to the many attempts at modeling ethical behavior in economics; for a definitive treatment, see the relevant entries in Peil and van Staveren, *Handbook of Economics and Ethics.*

2. Sen, "Rational Fools," 94.

3. Walsh, *Rationality, Allocation, and Reproduction,* 29–30.

4. Frankena, *Ethics,* 15; see Gaus's two-part article "What Is Deontology?" for a critical exposition of the term.

5. Such allowances are sometimes called *agent-relative prerogatives,* in that they permit an agent to say that doing *x* may be good, or that it would be good for someone to do *x,* but *I* shall not do it myself; contrast this with *agent-neutral obligations,* which bind any agent and do not allow for personal exceptions. (See Scheffler, *Rejection of Consequentialism.*) Sen deals with a similar concept, which he calls *evaluator relativity,* in "Rights and Agency" and "Evaluator Relativity and Consequential Evaluation."

6. The "trolley problem" is a famous philosophical thought experiment that illustrates this dilemma (and many more). See Thomson, "Trolley Problem," and *Realm of Rights,* chap. 7, for the most influential treatments; the original idea is credited to Philippa Foot (*Virtues and Vices,* 19–32).

7. Broome, "Deontology and Economics," 282.

8. Indeed, while Kant's moral theory is usually put forth as the archetype of deontological ethics, there are scholars who instead call it teleological (Ward, "Kant's Teleological Ethics") or at least compatible with consequentialism (Cummiskey, *Kantian Consequentialism*); see Guyer, "Ends of Reason and Ends of Nature," for a thorough treatment of the role of teleology in Kant's ethics. While teleology certainly plays a large role in motivating Kant's ethical system on the whole, the moral imperatives given to individual agents are nonetheless essentially deontological in nature.

9. The first term in the title of this book, *Grundlegung* in the original German, is translated variously as "groundwork," "grounding," or "foundation." I prefer and use the first, though the translation on which I rely uses the second.

10. *Groundwork,* 436–7.

11. I am not alone in this; for instance, Allen Wood also takes dignity as his starting point in his book *Kant's Ethical Thought.*

12. Korsgaard, *Self-Constitution,* 108. (We will see much more of Professor Korsgaard and *Self-Constitution* in Chapter 3.)

13. For discussions of the various meanings of autonomy (including Kant's), see Feinberg, *Harm to Self,* chap. 18; Gerald Dworkin, *Theory and Practice of Autonomy,* chap. 3; Hill, "Autonomy and Benevolent Lies," 29–37, and "Kantian Conception of Autonomy"; and Irwin, "Kantian Autonomy," 139–40.

14. This is hardly surprising, since many aspects of Kant's moral and political theories overlap (by intention). Sullivan's *Introduction to Kant's Ethics* even begins with Kant's political theory, and then draws analogies to it when detailing his moral theory; see Chapter 4 for more on this.

15. The concept of an agent's proper relationship to outside influences, particularly as it relates to social identities, will be discussed further in Chapter 3.

16. And even when an agent does follow her desires unthinkingly, she still made a choice to do so, assuming she has the capacity for autonomous choice, and so forth; see Oshana, "Wanton Responsibility."

17. Hume, *Treatise of Human Nature*, 415.

18. Irwin, "Kantian Autonomy," 138.

19. Korsgaard, *Self-Constitution*, 162, drawing from Kant's *Religion*, 32–9.

20. Hill, "Kantian Conception of Autonomy," 85.

21. See Hill, "Importance of Autonomy," and Guyer, "Kant on the Theory and Practice of Autonomy." In Chapter 3 in this book I discuss how an agent's actions constitute her identity, but only if she acts autonomously.

22. *Groundwork*, 436.

23. Ibid., 434; the persons/things distinction itself appears on 428. (See also Sullivan, *Immanuel Kant's Moral Theory*, 195–8.)

24. *Groundwork*, 428, 434; *Metaphysics of Morals*, 434–5.

25. For more on Kantian dignity, see Hill, "Humanity as an End in Itself," 47–50; Sullivan, *Immanuel Kant's Moral Theory*, chap. 14; and Holtman, "Autonomy and the Kingdom of Ends," 108–10.

26. Hill, "Social Snobbery and Human Dignity," 170. Also, Sullivan writes that "Kant's entire moral philosophy can be understood as a protest against distinctions based on the far less important criteria of rank, wealth, and privilege, and perpetuated by religious and political force and fear" (*Immanuel Kant's Moral Theory*, 197).

27. Hill, "Humanity as an End in Itself," 49.

28. This point is especially pertinent in reference to the discussion of Kaldor-Hicks efficiency in Chapter 4 of this book.

29. McCloskey, *Bourgeois Virtues*, 263. Later in the book (353), she attributes this caricature to (some) modern followers of Kant, not the magister himself, a statement which (as you can well imagine) I found wholly gratifying.

30. *Groundwork*, 402–404.

31. Naturally, much scholarly attention has been given to analyzing the categorical imperative. See Sullivan, *Introduction to Kant's Ethics*, chaps. 2–6, for an excellent introduction; Sullivan, *Immanuel Kant's Moral Theory*, part III, for an detailed summary; and Paton, *Categorical Imperative*, for an in-depth analysis.

32. Paton lists five formulations of the categorical imperative (*Categorical Imperative*, 129), but two of them are variations on two of the three "standard" ones. (I

discuss the variant of the first one below.) Also, Kant gave no official names or titles to his formulae, so I base mine on Sullivan, *Immanuel Kant's Moral Theory*, 149–50.

33. *Groundwork*, 421.

34. Ibid., 402–3, 422.

35. Through his innovative and original analysis of the Formula of Autonomy, Binmore seems to arrive at the same conclusion: that logical consistency alone cannot ground the categorical imperative (*Playing Fair*, 153–9).

36. *Groundwork*, 421.

37. Paton, *Categorical Imperative*, 151.

38. *Groundwork*, 427; see also Herman, "Obligatory Ends."

39. For the opposite understanding, see McCloskey, *Bourgeois Virtues*, 322.

40. Paton, *Categorical Imperative*, 76. Later, he writes that "it is no part of Kant's doctrine that the moral law can be applied without any regard to empirical knowledge of the facts of human life" (151). See also Sullivan, *Immanuel Kant's Moral Theory*, 159–60.

41. *Groundwork*, 412 (emphasis mine); see also *Metaphysics of Morals*, 216–7.

42. *Groundwork*, 429.

43. For instance, in his discussion of price and dignity in the *Groundwork*, Kant writes that "skill and diligence in work have a market price" (434); in the *Anthropology*, he writes that "all other good and useful properties of character have a price in exchange for others which have just as much use. Talent has a market price, since the sovereign or estate-owner can use a talented person in all sorts of ways. . . . But character has an inner value and it is above all price" (292). For more, see Sullivan, *Immanuel Kant's Moral Theory*, 196–7.

44. For more on this point, see the prisoners' dilemma discussion later in this chapter, as well as Chapter 5.

45. *Metaphysics of Morals*, 395.

46. *Groundwork*, 438.

47. Ibid., 436.

48. Herman, "Murder and Mayhem"; Korsgaard, "Right to Lie."

49. Korsgaard, "Right to Lie," 143.

50. Herman, "Murder and Mayhem," 117.

51. Ibid., 118.

52. *Groundwork*, 421n12.

53. Much of this discussion of perfect and imperfect duties admits of exceptions; for instance, we saw above that "do not kill," certainly a narrow, perfect duty, cannot result from the Formula of Autonomy.

54. *Metaphysics of Morals*, 390.

55. See Gregor, *Laws of Freedom*, chap. 7, and Hill, "Imperfect Duty and Supererogation," for an in-depth discussion of perfect and imperfect duty; we will revisit the topic of the latitude involved with imperfect duties in Chapter 3.

56. Gregor, *Laws of Freedom*, 98.

57. As we will see when discussing the prisoners' dilemma game, in a way this is true of perfect duties as well: they tell us what *not* to do, but they do not tell us what *to* do instead. Do not lie, certainly, but don't feel you must necessarily tell the truth either. (If you listen carefully, you can hear the collective sigh of relief from lawyers and politicians everywhere.)

58. *Metaphysics of Morals*, 454. This contrasts significantly with caricatures of Kant in which he is supposed to advocate an extreme version of altruism, where others' interests take absolute precedence over one's own, and extreme self-sacrifice is mandated. Instead, he wrote that "when I say that I take an interest in this human being's well-being only out of my love for all human beings, the interest I take is as slight as an interest can be. I am only not indifferent with regard to him" (*Metaphysics of Morals*, 451), hardly an endorsement of ascetic generosity. (We will return to this point in Chapter 3.)

59. For instance, Aristotle wrote that it is not enough for a virtuous person to do acts which are generous or honest, but she must actually *be* generous and honest; she must embody, not merely exhibit, virtues. (See Hursthouse, *On Virtue Ethics*, chap. 4, for a comparison of Aristotle and Kant on this point.)

60. *Groundwork*, 393.

61. Ibid., 394.

62. Ibid.

63. Ibid., 398. As you may well imagine, this passage is often cited by those who accuse Kant of neglecting the role of emotions in human life. Kant did acknowledge some instrumental role of moral sentiment, mainly to help promote the performance of duty in cases where self-love may be too strong, for these feelings can support—but never replace—the requirements of the moral law. In the best case scenario, moral sentiments are psychological manifestations of the moral law, and if so can be regarded as truly moral. But otherwise, if these sentiments are not identical to the moral law, it is possible they can lead us astray from what duty requires, and this is the danger of relying on them to guide moral action. On these points, see Sullivan, *Immanuel Kant's Moral Theory*, 132–3; Baron, *Kantian Ethics Almost Without Apology*, chap. 6; Sherman, "Place of Emotions in Kantian Morality"; and Sabini and Silver, "Emotion, Character, and Responsibility."

64. *Groundwork*, 397–8.

65. For a much more nuanced view of suicide from a Kantian point of view, see Hill, "Self-Regarding Suicide."

66. On this point, see Sullivan, *Immanuel Kant's Moral Theory*, 122–4.

67. O'Neill, "Kant: Rationality as Practical Reason," 104.

68. Kant, "An Answer to the Question: What Is Enlightenment?", 54–5.

69. O'Neill, "Kant After Virtue," 161. A characteristic passage from MacIntyre is: "In Kant's moral writings we have reached a point at which the notion

that morality is anything other than obedience to rules has almost, if not quite, disappeared from sight" (*After Virtue*, 219); see also Louden, "Kant's Virtue Ethics," in response to McIntyre and other critics.

70. *Groundwork*, 404.

71. *Critique of Pure Reason*, A133/B172.

72. Sullivan, *Introduction*, 40.

73. See Sullivan, *Immanuel Kant's Moral Theory*, 53.

74. Wood, *Kant's Ethical Thought*, 107. He adds, parenthetically, "Any moral theory that purports to offer one should *precisely thereby* have discredited itself in the eyes of any person of good judgment."

75. Louden, *Kant's Impure Ethics*, 25; on the interaction of Kant's anthropology and his ethics, see also Frierson, *Freedom and Anthropology in Kant's Moral Philosophy*.

76. Herman, "Practice of Moral Judgment," 77.

77. Ibid., 75.

78. Herman, "Bootstrapping," 170.

79. *Groundwork*, 389. (Yes, even the *Groundwork* discusses judgment.)

80. *Metaphysics of Morals*, 224.

81. In Chapter 3, I argue that a person's unique faculty for judgment (along with her will, to be discussed in the next chapter) defines who she is, and together they comprise her character, which serves as her most essential identity and renders her unique.

82. This wording is inspired by the jurisprudence of Ronald Dworkin (*Taking Rights Seriously*; *Law's Empire*), which informs my take on judgment; I plan to explore this much further in future work.

83. For more on social proximity, see Chapter 3.

84. Again, this is analogous to a Dworkinian judge balancing various principles relevant to a case at hand; see "Hard Cases."

85. Herman, "Making Room for Character," 54; see also Hill, "Moral Dilemmas, Gaps, and Residues," arguing that "having gaps . . . is not unqualifiedly a defect in a [moral] theory. Gaps may reflect important features of our moral experience that closure would distort" (382).

86. This game is alternatively referred to as the *prisoner's* dilemma and the *prisoners'* dilemma. I choose the latter to emphasize that the problem arises only in strategic, multi-player situations.

87. Sen, "Choice, Orderings, and Morality," 77. For a similar discussion of ethical behavior and the prisoners' dilemma game, see Minkler and Miceli, "Lying, Integrity and Cooperation."

88. Keeping the description of the game general avoids the complication of judging the intrinsic morality of the acts that characterize deviation and cooperation in any specific game. For instance, deviation in the standard bank robber

tale—telling the truth and cooperating with the authorities—is the more ethical choice from society's point of view, but deviation in a public good financing problem—free-riding—is not.

89. Binmore sees some inconsistency here, but it is not clear to me why; he writes that "the maxim [never use a strongly dominated strategy] presumably fails Kant's test because, if it were adopted as a universal law, people would not cooperate" (*Playing Fair*, 149).

90. Sen, "Choice, Orderings, and Morality," 76 (emphasis mine).

91. Indeed, Kant explicitly criticized the Golden Rule—"do unto others as you would have them do unto you"—for the same reason, that it is grounded in subjective inclination rather than objective duty (*Groundwork*, 430n). (See Wattles, *Golden Rule*, 83–6, for a discussion of Kant's critique of the Golden Rule.)

92. Bilodeau and Gravel, "Voluntary Provision of a Public Good," 646 (emphasis mine).

93. Wolfelsperger, "Sur l'Existence d'une Solution 'Kantienne' du Problème des Biens Collectifs"; and Ballet and Jolivet, "A Propos de l'Économie Kantienne."

94. *Groundwork*, 402–3; see Hill, "Promises to Oneself," for more detail on the Kantian ethics of promise-keeping, to oneself as well as to other people.

95. *Groundwork*, 429–30 (emphasis mine).

96. See O'Neill, "Between Consenting Adults"; Korsgaard, "Right to Lie"; and Chapter 5 of this book.

97. This statement holds even if the choice situation reflects incomplete information, or constraints resulting from legal or institutional coercion, neither of which are an agent's responsibility towards others, and therefore do not affect the respect with which one treats another person.

98. For an extension of this logic to antitrust law, see Chapter 4.

99. Interestingly, this is the view also taken by most modern utilitarian philosophers, with the prominent exception of Richard Brandt (see *Theory of the Good and the Right*, chap. 13). For a defense of the desire-based account of utility, see Griffin, *Well-Being*, chap. 1.

100. The common assumption of the self-interested economic agent is usually not recognized as an essential part of the rational choice model, but is undeniably useful in showing that some socially beneficial outcomes can arise out of the interaction of narrowly self-interested actors (captured in Adam Smith's famous "invisible hand" metaphor and modern general equilibrium theory, for example). See Walsh, *Rationality, Allocation, and Reproduction*, chap. 5, for an fascinating discussion and history of the self-interest assumption in economics.

101. Obviously, this is a very abbreviated summary of economic models of choice, as the myriad fine details are not essential for our purposes; for an insightful and critical treatment, see Hargreaves Heap et al., *Theory of Choice*.

102. Another argument against lexicographic preferences is based on the standard use of preferences in welfare economics to measure well-being, which is obviously complicated by having "supreme" preferences that must be satisfied before even the least expensive normal ones. But since I argue against the equivalence of well-being and preferences later, I choose not to emphasize this argument.

103. Gintis, *Bounds of Reason*, 73–4 (emphasis removed).

104. Sen makes a similar point, writing that even though a constraint can be modeled formally as a preference, such a preference is "a devised construction and need not have any intuitive plausibility *seen as preference.* A morally exacting choice constraint can lead to an outcome that the person does not, in any sense, 'desire,' but which simply mimics the effect of his self-restraining constraint" ("Maximization and the Act of Choice," 191).

105. Gintis, *Bounds of Reason*, 73. To similar effect, Minkler writes: "While preferences and principles are independent from one another, individuals still possess preferences over principles . . . to the extent that if I act on that principle I may receive positive utility" (*Integrity and Agreement*, 3); as we'll see in the next chapter, Amitai Etzioni also posits a (meaningful) utility gain from moral behavior. In "Limits of *Homo Economicus*," Gaus poses the same problem more generally as a conflict between principles and values, but also assumes a rate of exchange between them.

106. For further discussion of moral preferences versus constraints, see Goldfarb and Griffith, "Amending the Economist's 'Rational Egoist' Model, Part 2." In a more recent paper with Dowell ("Economic Man as a Moral Individual"), they offer a model which represents a compromise between normal moral preferences and lexicographic ones. In their model, a preference for morality enters the utility function in such a way that the "utility from consuming a given set of goods varies in a 'lumpy' or 'discontinuous' way with the concurrent moral content of the individual's behavior" (649). As a result, incentives below a certain level will not produce changes in moral behavior, but large ones may, depending on the size of the discontinuity representing the agent's aversion to immorality. (In a way, this mimics the outcome of the model of the will to be described in the next chapter.)

107. Goldfarb and Griffith, "Amending the Economist's 'Rational Egoist' Model, Part 2," 65. Or, as James Buchanan put it, "the ordering over goods cannot be separated from the means through which goods are expected to be secured" ("Choosing What to Choose," p. 85). Sen calls this *process significance*; see his "Maximization and the Act of Choice."

108. Kant, *Metaphysics of Morals*, 451; I think "permit" here is misleading, since treating yourself as an end would mandate, not simply allow, some degree of self-interested action. As Herman writes, "the Kantian charge against self-interest is not that it is inherently contrary to morality; it need not be. The problem lies in its tendency to be presumptive" ("Making Room for Character," 52). Con-

trast this with virtue ethicist Michael Slote, who writes that "Kant's conception of morality . . . provides no basis for assigning positive moral value to actions to the extent they merely promote the happiness or well-being of their agents" ("Some Advantages of Virtue Ethics," 440).

109. Dworkin, "Hard Cases."

110. See also Hill, "Moral Dilemmas, Gaps, and Residues."

111. Kant, "On a Supposed Right to Lie." I am afraid Kant shot himself in the foot with this one, and wasted innumerable hours of good scholars' time in attempting to hold his moral theory together in light of it.

CHAPTER 2

1. *Self-Constitution*, 1.

2. Ibid.

3. Davidson, *Essays on Action and Events*.

4. "Human Freedom and the Self," 34. Chisholm contrasts this view with the "Kantian approach" (with which he agrees), in which "there is no logical connection between wanting and doing, nor need there even be a causal connection" (34–5).

5. Velleman, "What Happens When Someone Acts?," 461.

6. On bounded rationality, see Simon, "A Behavioral Model of Rational Choice"; and on cognitive biases, see Kahneman and Tversky, "Prospect Theory."

7. Behavioral economics, inspired by Kahneman and Tversky's work among others, will come up again in Chapter 5.

8. See the introduction to Stroud and Tappolet, *Weakness of Will and Practical Irrationality*, for a summary of research on weakness of will; more on this topic later in this chapter.

9. Ainslie, *Breakdown of Will*, 17.

10. Lutz, *Economics for the Common Good*, 155.

11. Shackle, *Decision Order and Time in Human Affairs*, 272.

12. Davis, "Identity and Individual Economic Agents," 73. Davis's ideas regarding identity play an important role in the next chapter.

13. George, *Preference Pollution*, 23 (also invoking Frankfurt's "wanton" from "Freedom of the Will").

14. Brennan, "Voluntary Exchange and Economic Claims," 114.

15. Minkler, *Integrity and Agreement*, 21.

16. Wallace, "Addiction as Defect of the Will," 172. This is reminiscent of Thorstein Veblen's criticism of "the hedonistic conception of man [which] is that of a lightning calculator of pleasures and pains who oscillates like a homogeneous globule of desire of happiness under the impulse of stimuli that shift him about the area, but leave him intact" ("Why Economics Is Not an Evolutionary Science," 389).

17. Wallace, "Addiction," 174. Esheté makes a similar point, writing that when a "conflict among the desires is in part resolved by the differences in the strength of the desires . . . the individual is no more than the playground for different forces" ("Virtue and Freedom," 498).

18. Velleman, "What Happens When Someone Acts?," 461.

19. Ibid., 465–6.

20. Searle, *Rationality in Action*, 5.

21. Ibid., p. 14. Other gaps occur between decision and action—discussed further below—and between the initiation of an action extended in time and its continuation or completion.

22. Ibid., 62.

23. Recalling Velleman's language quoted above, Searle supposes a world in which our actions were determined by our intentions: "if that were how the world worked in fact, we would not have to *act on* our intentions; we could, so to speak, wait for them to act by themselves. We could sit back and see how things turned out. But we can't do that, we always have to act" (ibid., 232–3).

24. Ibid., 17.

25. Ibid., 74, 83, 95. See the next chapter for further discussion of the nature of the self.

26. It is important to note that this discussion does not presuppose free will in the metaphysical sense; agents' decisions may ultimately be determined physically, but on a different level than conscious choice. The agent has the distinct experience of making choices that do not necessarily follow directly from her beliefs and desires, which is inconsistent with *psychological* determinism only, not with physical determinism (Wallace, "Three Conceptions of Rational Agency," 59n31). As Holton writes, "all that is denied is that agents' choices are determined by their explicit psychological states: their beliefs, desires, and intentions. It is quite compatible with that that they are determined in other ways" (*Willing, Wanting, Waiting*, 170–1). Therefore, I do not discuss "agent causation," which in its strongest form holds that an agent is "a prime mover unmoved" (Chisholm, "Human Freedom and the Self"), although it is an implication of Kantian autonomy (but one that is unnecessary to my overall thesis).

27. Ryle, *Concept of Mind*, 63; Davidson, *Essays on Actions and Events*, 83.

28. Ross, *Economic Theory and Cognitive Science*, 257. For more on the debate over the nature of conscious will in light of recent psychological and neurological research, see Wegner, *Illusion of Conscious Will*, and Mele, *Effective Intentions*.

29. Ainslie, *Breakdown of Will*, 104.

30. See the references in note 104 below.

31. O'Shaughnessy, *Will*, 30.

32. Wallace, "Three Conceptions of Rational Agency," 58.

33. Wallace, "Normativity, Commitment, and Instrumental Reason," 83.

34. Holton, "How Is Strength of Will Possible?," 40, 49.

35. Searle, *Rationality in Action*, 13.

36. Ibid., 14. In their book on humanistic economics, Mark Lutz and Kenneth Lux agree with Searle that truly free choice "has no antecedents, no determining principles, and no maximization. We have no way of 'explaining' free choice precisely because it is free" (*Humanistic Economics*, 117).

37. *Critique of Practical Reason*, 122.

38. *Groundwork*, 408.

39. In previous work, I used the term "character" to denote strength of will, but no longer, as now I treat an agent's character as consisting of her judgment and strength of will together. To a lesser extent, I will also try to avoid the word "virtue" as Kant uses it, since it is easily confused with the more common use of the term in virtue ethics, though there is some connection. On this point, see Kant, *Metaphysics of Morals*, 403–6; Wood, *Kant's Ethical Thought*, 329–33; and the discussion of virtue ethics in the Introduction above.

40. For more on this, see Allison, *Kant's Theory of Freedom*, chap. 7; and Beck, *Commentary on Kant's Critique of Practical Reason*, 176–81, both of which discuss Kant's inconsistent and evolving usage of the terms. Note that *Wille* and *Willkür* are two aspects of the agent's will, which should not be misread as two separate wills or a version of the divided self; as Beck writes, "we must never suppose that there are two faculties related to each other in some external, coercive way. There is only one, but it has prima facie two kinds of freedom" (180). (I discuss these topics further in Chapter 3.)

41. Allison, *Kant's Theory of Freedom*, 129.

42. Kant, *Metaphysics of Morals*, 397. On Kant's theory of virtue as strength, see Mary Gregor, *Laws of Freedom*, 70–75; Paul Guyer, *Kant on Freedom, Law, and Happiness*, 306–11; and Stephen Engstrom, "Inner Freedom of Virtue" (and references therein, especially from 290n5).

43. *Religion*, 29.

44. Ibid.

45. *Metaphysics of Morals*, 408.

46. Technically, having an impure will involves mixing inclination with duty for otherwise moral ends, while depravity (or the "corruption of the human heart") involves putting aside the moral law altogether (see *Religion*, 29–30). Since I am not concerned here with the ultimate ends of the agent, I will use impurity of the will to refer to any influence of inclination on the determination of maxims (for whatever end).

47. *Metaphysics of Morals*, 408.

48. Ibid., 407–8.

49. Ibid., 408.

50. As Engstrom notes, affects "directly interfere with our choice of actions rather than of ends," while passions "directly interfere with our choice of ends, rather than of actions" ("Inner Freedom," 309n22).

51. *Metaphysics of Morals*, 408.

52. Ibid., 409 (emphasis removed); see also *Religion*, 253–4; Gregor, *Laws of Freedom*, 72–3; Engstrom, "Inner Freedom," 307–8, 310n24; and Seidler, "Kant and the Stoics on the Emotional Life."

53. While I hope my treatment is relatively faithful to *Wille* and *Willkür*, Kant's broader concept of will is much more daunting: "in most modern philosophy, it is a given that Kant's view of the will is the one to avoid" (Herman, "Bootstrapping," 156). I therefore make no claims regarding fidelity to Kant on this matter; see Herman, "Bootstrapping" and "Will and Its Objects" for further discussion.

54. Sen, "Rational Fools," 335–36.

55. See Davis, *Theory of the Individual in Economics*, chap. 4, for a survey of conceptions of multiple utilities or selves, and an exchange in the journal *Economics and Philosophy* for a spirited debate on the issue (Etzioni, "Case for a Multiple Utility Conception"; Brennan, "Methodological Assessment"; Lutz, "Utility of Multiple Utility"; and Brennan's brilliantly titled "Futility of Multiple Utility").

56. For an example of parallel orderings, see Etzioni, "Toward a Kantian Socio-Economics," 140–2, and *Moral Dimension*, chap. 3 (discussed further below); for an example of hierarchical preferences, see Frankfurt, "Freedom of the Will."

57. See below for more on metapreferences in relationship to the model of the will presented here.

58. Hill, "Self-Respect Reconsidered"; see also his "Promises to Oneself" and "Weakness of Will and Character," which is invoked below.

59. *Metaphysics of Morals*, 394.

60. It may even do so *asymptotically*. (I wanted to include something for the mathematical economist who may have picked up this book by mistake.)

61. See below for other examples of economic models of willpower that include a similar term as a decision variable in a deterministic model of choice.

62. For example, see the reports of success rates in dieting, such as those reported by Martin Seligman (*What You Can Change*), which, as Richard Holton points out, measures the difficulty of the task, not the likelihood of any particular person's success; the latter is not completely random, but rather largely a function of effort (*Willing, Wanting, Waiting*, 174).

63. Searle, *Rationality in Action*, 73.

64. A point made in a previous note is worth repeating: in the sense in which I use it, free choice is not dependent on free will in the metaphysical

sense. Free choice is compatible with physical determinism, but not psychological determinism.

65. Kant had no patience for those who *would* regard the choice of ice cream flavor as morally loaded: "But that human being can be called fantastically virtuous who allows *nothing to be morally indifferent* and strews all his steps with duties, as with mantraps . . . Fantastic virtue is a concern with petty details which . . . would turn the government of virtue into tyranny" (*Metaphysics of Morals*, 409).

66. See Baker, "Virtue and Behavior," for more reasoning along these lines.

67. Cooter, "Prices and Sanctions," also considers this issue, based on a model similar to that in Dowell et al., "Economic Man as a Moral Individual" (see chapter 1); Cooter posits a discontinuity in the agent's utility function where immoral action is concerned that creates an extra internal cost to sanctions. (Coincidentally, this example is very close to the one that Gary Becker credits with inspiring his initial analysis of the economics of crime; see Becker, "Economic Way of Looking at Life," 389-90.)

68. Hill, "Weakness of Will and Character."

69. Baumgarten, "Acting against Better Knowledge."

70. Steedman and Krause, "Goethe's *Faust*, Arrow's Possibility Theorem and the Individual Decision-Taker."

71. Etzioni, "Toward a Kantian Socio-Economics," 140–2, and *Moral Dimension*, chap. 3. In "Toward a Dual Motive Metaeconomic Theory," Lynne presents a similar model, inspired by Adam Smith rather than Kant (appropriately, since this framework is more in line with sentimentalism than deontology).

72. See note 63 in Chapter 1 for more on the role of moral sentiments.

73. George, *Preference Pollution*, 15–20; Frankfurt, "Freedom of the Will." This brief summary obscures the differences in how the two scholars represent the hierarchical structure of preferences; see *Preference Pollution*, 18–20. (See also 32–4 in same detailing the difference between metapreferences and multiple utilities or selves.)

74. *Preference Pollution*, 20. The possibility of partial freedom in George's model opens the door for external manipulation of one's preferences, which is the normative thesis of his book.

75. Cooter, "Lapses, Conflict, and Akrasia."

76. Minkler, *Integrity and Agreement*, 22.

77. Loewenstein, "Willpower," 53, 73 (emphasis mine).

78. Kim, "Hyperbolic Discounting and the Repeated Self-Control Problem."

79. However, in his model, Kim also posits a measure of "perceived willpower," which is endogenous to the agent, and which also affects resolve in action; this perceived willpower behaves much like the probability term in my model. (I discuss this aspect of his model at more length below.)

80. Elster, *Ulysses and the Sirens*, 44.

81. Taken to the extreme, this would support the view of situationists who deny global character traits (such as resolve) in favor of local ones that vary with respect to situational details; see Doris, *Lack of Character*.

82. "Strength of any kind can be recognized only by the obstacles it can overcome" (*Metaphysics of Morals*, 394).

83. Keep in mind that p_H is merely an estimation of the agent's resolve, not an exogenous factor deterministic of it; I try to assert this in the text above by referring primarily to changes in the agent's willpower, and only then to changes in her p_H, a mere reflection of the former.

84. However, I express reservations about this relationship below.

85. It may seem that the strength of the temptation should not matter, as this is a sensuous matter and is therefore of no regard to autonomous persons. But, insofar as weakness implies allowing inclination into decision-making, even temporarily, it may trigger consideration of sensuous matters; likewise, resistance to such factors may in turn signal a strengthening of character.

86. *Anthropology*, 267.

87. Not for nothing does Kant refer to passions as "cancerous stores for pure practical reason" (ibid., 266).

88. *Metaphysics of Morals*, 394.

89. Ibid., 409.

90. Ibid., 397.

91. Muraven and Baumeister, "Self-Regulation and Depletion of Limited Resources"; see also Baumeister and Heatherton, "Self-Regulation Failure: An Overview."

92. Holton, "Strength of Will," 49. In "Feeling of Doing," Bayne and Levy explore the phenomenology of agency, with particular attention to effort and Baumeister et al.'s work on it.

93. Muraven and Baumeister, "Self-Regulation and Depletion of Limited Resources," 247, 254. A more recent paper proposes that general decision-making (not just self-control situations) draws on this same limited psychological resource, resulting in "decision fatigue"; see Vohs et al., "Making Choices Impairs Subsequent Self-Control."

94. Heatherton and Baumeister, "Self-Regulation Failure: Past, Present, and Future," 93.

95. Baumeister and Heatherton, "Self-Regulation Failure: An Overview," 4.

96. Ibid., 6–9.

97. In "Willpower," Loewenstein offers a preliminary economic analysis of the allocation of limited willpower, along the same lines as the work of Baumeister and colleagues.

98. Ainslie, "Procrastination," 27. On the identification of procrastination with weakness of will, and the complications involved therein, see Stroud, "Is

Procrastination Weakness of Will?" (I address one of her concerns in note 122 below.)

99. As indicated above, see Stroud and Tappolet's introduction to *Weakness of Will and Practical Irrationality* for an overview of the literature, and Walker, "Problem of Weakness of Will," for an extensive discussion of various critiques of the concept. (The summary presented here draws significantly from these sources.)

100. Stroud and Tappolet, *Weakness of Will*, 8. Scholars have identified several degrees of weakness of will; the cases I have described fall into the category of *last ditch akrasia*, to use Pears's term (from *Motivated Irrationality*). Milder cases include *motivated irrational action*, in which case "the akrates' rebellious desire infects his prior reasoning and thinking in such a way that his contemplated action seems to him warranted, and he acts accordingly" (Walker, "Problem," 653). In last ditch *akrasia*, the agent's reasoning is not corrupted and clearly advises against the act, implying a greater conflict between reason and action.

101. See, for instance, Audi, "Weakness of Will and Rational Action"; and Searle, *Rationality in Action*, chap. 7.

102. The various arguments against the intentionality of akratic acts trace back to Davidson, "How Is Weakness of Will Possible?"; see Walker, "Problems," 658–66, for detailed discussion.

103. Pugmire, "Motivated Irrationality," Watson, "Skepticism About Weakness of Will," and Kubara, "Acrasia," all argue that akratic action is unfree (albeit for different reasons).

104. For instance, see Wallace, "Addiction as Defect of the Will"; Gjelsvik, "Addiction, Weakness of the Will, and Relapse"; and many of the essays in Elster, *Addiction*.

105. The classic work by economists on self-control includes Strotz, "Myopia and Inconsistency"; Schelling, *Choice and Consequence*; and Thaler and Shefrin, "Economic Theory of Self-Control." Economists have also been influenced in this area by the work of philosopher Jon Elster (*Ulysses and the Sirens*) and psychiatrist George Ainslie (*Breakdown of Will*), whose work on procrastination will be discussed more below.

106. Searle, *Rationality in Action*, 232 (and chap. 7 in general).

107. Korsgaard, *Self-Constitution*, 2–3.

108. See Heath and Anderson, "Procrastination and the Extended Will," for more on external mechanisms for coping with procrastination.

109. See Ross, "Economic Models of Procrastination," for a more detailed examination of—well, you know.

110. Akerlof, "Procrastination and Obedience," 1.

111. O'Donoghue and Rabin, "Doing It Now or Later," 103n2.

112. Ibid., 103.

113. O'Donoghue and Rabin, "Incentives for Procrastinators."

114. O'Donoghue and Rabin, "Choice and Procrastination."

115. O'Donoghue and Rabin, "Procrastination on Long-Term Projects."

116. Fischer, "Read This Paper Later."

117. Fischer, "Read This Paper Even Later."

118. Andreou, "Understanding Procrastination," 183; but again, see Stroud, "Is Procrastination Weakness of Will?" for important qualifications.

119. Korsgaard, *Self-Constitution*, 69.

120. See Hill, "Weakness of Will and Character." This assumes that the task in question is not contrary to duty itself; if it were, procrastination in performance of the task would compound one violation of duty on top of another, and therefore still show a lack of character, despite any beneficial effects from delaying the wrongful act. (I thank Chrisoula Andreou for pointing out this possibility.)

121. Ibid., 134.

122. Ibid., 135. For more on rational reconsideration, see Bratman, *Intentions, Plans, and Practical Reason*, chap. 5, and "Planning and Temptation"; and Holton, *Willing, Wanting, Waiting*, 73–8.

123. Ibid., 136. This concept of weakness of will is similar to that of Richard Holton, who argues that weakness of will is properly understood as failure to carry out plans, not acting against better judgment (or *akrasia*). (See Holton, *Willing, Wanting, Waiting*, chap. 4.) Holton's point is also emphasized by Stroud ("Is Procrastination Weakness of Will?") in questioning the identification of procrastination with weakness of will; I think my model is general enough to encompass both understandings.

124. This assumes that said incentives do not change enough to make delay the overall best choice, both prudentially and ethically—if so, the nature of higher path itself would change, and choosing delay would no longer qualify as procrastination, but rather prudent delay.

125. I am not ruling out rational reconsideration that may legitimately affect judgment; see note 121 above.

126. In statistical language, we could say that, in this case, her lapses (or "errors") are independent and identically distributed. (I try to offer a little something for everybody.)

127. Ainslie, *Breakdown of Will*, chap. 7, and "Procrastination."

128. For a recent formalization of this idea, see Bénabou and Tirole, "Willpower and Personal Rules."

129. However, Ainslie counsels against excessive reliance on willpower; see *Breakdown of Will*, chaps. 9–11.

130. Kim, "Hyperbolic Discounting."

131. Ibid., 346, 349.

132. Ibid., 350.

133. See Doris, *Lack of Character*, for the modern focal point of the debate over character-based virtue ethics and situationist critiques thereof. I think this also touches on the debate regarding moral particularism, the view that moral decisions can be made on a case-by-case with no need for general principles; without the principles that help comprise our judgment (and therefore contribute to our character), again I ask, who are we, and what makes us unique? (For arguments for particularism, see Dancy, *Ethics Without Principles*, and for arguments for generalism, see McKeever and Ridge, *Principled Ethics*.) I hope to develop these thoughts further in future work.

CHAPTER 3

1. Gary Watson puts this in terms of acting on the basis on one's valuations (arising from judgment) rather than from one's motivations (arising from desire); see his "Free Agency," especially 215–6.

2. Davis, "Atomism, Identity Criteria, and Impossibility Logic," 83.

3. Reath, "Legislating for a Realm of Ends," 192.

4. I do not have much to say regarding *methodological individualism*, the modeling strategy that attempts to explain all social phenomena by reference to individuals, since my immediate concerns are not methodological, and so much in this debate hinges on the understanding of the individual, especially whether that understanding includes relationships with other persons. Generally, I am sympathetic to Geoffrey Hodgson's view that "all satisfactory and successful explanations of social phenomena (including in economics) involve interactive relations between individuals," but that methodological individualism hardly seems like an appropriate name for such theories ("Meanings of Methodological Individualism," 217). Nonetheless, according to Hodgson, Friedrich von Hayek held such a view under that very name, maintaining that "society consists not merely of individuals, but also of interactions between individuals, plus interactions between individuals and other aspects of their environment including, presumably, both the natural world and other socio-economic systems" ("Meanings," 215, referring to Hayek, *Studies in Philosophy, Politics and Economics*, 70–1). See also Zwirn, "Methodological Individualism or Methodological Atomism," who makes similar claims regarding Hayek, and argues that the term *methodological atomism* should be used for the mainstream view, which omits social factors, while methodological individualism should be reserved for accounts like that of Hayek.

5. Davis, "Conception of the Socially Embedded Individual," 92. See also Davis, *Theory of the Individual in Economics*, chap. 6.

6. See Hargreaves Heap, "Individual Preferences and Decision-Making," for a brief survey of social preferences. For more on the compatibility of autonomy with concern, care, and community, see Hill, "Importance of Autonomy," and Oshana, "Autonomy Bogeyman."

7. Lutz, *Economics for the Common Good*, 6.

8. Granovetter, "Economic Action and Social Structure," 58.

9. Davis, *Theory of the Individual*, 108; Lutz, *Economics*, 6.

10. Hodgson, "Meanings," 218 (emphasis mine).

11. To be sure, on methodological grounds, Vilfredo Pareto did say that "the individual can disappear, provided he leaves us [a] photograph of his tastes" (*Manual of Political Economy*, 120), quoted in Rizvi, "Adam Smith's Sympathy," 249.

12. For a survey, see Davis, *Theory of the Individual*, 117–27.

13. Frankfurt, *Necessity, Volition, and Love*, 132.

14. Dworkin, "Hard Cases."

15. What can I say—once you're a Jet . . .

16. In no way am I implying that these changes are necessarily bad; I imagine every new parent must have said, at some point, "I was never the same after my child was born." (And they do not mean just extra pounds or less hair!)

17. On *Gesinnung*, see Allison, *Kant's Theory of Freedom*, 136–45, and Munzel, *Kant's Conception of Moral Character*. Munzel chooses the translate the term— "one of the most difficult words to render in English"—as "comportment of mind," which "is intended to convey the specific sense thereof as one's mental bearing, informed by principles one consistently adopts in setting and pursuing one's purposes and in guiding one's choice making" (xvi–xvii).

18. Allison, *Kant's Theory of Freedom*, 136–7. Note the relevance of the second sentence to my brief comments regarding situationism at the end of the last chapter.

19. Korsgaard, "Personal Identity and Unity of Agency," 378.

20. For more discussion on the relationship between the two topics, see the essays in Mackensie and Atkins, *Practical Identity and Narrative Agency*. In this discussion I do not rely on Kant's own discussion of personal identity, which is largely metaphysical and not relevant to my treatment of character; on these neglected issues, see Ameriks, *Kant's Theory of Mind*, chap. 4; and Kitcher, "Kant on Self-Identity" and "Kant's Philosophy of the Cognitive Mind."

21. Darwall, "Scheffler on Morality," 254, responding to Parfit, "Later Selves and Moral Principles." (Lest there be any confusion, the bulk of Darwall's article deals with Scheffler's arguments in "Ethics, Personal Identity, and Ideals of the Person" regarding Parfit; only the last paragraph, quoted above, deals with Parfit directly.) See also Shoemaker, "Utilitarianism and Personal Identity."

22. Darwall, "Scheffler on Morality," 254–5.

23. Darwall, *Impartial Reason*, 101–2.

24. Korsgaard, *Self-Constitution*, 25 (emphasis mine). Korsgaard is not the only philosopher to have argued for self-constitution, though her conception of it is unique; for a list of other adherents, see Velleman, "Self as Narrator," 203n1, and for a critical survey, see Berofsky, "Identification, the Self, and Autonomy."

25. Munzel uses similar language in describing "the role of maxims as in fact constituting principles formative of character, as being (literally speaking) 'character-building devices'" (*Kant's Conception of Moral Character*, 68).

26. Korsgaard, *Self-Constitution*, 42–4.

27. Ibid., 43.

28. Feinberg, *Harm to Self*, 35; see more generally 33–5 on autonomy as self-determination.

29. Gerald Dworkin, "Autonomy and Behavioral Control," 24. (See also Oshana, "Autonomy and Free Agency," 196–8, and Herman, "Responsibility and Moral Competence," 91–7.) Note also the similarity with economic conceptions of business competition (to be discussed more in Chapter 4): mainstream economists treat competition as a fixed equilibrium determined by certain initial conditions, whereas Austrian economists see it as a continual process of discovery, innovation, and equilibration that never actually ends in an equilibrium but is always heading toward one until the next change in market conditions alters where the hypothetical equilibrium is. (For instance, see Ikeda, "Market Process.")

30. In this sense, she achieves integrity in the formal sense of coherence and continuity, as opposed to more substantive understandings (implying specific moral values); see McFall, "Integrity," on the various meanings of the term, and Minkler, *Integrity and Agreement*, for a comprehensive discussion of substantive integrity (specifically, honesty) within economics. Korsgaard can be read as arguing that formal coherence as an agent implies substantive morality according to Kantian principles.

31. Korsgaard, *Self-Constitution*, chap. 7.

32. Ibid., 135, drawing on Plato's *Republic*, book 1.

33. Korsgaard, *Self-Constitution*, 126.

34. Ibid., 214.

35. The most well-known conception of this, perhaps, is George Ainslie's *picoeconomics* (see *Picoeconomics* and *Breakdown of the Will*). See also the papers in Elster, *Multiple Self* (including an early presentation of picoeconomics by Ainslie); Lynne, "Divided Self Models"; Davis, *Theory of the Individual*, chap. 4; and Bazin and Ballet, "Basic Model of Multiple Self." Etzioni argues that Kantian decision-making itself is best represented by multiple selves: "by Kantians, the self is divided, one part standing over the other, judging it and deciding whether or not to yield to any particular desire" ("Toward a Kantian Socio-Economics," 140). It is unclear how literally he meant this (a problem common to much of the multiple selves literature), but cer-

tainly Kant did not posit separate selves, but a single will which strikes the appropriate balance between duty and inclination (see note 40 in Chapter 2).

36. Elster, *Multiple Self,* 30–1 (emphasis in original).

37. This can be taken in the context of the debates between communitarians and John Rawls over the extent that society shapes the individual; see Bell, "Communitarianism," section 2.

38. Korsgaard, *Sources of Normativity,* 101.

39. Korsgaard, *Self-Constitution,* 23.

40. Ibid., 120. As Kant writes in the *Religion,* "freedom of the power of choice has the characteristic, entirely peculiar to it, that it cannot be determined to action through any incentive *except so far as the human being has incorporated it into his maxim*" (23–4).

41. Korsgaard, *Self-Constitution,* 139, based on Plato, *Republic,* 437c; this also relates to the discussion of volitionism and "gaps" in Chapter 2.

42. Sen, *Rationality and Freedom,* 36; on this, see also Charles Taylor's conception of "strong evaluation" in *Sources of the Self,* and Davis, "Identity and Commitment."

43. On the latter point, see David George's frank description of his acknowledged love for junk food in *Preference Pollution,* 8–11.

44. Davis, *Theory of the Individual,* 114.

45. Davis, "Identity and Individual Economic Agents."

46. Davis, "Conception of the Socially Embedded Individual," 94.

47. Davis, *Theory of the Individual,* 114.

48. Ibid.

49. Oshana, "Autonomy and Free Agency," 196.

50. Herman, "Moral Improvisation," 298.

51. Davis, "Collective Intentionality and Individual Behavior," and *Theory of the Individual,* chap. 7.

52. Gilbert, *Walking Together.*

53. See, for instance, Schmid, "Rationalizing Coordination."

54. See, for instance, Gilbert, *Walking Together,* chap. 6: "When a goal has a plural subject [as opposed to the shared personal goal of the participants], each of a number of persons . . . has, in effect, offered his will to be part of a pool of wills that is dedicated, as one, to that goal" (185). But she explicitly disavows any notion of a group mind: "human beings create joint commitments together and thereby constitute plural subjects" (*Sociality and Responsibility,* 3).

55. See Tuomela, *Importance of Us.* The characterizations of the last two viewpoints comes from Schulte-Ostermann, "Agent Causation and Collective Agency," 192.

56. Davis, *Theory of the Individual,* 130.

57. Ibid., 134.

58. I would be remiss if I neglected to mention *team reasoning*, a conception of collective action that emphasizes processes of rational decision-making over the nature of agency; see Gold and Sugden, "Theories of Team Agency," for a comprehensive summary of the various approaches to team agency, as well as their relationships to the conceptions of plural agency described above.

59. Louden, *Kant's Impure Ethics*, 172. See also Herman: "if autonomy is a source of dignity, it seems equally to be the source of a kind of autarchic individualism, supporting a conception of persons as radically separate from one another" ("Cosmopolitan Kingdom of Ends," 52).

60. Sullivan, *Immanuel Kant's Moral Theory*, 199.

61. Berlin, "Two Concepts of Liberty." (The role of negative liberty in Kant's political philosophy will be addressed in the next chapter.)

62. Kant, *Metaphysics of Morals*, 464.

63. In other words, the Vulcan salutation "Live long and prosper" from *Star Trek* was particularly ironic; a race ruled by logic may live long, but true prosperity would likely elude it.

64. Gregor too considers that "Kant's ethics is primarily a study of [imperfect] duties," and blames the characterization of his ethics as "legalistic" for overlooking this (*Laws of Freedom*, 95).

65. Kant, *Metaphysics of Morals*, 453.

66. Ibid., 449 (emphasis removed).

67. Ibid., 449–50. It is important to note also that the duty of beneficence does not extend to concern for another person's moral character; we certainly have a duty not to corrupt others, but no positive duty to look out for others' virtue. (See ibid., 386, 393–4, and Sullivan, *Immanuel Kant's Moral Theory*, 205.)

68. At times, however, Kant seemed to lean toward a maximizing conception; see Baron, *Kantian Ethics Almost without Apology*, 95–8, where she rejects this as an inaccurate and inconsistent picture of Kant's views.

69. Singer, "Famine, Affluence, and Morality"; Veblen, "Why Economics Is Not an Evolutionary Science." Kant does, however, say that the rich have a stronger obligation to help others, though their beneficence is less meritorious than a similar act on the part of a less wealthy person (*Metaphysics of Morals*, 453). Nonetheless, beneficence is an imperfect duty for all, rich and poor.

70. Kant, *Metaphysics of Morals*, 448–9.

71. Ibid., 454; this is also relevant to the critique of "libertarian paternalism" given in Chapter 5 of this book.

72. On the degree and kind of latitude allowed with respect in imperfect duty, see Baron, *Kantian Ethics Almost Without Apology*, chap. 3; Herman, "Scope of Moral Requirement"; Sherman, *Making a Necessity of Virtue*, chap. 8; and Baron and Fahmy, "Beneficence and Other Duties of Love" (as well as the references

given in note 55 in Chapter 1). Related to this is the issue of supererogation (acting above and beyond the demands of morality) and whether Kant can accommodate the concept; this is a primary theme of Baron's *Kantian Ethics* (and references therein).

73. This includes being purposefully attentive to the sufferings of others: "It is therefore a duty not to avoid the places where the poor who lack the most basic necessities are to be found but rather to seek them out" (Kant, *Metaphysics of Morals*, 457).

74. *Groundwork*, 438.

75. Ibid., 433.

76. See Paton, *Categorical Imperative*, 194–5, on moral progress and the kingdom of ends; in particular, "one great merit of Kant's system is that it puts into a true perspective the spirit, as opposed to the letter, of the moral law" (194).

77. *Groundwork*, 434. The reader may note the similarity between the Kantian concept of universal legislation based on impersonal concerns and John Rawls's concept of hypothetical decision-making behind the "veil of ignorance" (*Theory of Justice*).

78. Indeed, Herman suggests that "if one thinks of Kantian morality as inherently social it is hard to see what the idea of a kingdom of ends adds" ("Cosmopolitan Kingdom of Ends," 66).

79. Kant, "Idea for a Universal History," 20; also, "the human being is a being meant for society (though he is also an unsociable one)" (*Metaphysics of Morals*, 471). (For more on this, see Wood, *Kant's Ethical Thought*, 213–5, and Kneller, "Introducing Kantian Social Theory.")

80. Kant, "Idea for a Universal History," 21.

81. Kant, *Religion*, 97.

82. Sullivan, *Immanuel Kant's Moral Theory*, 214–6.

83. Of course, as we shall see in Chapter 4, this is the standard assumption made in neoclassical law and economics, corresponding to Oliver Wendell Holmes's "bad man" (from "The Path of the Law"); see Cooter, "Models of Morality in Law and Economics," and Gordon, "The Path of the Lawyer" (including the wonderful term *Homo law-and-economicus*).

84. Kant, *Religion*, 95.

85. For an application of this idea to the improvement of public debate (about which Kant was passionate), see Rossi, "Public Argument and Social Responsibility."

86. The similarities between Smith and Kant have been explored most intensively and thoroughly by Samuel Fleischacker; see his "Philosophy in Moral Practice," "Values Behind the Market," and *Third Concept of Liberty*.

87. *Theory of Moral Sentiments*, I.i.5.5. See Evensky, *Adam Smith's Moral Philosophy*, 12–6, for more on Smith's vision of the ideal progress of humankind,

corresponding (politically) to "the liberal plan of equality, liberty, and justice" (*Wealth of Nations*, IV.9.3).

88. Young, *Economics as a Moral Science*, 25.

89. Fleischacker, *On Adam Smith's* Wealth of Nations, 91 (emphasis in original).

90. See ibid., 55–7, on Smith's moral/political assessment of capitalism. Also, Smith's conception of self-interest (or self-love) is very different from that of the modern economist; on this see Wight, "Adam Smith and Greed," and McCloskey, "Adam Smith."

91. Furthermore, as Deirdre McCloskey explains in *Bourgeois Virtues*, actual markets also support virtue, not just in the minimal aspect of respect described in the sketch of markets above, but in a strongly positive sense, incorporating not just prudence, justice, temperance, but also faith, hope, and love.

92. See Fleischacker, *Third Concept of Liberty*, 137–8, and references to *WN* therein.

93. See *Theory of Moral Sentiments*, VI.ii.1, for Smith's description of the diminution of sympathy and benevolence as social distance increases, what Young calls "a kind of inverse square law" (*Economics as a Moral Science*, 71), which is also very similar to Kant's views on social distance and beneficence, discussed below (see also Herman, "Scope of Moral Requirement," 205–8).

94. *Wealth of Nations*, IV.9.51. This is also what David Gauthier means in *Morals by Agreement* when he refers to the market as a "morally free zone": "in understanding the perfect market as a morally free zone we shall be led back to its underlying, antecedent morality" (84–5)—that is, mutually agreed-upon constraints on behavior corresponding to what Smith called the "laws of justice" that thereby define the boundaries of the market. How Gauthier breaks from both is by claiming that the market is the ideal model for an ethical society, and morality is necessary only where markets are not possible (see *Morals by Agreement*, chap. VIII).

95. Kant, *Metaphysics of Morals*, 458.

96. Wight, "Adam Smith's Ethics," 156.

97. As Aristotle wrote, "if people are friends, they have no need of justice" (*Nicomachean Ethics*, 1155a); however, Sherman claims that Kant would have said the opposite, based on our "unsocial sociability" and the possibility of betrayal of respect between friends ("Virtues of Common Pursuit," 20). See also Korsgaard, "Creating the Kingdom of Ends," 189–97 on the close relationship between Aristotle's and Kant's conceptions of friendship, as well as the references in the next note.

98. Wood, *Kant's Ethical Thought*, 275 (more generally, 275–82); see also Kant, *Metaphysics of Morals*, 469–73, and Paton, "Kant on Friendship." This criticism of Kant regarding friendship often comes from virtue ethicists, who have written much more about friendship than Kant has; Aristotle's *Nicomachean Ethics*

(books 8 and 9) is the starting point (and, frequently, the stopping point as well) of any philosophical discussion of friendship. (See also Sherman, *Fabric of Character*, chap. 4; Badhwar, *Friendship* [especially her introduction]; and McCloskey, *Bourgeois Virtues*, chap. 8. For a popular account informed by philosophy as well as other fields, I highly recommend Joseph Epstein's *Friendship: An Exposé*.) Consequentialists, naturally, have the hardest time explaining friendship; see, for instance, the critical work of Kapur, "Why It Is Wrong to Always Be Guided by the Best," and Stocker, "Schizophrenia of Modern Ethical Theories."

99. Kant, *Metaphysics of Morals*, 451.

100. Ibid.

101. Ibid., 452. For a more thorough treatment of impartiality and love in a Kantian context, see Velleman, "Love as a Moral Emotion."

102. Korsgaard, "Creating the Kingdom of Ends," 189.

103. This applies to commitments we make to ourselves also; see the discussion of duties of self-respect and weakness of will in Chapter 2.

104. Korsgaard, "Creating the Kingdom of Ends," 192.

105. For a detailed look at how autonomy plays into family relations and friendships, see Kupfer, *Autonomy and Social Interaction*, chap. 4.

106. Hume, *Treatise of Human Nature*, 521.

107. Gintis, "Strong Reciprocity and Human Sociality," 169; see also various chapters in Gintis et al., *Moral Sentiments and Material Interests*, in particular the first chapter (by the editors).

108. Gintis, "Strong Reciprocity and Human Sociality," 169.

109. Sen, "Foreword," x.

CHAPTER 4

1. Sullivan, *Immanuel Kant's Moral Theory*, 258.

2. Kant, *Metaphysics of Morals*, 230.

3. See also Sullivan, *Immanuel Kant's Moral Theory*, 247–8.

4. Ripstein, *Force and Freedom*, 9.

5. *Metaphysics of Morals*, 231.

6. Reiss, "Introduction," 23.

7. Kersting, "Kant's Concept of the State," 153.

8. Kant, "On the Proverb," 290–1. There is one well-known exception in Kant's large body of work in which he seems to relax this and endorse a limited form of the modern welfare state; see *Metaphysics of Morals*, 326, as well as Murphy, *Kant: The Philosophy of Right*, 123–5 for a discussion of it that acknowledges its inconsistency, but nonetheless develops (what he calls) a "provisional account" of a Kantian basis for positive welfare payments. See also Ripstein, *Force and Freedom*, chap. 9, for an argument for a welfare state

based on equal opportunity (which he considers an essential aspect of right or justice) rather than consequences; and Wood, *Kantian Ethics*, 196, makes a similar argument.

9. Once again, this role of the state emphasizes what Berlin called *negative liberty*; see Berlin, "Two Concepts of Liberty."

10. In modern times, Richard Epstein's *Skepticism and Freedom* is a representative presentation of a classical liberal argument; James Otteson's *Actual Ethics* is an excellent defense of classical liberalism based on Kantian personhood (with aspects of Aristotelianism as well); and for a more economics-focused treatment, informed by Kant, John Rawls, and James Buchanan, see Timothy Roth, *Ethics and Economics of Minimalist Government* and *Equality, Rights and the Autonomous Self.*

11. Kant laid out the bulk of his political philosophy in the first half of the *Metaphysics of Morals*, known as the "Doctrine of Right"; see especially 229–36 on his justification of, and limitations on, state power. For further discussion of Kant's political philosophy, see Sullivan, *Immanuel Kant's Moral Theory*, chaps. 16–17; Murphy, *Kant: The Philosophy of Right*; and Ripstein, "Kant on Law and Justice" and *Force and Freedom*.

12. See Sen, "Utilitarianism and Welfarism," for a detailed analysis of these two separate but related concepts; for present purposes, I use the former term for the ethical system, and the latter for the policy-oriented application of it.

13. For the definitive analysis, see Little, *Critique of Welfare Economics*, which begins with an open acknowledgment and elucidation of the utilitarian nature of welfare economics (without directly challenging it). (For general surveys, see Graaff, *Theoretical Welfare Economics*, and Boadway and Bruce, *Welfare Economics*.)

14. This, in fact, is the central point of Kaplow and Shavell's *Fairness Versus Welfare*, discussed below.

15. This understanding of consent will be questioned in the next chapter.

16. Pigou, *Economics of Welfare*.

17. On this, see the comment by Richard Posner in note 84 below. Ambiguity on that point leads some economists-of-crime to refer to the crime that society cannot prevent as its "demand for crime"—formally accurate, perhaps, but woefully inappropriate and frighteningly misleading.

18. Coase, "Problem of Social Cost."

19. Or, for that matter, when the car in front of him is traveling *exceptionally* slowly while the driver shaves or applies make-up in the rearview mirror?

20. For more on offense and its relation to harm and the criminal law, see Feinberg, *Offense to Others*.

21. The discussion of market failure herein closely parallels Austrian arguments; see, for instance, Kirzner, *Market Theory and the Price System*, and Cordato, *Welfare Economics and Externalities*. For a critical analysis of the term "mar-

ket failure" from the perspective of transaction costs, see Zerbe and McCurdy, "Failure of Market Failure."

22. Notable exceptions include Dominick Armentano (*Antitrust Policy*, chap. 6; *Antitrust and Monopoly*, chap. 9) and Walter Block ("Total Repeal of Antitrust Legislation"), who draw on the work of Israel Kirzner and Murray Rothbard, respectively. A recent philosophical treatise on antitrust dismisses (with prejudice) any ethical problems with interventionist policy: "it is uncontroversial that there are circumstances in which the public interest justifies the state in infringing liberty or autonomy: think of the liberty of *convicted murderers*" (Black, *Conceptual Foundations of Antitrust*, 56, emphasis mine—witness the dangers of consequentialist moral equivalence).

23. Posner, *Antitrust Law*, ix (emphasis mine).

24. Epstein, "Private Property and the Public Domain."

25. Note that the maxim is stated as the right to merger, not simply merger itself; certainly, if every firm merged into it, that would make any further merger impossible, which would seem to contradict itself. But we are not asking if every firm should merge, but only if they should be able to merge if it is in their interests to do so.

26. Of course, any nonnegotiable price set by a seller is a restriction of terms.

27. Deceit and coercion will be discussed at much more length in the next chapter.

28. To be fair, one could argue that since the limited-liability corporation exists as an artificial creation of the state for consequentialist ends, the state has exceptional rights to regulate its behavior to promote those same ends; see Crane, "Lochnerian Antitrust."

29. For an excellent introduction to the various schools of law and economics, see Mercuro and Medema, *Economics and the Law* (2nd ed.); I limit my comments to neoclassical law and economics, the most prominent approach to the subject, and the most accepting of traditional welfare economics. Also, for an in-depth exposition on the legacy of utilitarian Jeremy Bentham as represented by economic imperialism (with particular emphasis on Gary Becker and law and economics), see Hurtado, "Jeremy Bentham and Gary Becker."

30. Fletcher, *Basic Concepts of Legal Thought*, 162.

31. Posner, "Economic Approach to Law," 777 (emphasis mine).

32. However, many of the ideas in this section can be stated in terms of more general, nonconsequentialist systems of ethics; indeed, many of the critics of law and economics cited in this chapter would not be considered Kantians, though their writings are quite consistent with a Kantian approach. Indeed, in their recent book *Law, Economics, and Morality*, Zamir and Medina argue many of the same points I do, but they do so chiefly in terms of *threshold deontology*, which

recommends following absolute rules until the negative consequences reach a threshold level, rather than Kantian deontology *per se* (though it is addressed throughout the book). (On threshold deontology, see Moore, "Torture and the Balance of Evils," for the seminal discussion, and Alexander, "Deontology at the Threshold," for criticism.)

33. Fletcher, "Fairness and Utility," 573.

34. For instance, both Weinrib (*Idea of Private Law*) and Wright ("Right, Justice, and Tort Law") interpret tort law in terms of a Aristotelian-Kantian conception of corrective justice; see Weinrib, "Corrective Justice," for a brief overview. Coleman (*Practice of Principle*) argues that tort law does not serve corrective justice instrumentally, but rather embodies it; in other words, the practice of tort law helps define corrective justice.

35. All in-text page-number citations in this section refer to *Fairness Versus Welfare*.

36. The authors also complain that fairness is often not well-defined (45), but certainly particular notions of justice and rights are (though not decisively). See also Waldron, "Locating Distribution," for a critical discussion of the authors' use of the term "fairness."

37. They are not alone, of course; in "Can Law and Economics Be Both Practical and Principled?," Hoffman and O'Shea discuss prominent utilitarians' reactions to discovering that not all people—even their own students—accept efficiency as the highest end.

38. "Of course, the foregoing observation [concerning including tastes for fairness in welfare evaluation] could easily be taken too far—for example, by defining each individual's well-being as equivalent to the degree to which a policy satisfies some notion of fairness that is *not conventionally understood* to have anything to do with individual's well-being" (23n14, emphasis added). We will challenge this "convention" in the next chapter.

39. This resembles the arguments of proponents of behavioral law and economics and "libertarian paternalism," to be discussed in the next chapter. See also Hoffman and O'Shea, "Can Law and Economics," who introduce the concept of "law-related preferences—preferences about the content and fairness of the legal system" (339), which would complicate matters further for preference-based legal analysis such as Kaplow and Shavell use.

40. As examples of the former, see Coleman, "Grounds of Welfare," and Ferzan, "Some Sound and Fury"; for the latter, see Chang, "Liberal Theory of Social Welfare."

41. Coleman, "Economics and the Law," 662; see also Baker, "Ideology of the Economic Analysis of Law," and Leff, "Economic Analysis of Law," 477–81.

42. Calabresi and Bobbitt, *Tragic Choices*.

43. Kronman, "Wealth Maximization," 238 (emphasis mine).

44. The phrase "mimic the market" was coined by Richard Posner; see, for instance, his *Economic Analysis of Law*, 250.

45. Posner, "Ethical and Political Basis of the Efficiency Norm," 492–7.

46. Coleman, "Efficiency, Utility, and Wealth Maximization," 118–21; see also Ronald Dworkin, "Why Efficiency?," 275–80, as well as Veljanovski, "Wealth Maximization, Law and Ethics,"12–6. Kronman is more accepting of the notion of *ex ante* compensation, but is concerned (as is Posner) with its realization in practical terms: "how are we to distinguish those cases in which there has been *ex ante* compensation from those in which there has not?" ("Wealth Maximization," 237).

47. Posner, *Economics of Justice*, 97–8.

48. Ibid., 98.

49. Posner, "Value of Wealth," 251. Some scholars frame the issue of *ex ante* compensation in terms of *hypothetical consent*; see Brudney, "Hypothetical Consent," and Wennberg, "Modelling Hypothetical Consent." (Hardin refers to it as *institutional consensualism*; see "Morality of Law and Economics," pp. 361–4.) In "Wealth Maximization," Veljanovski analyzes Posner's writings on both private and public law through the lens of his view of consent.

50. One could argue that if one party values a right at $100, but does not want to sell to another party who values it at $200, the potential seller's valuation is incorrect, and is actually higher than $200, which then "explains" the decision. But the reluctant seller may have other reasons not to sell that are immeasurable in monetary terms, such as a personal dislike for the buyer that drive him to block a sale at any price. It is not that she now values the right at infinite value; rather she has something akin to a desire-independent reason not to sell. (I discuss this more in the next chapter.)

51. Dworkin, *Taking Rights Seriously*.

52. Dworkin, "Is Wealth a Value?," 243.

53. Posner, *Economics of Justice*, 70.

54. Dworkin, "Is Wealth a Value?," 252.

55. No, that is not a typo; see Posner, *Economics of Justice*, 71. Posner must be given credit for recognizing some limitations of this approach: when discussing the economic analysis of rape law, which is not conclusively supportive of an unqualified prohibition, he admits "the fact that any sort of rape license is even thinkable within the framework of the wealth-maximization theory that guides so much of the analysis in this book is a *limitation on the usefulness of that theory*" (*Economic Analysis of Law*, 238, emphasis mine).

56. Dworkin, "Is Wealth a Value?," 251–2.

57. While perfectly understandable, please do not allow Brad's taste in philosophers to bias your judgment in this case.

58. The party who bears the cost of the solution does, of course, depend on the assignment of the right; but if the right is assigned in a just manner, the burdens can be considered to be justly distributed as well.

59. And, inside of utilitarians and legal economists, it's too dark to use a calculator. (With apologies to Groucho Marx.)

60. Posner, *Economics of Justice*, 98.

61. This only holds for perfect duties such as "do not steal" and "do not kill"; recall that imperfect duties, such as general duties of beneficence, imply no correlative rights, but neither do they lie within the domain of the law.

62. Calabresi, *Cost of Accidents*.

63. Coase, "Problem of Social Cost," 2 (emphasis mine).

64. Epstein, "Theory of Strict Liability," 165.

65. Ibid.

66. Page, "Responsibility, Liability, and Incentive Compatibility," 252. The concept of nonreciprocal harm ultimately has its roots in the Aristotelian concept of *corrective justice*; see Aristotle's *Nicomachean Ethics*, 1131–2, for the original statement. See also Posner, "Concept of Corrective Justice," for an interesting discussion of the use of the term in law and economics; and Wright, "Right, Justice, and Tort Law," for the links between Aristotle's corrective justice and Kant's later formulation.

67. Posner, "Strict Liability," 216.

68. Wright, "Rights," 176.

69. Posner, "Strict Liability," 218.

70. Ibid., 220n35.

71. Page, "Responsibility."

72. Coleman, "Efficiency, Auction, and Exchange," 81.

73. See Shavell, *Economic Analysis of Accident Law*.

74. See Mercuro and Medema, *Economics and the Law*, 138–44.

75. For a similar argument, see Friedmann, "Efficient Breach Fallacy."

76. *Kelo v. City of New London*, 545 U.S. 469, 125 S Ct 24 (2005). For an analysis of the legal, political, and economic aspects of this case, see Somin, "Controlling the Grasping Hand," and Epstein, "Public Use in a Post-*Kelo* World."

77. *Kelo*, 125 S Ct at 2677 (O'Connor dissenting); see also Somin, "Controlling the Grasping Hand," 231–2 on O'Connor's comments.

78. A key influences on the economic approach to crime was the criminology of Cesare Beccaria, *On Crimes and Punishments*, which also influenced Jeremy Bentham (for instance, see *Principles of Morals and Legislation*, 179).

79. In his paper "Theft as a Paradigm for Departures from Efficiency," Dan Usher lists "four efficiency costs of the existence of theft: loss of [social value of] labour of the thief, loss of the labour of the victim who protects himself, destruc-

tion of product [lost in act of theft], and deadweight loss in underproduction of stealable goods" (237).

80. Klevorick, "Legal Theory," 908.

81. Klevorick's argument is more complex than this brief summary; see Coleman, "Crimes, Kickers, and Transaction Structures," and Fletcher, "Transaction Theory of Crime?," for commentary. His theory builds on previous work by Calabresi and Melamed ("Property Rules, Liability Rules, and Inalienability") as well as Posner ("Economic Theory of the Criminal Law"), who writes that "the major function of criminal law . . . is to prevent people from bypassing the system of voluntary, compensated exchange . . . in situations where, because transaction costs are low, the market is a more efficient method of allocating resources than forced exchange" (1195).

82. Klevorick, "Economic Analysis of Crime," 301–4.

83. Coleman, "Crimes, Kickers," 165. This statement foreshadows Coleman's later work (*Practice of Principle*) on the economics of tort law, which he criticizes for (among other things) not accounting for the bilateral relationship between injurer and victim.

84. Morris, "Decline of Guilt," 73. Of course, "acceptable" would mean "efficient," as in Richard Posner's lament that retributivist punishments may be suboptimal, "but this is not say that there would be too much crime. There might rather be too little" (*Economics of Justice*, 215).

85. This is not to say, of course, that there can be no other justifications; for example, rehabilitation can be understood to be oriented toward the dignity and autonomy of the prisoner.

86. On retributivism, see Duff, *Punishment, Communication, and Community*, chap. 1; Ten, *Crime, Guilt, and Punishment*, chap. 3; and Zaibert, *Punishment and Retribution*.

87. However, Moore ("Justifying Retributivism") does argue that retributivism can be reconciled with consequentialism; see also Cahill, "Real Retributivism," and Markel, "Are Shaming Punishments Beautifully Retributive?"

88. Posner, "Retribution," 92.

89. Ibid., 83.

90. *Fairness Versus Welfare*, 366 (of course, they fail to reflect on the alignment between their welfarism and their own "tastes" for well-being). On a similar note, referring to evidence that juries often determine punitive damages based on blame and condemnation than optimal deterrence, Cass R. Sunstein ("On the Psychology of Punishment") links such retributivist inclinations to "outrage." While he stops short of calling such opinions "irrational," he does predict dire consequences for a trial system that takes them into account. (On the crucial distinction between retribution and revenge, see Murphy and Coleman, *Philosophy of Law*, 120–1, and Nozick, *Philosophical Explanations*, 366–8.)

91. Wittman, "Punishment as Retribution"; John R. Harris, "On the Economics of Law and Order," also incorporates the cost of punishing innocents into an economic model of crime, but without mentioning retributivism.

92. For another take on this problem, see Cahill, "Real Retributivism."

93. On Hegel's retributivism, see his *Philosophy of Right*; for Kant's primary writings on punishment, see *Metaphysics of Morals*, 331–7. Space prohibits a comprehensive discussion of Kant's stance on punishment here, but suffice it to say that things are not as clear as his reputation implies. For instance, Murphy, "Does Kant Have a Theory of Punishment?," questions the consistency of Kant's scattered comments on punishment; and Byrd, "Kant's Theory of Punishment," argues that Kant supported a "hybrid" theory of punishment that holds deterrence to be a motivation for punishment, while retributivist concerns justify and restrain it. (Other proponents on such a view include Hart, *Punishment and Responsibility*, and Rawls, "Two Concepts of Rules"; Avio integrates a hybrid theory of punishment with an economic model in "Economic, Retributive and Contractarian Conceptions of Punishment.")

94. Kant, *Metaphysics of Morals*, 331.

95. Murphy, "Marxism and Retribution," 219.

96. Kant, *Metaphysics of Morals*, 334–5.

97. Braithwaite and Pettit, *Not Just Deserts*.

98. Kant, *Metaphysics of Morals*, 331. Later, he writes even more clearly, "justice ceases to be justice if it can be bought for any price whatsoever" (332).

99. Kipnis, "Criminal Justice and the Negotiated Plea," 106.

100. See Morris, "Decline of Guilt," 72. He never implicates the law and economics movement directly in this, but he definitely leaves such an impression, citing "an approach that subordinates principle to the realization of social goals, a mode of thinking that focuses, not upon exculpation of the innocent and conviction of the guilty, that is, upon justice, but upon keeping social disruption at the acceptable level . . . . Such an ideology provides the justification for conviction of the innocent, nonprosecution of the guilty, and disregard for principles of proportionality. It smacks of Wilde's cynic knowing the price of everything and the value of nothing" (73), which is a well-known criticism of economists.

101. See Cahill, "Real Retributivism."

102. See Austin, *Province of Jurisprudence Determined*; his "command theory of law" was thoroughly criticized by Hart (*Concept of Law*, chaps. 2–4) but still lingers in common discourse. (See Kornhauser, "Normativity of Law," on its continued influence on law and economics.)

103. Holmes, "Path of Law," 459; see Minow, "Path as Prologue," on Holmes's influence on law and economics, and Leiter, "Holmes, Economics, and Classical Realism," for a critical perspective on Holmes and economics.

104. Becker, "Crime and Punishment."

105. For a specific example, see the discussion of prices and sanctions in Chapter 2. On a related point, Cameron, "Subjectivist Perspective on the Economics of Crime," emphasizes the subjective nature of individual decision-making processes, which has particular relevance to criminal choice.

106. Lutz, *Economics for the Common Good*, 160.

107. Hart, *Concept of Law*, 82–91.

108. Ibid. In "Intrinsic Value of Obeying a Law," Robert Cooter models this distinction using preferences (external point of view) and constraints (internal point of view), similar to the modeling of imperfect and perfect duty in Chapter 1 of this book.

109. See also Martha Nussbaum, "Flawed Foundations," 1211–12.

110. Hill, "Punishment, Conscience, and Moral Worth."

111. Ibid., 360.

112. Weakness of will is one of the central innovations of *behavioral law and economics*, which criticizes key rationality assumptions made in the standard literature; see the next chapter for more.

CHAPTER 5

1. O'Donoghue and Rabin's work on procrastination, summarized in Chapter 2, is in this same spirit.

2. In "Choice, Consent, and Cycling," Katz questions Kaplow and Shavell's devotion to Pareto superiority, concluding that "the Pareto principle, our most uncontroversial measure of welfare and the economist's term for freedom of contract, sometimes has to yield to fairness for reasons which, though quite different from the familiar ones, are nevertheless not in the least recondite but rather command universal assent" (670).

3. Griffin, *Well-Being*, 147.

4. Coleman, "Efficiency, Auction, and Exchange," 93.

5. Blaug, *Methodology of Economics*, 127–8.

6. Sen, "Liberty, Unanimity, and Rights."

7. For instance, Posner claims that "consent, an ethical criterion congenial to the Kantian emphasis on treating people as ends rather than means . . . is the operational basis of Pareto superiority" (*Economics of Justice*, 89).

8. I assume the ideal case that such consent is freely given, in the absence of coercion or deception, and that this can be verified at little or no cost. In such cases, an agent's consent can reasonably be taken to represent, fully and clearly, the true choice and intention of the agent. See Feinberg, *Harm to Self*, 180–6, on the complexities of consent; O'Neill, "Between Consenting Adults," 106–9, on problems with interpreting consent as genuine; West, "Authority, Autonomy, and

Choice," for a critique of the presumed moral authority to consent; and Posner, "Ethical Significance of Free Choice," for a reply.

9. For an analysis of the normative power of consent along broadly Kantian grounds, see Hurd, "Moral Magic of Consent." Also, I am claiming only that consent is necessary to ensure respect for dignity, but not that it is sufficient to steer right action; see Katz, "Choice, Consent, and Cycling," for some problematic implications of respecting consent *too* much (such as consenting to the transfer of inalienable rights).

10. See Griffin, *Well-Being*, 147; Coleman, "Efficiency, Utility and Wealth Maximization," 97; and Posner, *Economics of Justice*, 88, among others. Technically, this is the strong Pareto principle; the weak Pareto principle demands that all parties be made better off. This distinction is not relevant to this discussion, and I will be referencing the strong version throughout.

11. See, for instance, Hausman and McPherson, *Economic Analysis, Moral Philosophy, and Public Policy*, 119–20.

12. For instance, see ibid., 65; Broome, *Weighing Goods*, 152; Sen, "Impossibility of a Paretian Liberal," 286, and Arrow, *Social Choice and Individual Values*, 96. (The last two are definitions of the weak Pareto principle specifically, but my point is simply that they are defined in terms of preferences, not general well-being.)

13. As Sen memorably wrote in criticism of traditional utility theory, a person's preference ranking "is supposed to reflect his interests, represent his welfare, summarize his idea of what should be done, and describe his actual choices and behavior" ("Rational Fools," 99). On the shortcomings of preferences as a measure of well-being, see also Sagoff, "Should Preferences Count?" and "Values and Preferences."

14. Rational choice models of addiction, such as Becker and Murphy's ("A Theory of Rational Addiction"), imply that addiction maximizes discounted lifetime utility, but this does not necessarily correlate with well-being in a richer sense. (I thank John Davis for suggesting this contrast.)

15. The policy relevance of such preferences will be considered below.

16. In this case, Pareto judgments would be overdetermined in a way, similar to the double-counting problem with preference-utilitarianism identified by Ronald Dworkin (*Taking Right Seriously*, 234–7).

17. Calabresi, "Pointlessness of Pareto," 1216–7; Sager, "Pareto Superiority, Consent, and Justice," 917–8.

18. For an influential discussion of idealized preferences, see Griffin, *Well-Being*, 11–17; for the controversies regarding them, see Sen and Williams, *Utilitarianism and Beyond*, 9–11, and Hausman and McPherson, *Economic Analysis*, 80–1.

19. Commenting on hypothetical consent based on ideal conditions and preferences, Thomson writes "the theorists argue from 'It is to their advantage' to

'The rules are just' via the intermediary 'They would consent to the rules'; but the intermediary is mere epiphenomenon" (*Realm of Rights*, 188–9n5).

20. See Sugden, "Capability, Happiness, and Opportunity," for a critique of normative analysis based on capabilities and happiness, along the same lines as the argument presented here regarding Pareto.

21. Coleman, "Foundations of Constitutional Economics," 137; elsewhere, he writes, "people sometimes choose to do what they do not prefer to do, and do not do what they would otherwise prefer to do, often because they think it wrong to act as they would otherwise prefer. So we cannot infer choice from preference. We could of course infer choice (or consent) from preference, but only if we build the notion of choice into the definition of what it is to have a preference" ("Grounds of Welfare," 1518).

22. Calabresi, "Pointlessness of Pareto," 1215n14.

23. Coleman, "Grounds of Welfare," 1517.

24. Dworkin, "Why Efficiency?," 276; see also Coleman, "Normative Basis of Economic Analysis," 1120–23, and "Economics and the Law," 674.

25. Walsh, *Rationality, Allocation, and Reproduction*, 199.

26. This theme is pervasive in Coleman's writings; for instance, see "Normative Basis of Economic Analysis," 1125–26, and "Foundations of Constitutional Economics," 137–8. Along similar lines, Shaw, "Pareto Argument and Inequality," provides an example of a Pareto improvement involving rights violations, and considers various responses to it. For recent work on incorporating procedural considerations into models of choice, see Sen, "Maximization and the Act of Choice"; Sandbu, "Valuing Processes"; and Dolan et al., "It Ain't What You Do, It's the Way That You Do It."

27. Coleman, "Foundations of Constitutional Economics," 136–9. More recently, in the context of personhood and dignity, he writes that "any plausible theory of what is valuable to a person would include the ability to act on the basis of one's preferences and desires. But that is because autonomous action is valuable to persons understood as planning agents who bear a special relationship of ownership and responsibility to how their life goes, and not because people have a taste for autonomy" ("Grounds of Welfare," 1542). (See also Lawson, "Efficiency and Individualism," 91–2.)

28. Coleman, "Foundations of Constitutional Economics," 139.

29. For an exploration of the general concept of coercion, see Nozick, "Coercion," and for an explicitly normative version, see Wertheimer, *Coercion*.

30. Kant, *Groundwork*, 429–30, emphasis mine; also, more generally, "every will, even the private will of each person directed to himself, is restricted to the condition of agreement with the autonomy of the rational being, namely, that it should be directed to no purpose which would not be possible by a law which could issue from the will of the subject who is the passive recipient of the action" (*Critique of Practical Reason*, 87).

31. Korsgaard, "Right to Lie," 138.

32. Ibid., 140–1; see also O'Neill, "Between Consenting Adults," 110–4.

33. Korsgaard, "Right to Lie," 140.

34. Kronman, "Wealth Maximization," 235.

35. O'Neill, "Between Consenting Adults," 110–1.

36. See Hausman and McPherson, *Economic Analysis*, 125–8.

37. In *Taking Rights Seriously* (234–7), Ronald Dworkin uses the terms *personal* and *external* preferences to distinguish between preferences over one's own goods and activities and preferences over the goods and activities of others; but he admits that distinguishing between them, while important for political decision-making, is not always possible.

38. See Feinberg, *Offense to Others*, for a detailed discussion of offense as injury; he argues that for an offense to be considered truly harmful, the aversion to the offense must be unavoidable and (fairly) universally shared (rather than idiosyncratic).

39. A related discussion concerns the delineation of this sphere of privacy, but for the sake of the discussion at hand, I will just assume that such a sphere does exist. I think most would agree that there is such a sanctified realm, no matter how narrow or broad each of us may define it, and the precise definition of it is not relevant here (though it is of great importance otherwise, as evidenced by many perpetual political debates regarding personal freedoms).

40. Mill, *On Liberty*, 5–6.

41. Nozick, *Anarchy, State, and Utopia*, 164–6.

42. Korsgaard, "Right to Lie," 142.

43. For the broader approach to behavioral economics, see Altman, *Handbook of Contemporary Behavioral Economics*; in his introduction, Altman makes clear that in behavioral economics, "assumptions can be of a psychological, sociological, or institutional type—it is not only psychology that is important to behavioral economics" (xv).

44. Camerer and Loewenstein, "Behavioral Economics," 3.

45. See Jolls, Sunstein, and Thaler, "Behavioral Approach to Law and Economics," and Korobkin and Ulen, "Law and Behavioral Science." The former essay is included in Sunstein, *Behavioral Law & Economics*, an early collection of literature related to the (then) nascent field; for a more recent collection, see Parisi and Smith, *Law and Economics of Irrational Behavior*.

46. Their seminal academic contribution to BLE (besides the paper with Jolls cited in the previous note) is Sunstein and Thaler, "Libertarian Paternalism Is Not an Oxymoron." (A condensed version published in an economics journal, presumably designed paternalistically to account for irrational impatience on the part of economists, is Thaler and Sunstein, "Libertarian Paternalism.") For another important contribution to the policy ramifications of BLE, a bit more re-

served and with more emphasis on distributional concerns, see Camerer et al., "Regulation for Conservatives."

47. It is unclear how consistent this definition of "soft paternalism" is with those outside the BLE literature. For instance, Feinberg defines soft paternalism as holding "that the state has the right to prevent self-regarding harmful conduct . . . *when but only when* that conduct is substantially nonvoluntary, or when temporary intervention is necessary to establish whether it is voluntary or not" (*Harm to Self*, 12; see also chaps. 20 and 21 on voluntariness and failures thereof). To be consistent, BLE would have to maintain that choice made in the presence of cognitive biases or failures is nonvoluntary, a claim I have not encountered as such, but which may require further discussion.

48. Sunstein and Thaler, "Libertarian Paternalism," 1159–60.

49. Ibid., 1162.

50. For a "slippery slope" argument against libertarian paternalism, see Whitman and Rizzo, "Paternalist Slopes."

51. Sunstein and Thaler, "Libertarian Paternalism," 1162. Some use the term "interests": "To the extent that the errors identified by behavioral research lead people not to behave in their own best interests, paternalism may prove useful" (Camerer et al., "Regulation for Conservatives," 1212), though their use of the term is not explained, and they fall back on standard "objective" interests such as health and wealth. Camerer et al. do, however, acknowledge the possibility of non-wealth interests, using the example of buying extended warranties, which is generally thought to be irrational: "if informed consumers continue to purchase the warranties, then it is quite possible that they have good reason to do so, however *unfathomable* that decision may seem to an economist" (1254, emphasis mine).

52. As Sunstein and Thaler write, "We are emphasizing, then, the possibility that people's preferences, in certain domains and across a certain range, are influenced by the choices made by planners. . . . Across a certain domain of possibilities, consumers will often lack well-formed preferences, in the sense of preferences that are firmly held and preexist the director's own choices about how to order the relevant items. If the arrangement of the alternatives has a significant effect on the selections the customers make, then their true 'preferences' do not formally exist" ("Libertarian Paternalism," 1164).

53. On the difficulty of choosing an adequate concept of welfare or well-being on which to base paternalistic policies, see Loewenstein and Haisley, "Economist as Therapist."

54. Trout, "Paternalism and Cognitive Bias," 433.

55. Sugden, "Why Incoherent Preferences Do Not Justify Paternalism," 232.

56. Brock, "Paternalism and Autonomy," 559.

57. In "Philosophical Dimensions of the Doctrine of Unconscionability," Philip Bridwell argues (much in the spirit of the previous chapter) that courts

should invalidate contracts only when they violate negative freedom (through deceit or coercion), not positive freedom, violation of which in any given case is open to arbitrary judicial interpretation. See also Pincione, "Welfare, Autonomy, and Contractual Freedom," particularly section II, and Epstein, "Unconscionability: A Critical Reappraisal," particularly section IV on substantive unconscionability. (Shiffrin critically analyzes the paternalistic interpretation of the unconscionability doctrine in "Paternalism, Unconscionability Doctrine, and Accommodation.")

58. Sunstein and Thaler, "Libertarian Paternalism," 1162. However, see Mitchell, "Libertarian Paternalism Is an Oxymoron," 1247n8, for criticism of the various cognitive biases and failures at the heart of BLE and libertarian paternalism. Richard Posner argues that many of BLE's "irrationalities" can be modeled with standard rational choice theory; see "Rational Choice, Behavioral Economics, and the Law," in response to Jolls et al., "Behavioral Approach"). (See also Mitchell, "Taking Behavioralism Too Seriously?")

59. See note 51. When debating this issue with a colleague, who asserted that eating donuts was not in my best interests and therefore I should be "nudged" against them, I argued that for all she knew, I may be a severe melancholic, whose only joy from life comes from little fried rings of dough; or perhaps eating them may remind me of a beloved grandfather, who took me to the donut shop every third Sunday and shared stories of his childhood with me; or perhaps I use them as an internal incentive mechanism to prod me on to finishing a book manuscript; or perhaps I only have six months to live (not due to a donut-related illness), and donuts help me enjoy my last months on this earth. None of these were true (even the book manuscript part, honest), but my point was that any of them could have been true, and would betray her "knowledge" of my "true interests."

60. Trout, "Paternalism and Cognitive Bias," 394.

61. Claire A. Hill, "Anti-Anti-Anti-Paternalism," 450.

62. Gerald Dworkin, *Theory and Practice of Autonomy*, 77–8.

63. Sunstein and Thaler, "Libertarian Paternalism," 1168. For an neuroeconomic argument in support of this contention, see Camerer, "Wanting, Liking, and Learning."

64. Buchanan, "Positive Economics, Welfare Economics, and Political Economy," 126.

65. Posner, "Rational Choice, Behavioral Economics, and the Law," 1575. Also, Claire Hill writes that BLE advocates "sometimes speak as though they have access to the knowledge of what people really want apart from what they choose. This position is ultimately untenable. . . . As convenient and tempting as it may be to extrapolate from our own introspection that others want what we do, or should, want, we simply have no access to others' beliefs and desires" ("Anti-Anti-Anti-Paternalism," 448).

66. Mitchell, "Libertarian Paternalism Is an Oxymoron," 1260 (emphasis mine).

67. Sunstein and Thaler, "Libertarian Paternalism," 1185.

68. Ibid., 1172–3.

69. Ronald Dworkin, "Why Efficiency?," 276.

70. See Amir and Lobel, "Stumble, Predict, Nudge," who generally sympathize with Sunstein and Thaler's program, but nonetheless argue that their "assumption that, absent irrationalities, every individual would agree that future savings and improved long-term health are better than immediate satisfaction and gratification seems problematic" (2120).

71. Loewenstein and Haisley, "Economist as Therapist."

72. As Hausman and Welch write, "to the extent that [nudges] are attempts to undermine [the] individual's control over her own deliberation, as well as her own ability to assess for herself her alternatives, they are *prima facie* as threatening to liberty . . . as is coercion" ("Debate," 130). One could say, even, that libertarian (or "soft") paternalism is worse because of its covert nature. Cigarette taxes are obvious "nudges" too, and are less manipulative for their overt nature. Hiding the cigarette rack in the back of the grocery store is crafty and presumptuous, taking advantage of cognitive dysfunction, and therefore much more insulting. Furthermore, as Edward Glaeser notes, "persuasion lies at the heart of much of soft paternalism, and it is not obvious that we want governments to become more adept at persuading voters or for governments to invest in infrastructure that will support persuasion" ("Paternalism and Psychology," 135; see also 155–6).

73. O'Neill, "Between Consenting Adults," 110. On this point, see also Korsgaard, who writes that "it is important to see that [Kant does] not mean simply that the other person *does not* or *would not* assent to the transaction or that she does not happen to have the same end I do, but strictly that she *cannot* do so: that something makes it impossible" ("Right to Lie," 138).

74. *Theory and Practice of Autonomy*, 123 (emphasis mine).

75. Ibid., 88.

76. Ibid., 123–4.

77. Sunstein and Thaler, "Libertarian Paternalism," 1164.

78. Mitchell adds that, if manipulation were inevitable, it would be so only "so long as individuals remain subject to these irrational influences," which is to say only if these "influences" themselves were inevitable and incurable ("Libertarian Paternalism Is an Oxymoron," 1251, emphasis removed; see 1248–60 in general on the supposed inevitably of paternalistic manipulation). Posner makes a similar point, accusing BLE of "treat[ing] the irrationalities that form the subject matter of behavioral economics as unalterable constituents of human personality. All their suggestions for legal reform are of devices for getting around, rather than dispelling, our irrational tendencies" ("Rational Choice,

Behavioral Economics, and the Law," 1575). Hausman and Welch go one step further and question if the "irrationalities" emphasized by BLE are truly irrational ("Debate," 126).

79. Indeed, Klick and Mitchell argue that accommodation of cognitive biases, rather than efforts to combat and lessen them, may make the biases themselves worse ("Government Regulation of Irrationality").

80. See Mitchell, "Libertarian Paternalism Is an Oxymoron," 1260–69, on BLE's favoring of welfare over liberty in its paternalism.

81. Sunstein and Thaler, "Libertarian Paternalism," 1173.

82. Ironically, Sunstein and Thaler come to the same conclusion with regards to automatic enrollment in parking plans, but their argument is based on saving people from their forgetfulness; see ibid., 1171.

83. Sugden, "Incoherent Preferences," sections 5 and 6.

84. Ibid., 247.

85. Kant, *Metaphysics of Morals*, 454.

Bibliography

Ainslie, George. *Breakdown of Will*. Cambridge: Cambridge University Press, 2001.

———. "The Dangers of Willpower." In *Getting Hooked: Rationality and Addiction*, edited by Jon Elster and Ole-Jørgen Skog, 65–92. Cambridge: Cambridge University Press, 1999.

———. *Picoeconomics: The Strategic Interaction of Successive Motivational States Within the Person*. Cambridge: Cambridge University Press, 1992.

———. "Procrastination: The Basic Impulse." In *The Thief of Time: Philosophical Essays on Procrastination*, edited by Chrisoula Andreou and Mark D. White, 11–27. Oxford: Oxford University Press, 2010.

Akerlof, George A. "Procrastination and Obedience." *American Economic Review* 81 (2) (1991): 1–19.

Alexander, Larry. "Deontology at the Threshold." *University of San Diego Law Review* 37 (2000): 893–912.

Allison, Henry. *Kant's Theory of Freedom*. Cambridge: Cambridge University Press, 1990.

Altman, Morris, ed. *Handbook of Contemporary Behavioral Economics: Foundations and Developments*. Armonk, NY: M. E. Sharpe, 2006.

Ameriks, Karl. *Kant's Theory of Mind*. New ed. Oxford: Oxford University Press, 2000.

Amir, On, and Orly Lobel. "Stumble, Predict, Nudge: How Behavioral Economics Informs Law and Policy." *Columbia Law Review* 108 (2008): 2098–2138.

Andreou, Chrisoula. "Understanding Procrastination." *Journal for the Theory of Social Behaviour* 37 (2007): 183–93.

Aristotle. *Nicomachean Ethics*. Translated by Terence Irwin. Indianapolis, IN: Hackett Publishing Company, 1985.

Armentano, Dominick T. *Antitrust and Monopoly: Anatomy of a Market Failure*. Oakland, CA: The Independent Institute, 1990.

———. *Antitrust Policy: The Case for Repeal*. Washington, DC: Cato Institute, 1986.

Arrow, Kenneth. *Social Choice and Individual Values*. New Haven, CT: Yale University Press, 1951.

Audi, Robert. "Weakness of Will and Rational Action." In *Action, Intention, and Reason*, 319–33. Ithaca, NY: Cornell University Press, 1993.

Austin, John. *The Province of Jurisprudence Determined*. Edited by Wilfrid E. Rumble. Cambridge: Cambridge University Press, 1995.

Avio, Kenneth L. "Economic, Retributive and Contractarian Conceptions of Punishment." *Law and Philosophy* 12 (1993): 249–86.

Badhwar, Neera Kapur, ed. *Friendship: A Philosophical Reader*. Ithaca, NY: Cornell University Press, 1993.

Baker, C. Edwin. "The Ideology of the Economic Analysis of Law." *Philosophy and Public Affairs* 5 (1975): 3–48.

Baker, Jennifer A. "Virtue and Behavior." In *Ethics and Economics: New Perspectives*, edited by Mark D. White and Irene van Staveren, 64–85. London: Routledge, 2009.

Ballet, Jerôme, and Patrick Jolivet. "A Propos de l'Économie Kantienne." *Social Science Information* 42 (2003): 185–208.

Baron, Marcia. *Kantian Ethics Almost Without Apology*. Ithaca, NY: Cornell University Press, 1995.

———, and Melissa Seymour Fahmy. "Beneficence and Other Duties of Love in *The Metaphysics of Morals*." In *The Blackwell Guide to Kant's Ethics*, edited by Thomas E. Hill, Jr., 211–28. Chichester, UK: Wiley-Blackwell, 2009.

Baumeister, Roy F., and Todd F. Heatherton. "Self-Regulation Failure: An Overview." *Psychological Inquiry* 7 (1996): 1–15.

Baumgarten, Hans-Ulrich. "Acting Against Better Knowledge: On the Problem of the Weakness of the Will in Plato, Davidson, and Kant." *The Journal of Value Inquiry* 36 (2002): 235–52.

Bayne, Tim, and Neil Levy. "The Feeling of Doing: Deconstructing the Phenomenology of Agency." In *Disorders of Volition*, edited by Natalie Sebanz and Wolfgang Prinz, 49–68. Cambridge, MA: MIT Press, 2006.

Bazin, Damien, and Jerôme Ballet. "A Basic Model for Multiple Self." *Journal of Socio-Economics* 35 (2006): 1050–60.

Beccaria, Cesare. *On Crimes and Punishments*. Translated by David Young. Indianapolis, IN: Hackett, 1986 (originally 1764).

Beck, Lewis White. *A Commentary on Kant's Critique of Practical Reason*. Chicago: University of Chicago Press, 1960.

Becker, Gary S. "Crime and Punishment: An Economic Approach." *Journal of Political Economy* 76 (1968): 169–217.

———. "The Economic Way of Looking at Life." *Journal of Political Economy* 101 (1993): 385-409.

————, and Kevin M. Murphy. "A Theory of Rational Addiction." *Journal of Political Economy* 96 (1988): 675–700.

Bell, Daniel. "Communitarianism." In *Stanford Encyclopedia of Philosophy*, http:// plato.stanford.edu/entries/communitarianism/, 2009.

Bénabou, Roland, and Jean Tirole. "Willpower and Personal Rules." *Journal of Political Economy* 112 (2004): 848–86.

Bentham, Jeremy. *The Principles of Morals and Legislation*. Buffalo, NY: Prometheus Books, 1988 (originally 1781).

Berlin, Isaiah. "Two Concepts of Liberty." In *Liberty: Incorporating* Four Essays on Liberty, edited by Henry Hardy, 166–217. Oxford: Oxford University Press, 2002.

Berofsky, Bernard. "Identification, the Self, and Autonomy." In *Autonomy*, edited by Ellen Frankel Paul, Fred D. Miller, Jr., and Jeffrey Paul, 199–220. Cambridge: Cambridge University Press, 2003.

Bilodeau, Marc, and Nicholas Gravel. "Voluntary Provision of a Public Good and Individual Morality." *Journal of Public Economics* 88 (2004): 645–66.

Binmore, Ken. *Playing Fair*. Cambridge, MA: MIT Press, 1994.

Black, Oliver. *Conceptual Foundations of Antitrust*. Cambridge: Cambridge University Press, 2005.

Blaug, Mark. *The Methodology of Economics (or How Economists Explain)*. 2nd ed. Cambridge: Cambridge University Press, 1992.

Block, Walter. "Total Repeal of Antitrust Legislation: A Critique of Bork, Brozen, and Posner." *The Review of Austrian Economics* 8 (1994): 35–70.

Boadway, Robin W., and Neil Bruce. *Welfare Economics*. Oxford: Basil Blackwell, 1984.

Bork, Robert H. *The Antitrust Paradox: A Policy at War with Itself*. Revised ed. New York: Free Press, 1993.

Braithwaite, John, and Philip Pettit. *Not Just Deserts: A Republican Theory of Criminal Justice*. Oxford: Clarendon Press, 1990.

Brandt, Richard B. *A Theory of the Good and the Right*. Amherst, NY: Prometheus Books, 1979.

Bratman, Michael E. *Intention, Plans, and Practical Reason*. Cambridge, MA: Harvard University Press, 1987.

————. "Planning and Temptation." In *Faces of Intention: Selected Essays on Intention and Agency*, 35–57. Cambridge: Cambridge University Press, 1999.

Brennan, Timothy J. "The Futility of Multiple Utility." *Economics and Philosophy* 9 (1993): 155–64.

————. "A Methodological Assessment of Multiple Utility Frameworks." *Economics and Philosophy* 5 (1989): 189–208.

————. "The Trouble with Norms." In *Social Norms and Economic Institutions*, edited by Kenneth J. Koford and Jeffrey B. Miller, 85-94. Ann Arbor: University of Michigan Press, 1997.

————. "Voluntary Exchange and Economic Claims." In *Research in the History of Economic Thought and Methodology*, vol. 7, edited by Warren J. Samuels, 105–24. Greenwich, CT: JSI Press, Inc., 1990.

Bridwell, Philip. "The Philosophical Dimensions of the Doctrine of Unconscionability." *University of Chicago Law Review* 70 (2003): 1513–31.

Broadie, Alexander, and Elizabeth M. Pybus. "Kant and Weakness of Will." *Kant-Studien* 73 (1982): 406–12.

Brock, Dan W. "Paternalism and Autonomy." *Ethics* 98 (1988): 550–65.

Broome, John. "Deontology and Economics." *Economics and Philosophy* 8 (1992): 269–82.

————. *Weighing Goods.* Oxford: Blackwell, 1991.

Brudney, Daniel. "Hypothetical Consent and Moral Force." *Law and Philosophy* 10 (1991): 235–70.

Buchanan, James M. "Choosing What to Choose." In *Moral Science and Moral Order*, vol. 17 of *The Collected Works of James M. Buchanan,* 80–95. Indianapolis, IN: Liberty Fund, 2001.

————. "Positive Economics, Welfare Economics, and Political Economy." *Journal of Law and Economics* 2 (1959): 124–38.

Byrd, B. Sharon. "Kant's Theory of Punishment: Deterrence in Its Threat, Retribution in Its Execution." *Law and Philosophy* 8 (1980): 151–200.

Cahill, Michael T. "Real Retributivism." *Washington University Law Review* 85 (2007): 815–70.

Calabresi, Guido. *The Cost of Accidents: A Legal and Economic Analysis.* New Haven, CT: Yale University Press, 1970.

————. "The Pointlessness of Pareto: Carrying Coase Further." *Yale Law Journal* 100 (1991): 1211–37.

————, and Philip Bobbitt. *Tragic Choices.* New York: W. W. Norton, 1978.

————, and A. Douglas Melamed. "Property Rules, Liability Rules, and Inalienability: One View of the Cathedral." *Harvard Law Review* 85 (1972): 1089–1128.

Camerer, Colin F. "Wanting, Liking, and Learning: Neuroscience and Paternalism." *University of Chicago Law Review* 73 (2006): 87–110.

————, Samuel Issacharoff, George Loewenstein, Ted O'Donoghue, and Matthew Rabin. "Regulation for Conservatives: Behavioral Economics and the Case for 'Asymmetric Paternalism.'" *University of Pennsylvania Law Review* 151 (2003): 1211–54.

————, and George Loewenstein. "Behavioral Economics: Past, Present, Future." In *Advances in Behavioral Economics*, edited by Colin F. Camerer, George Loewenstein, and Matthew Rabin, 3–51. Princeton, NJ: Princeton University Press, 2004.

Cameron, Samuel. "A Subjectivist Perspective on the Economics of Crime." *Review of Austrian Economics* 3 (1989): 31–43.

Chang, Howard F. "A Liberal Theory of Social Welfare: Fairness, Utility, and the Pareto Principle." *Yale Law Journal* 110 (2000): 173–235.

Chisholm, Roderick M. "Human Freedom and the Self." In *Free Will*, 2nd ed., edited by Gary Watson, 26–37. Oxford: Oxford University Press, 2003.

Coase, Ronald H. "The Problem of Social Cost." *Journal of Law and Economics* 3 (1960): 1–44.

Coleman, Jules L. "Crimes, Kickers and Transaction Structures." In *Markets, Moral and the Law*, 153–65. Cambridge: Cambridge University Press, 1988.

———. "Economics and the Law: A Critical Review of the Foundations of the Economic Approach to Law." *Ethics* 94 (1984): 649–79.

———. "Efficiency, Auction and Exchange." In *Markets, Morals and the Law*, 67–94. Cambridge: Cambridge University Press, 1988.

———. "Efficiency, Utility and Wealth Maximization." In *Markets, Morals and the Law*, 95–132. Cambridge: Cambridge University Press, 1988.

———. "The Foundations of Constitutional Economics." In *Markets, Moral and the Law*, 133–50. Cambridge: Cambridge University Press, 1988.

———. "The Grounds of Welfare." *Yale Law Journal* 112 (2003): 1511–43.

———. "The Normative Basis of Economic Analysis: A Critical Review of Richard Posner's 'The Economics of Justice.'" *Stanford Law Review* 34 (1982): 1105–31.

———. *The Practice of Principle: In Defence of a Pragmatist Approach to Legal Theory*. Oxford: Oxford University Press, 2001.

Cooter, Robert D. "The Intrinsic Value of Obeying a Law: Economic Analysis of the Internal Viewpoint." *Fordham Law Review* 75 (2006): 1275–85.

———. "Lapses, Conflict, and Akrasia in Torts and Crimes: Towards an Economic Theory of the Will." *International Review of Law and Economics* 11 (1991): 149–64.

———. "Models of Morality in Law and Economics: Self-Control and Self-Improvement for the 'Bad Man' of Holmes." *Boston University Law Review* 78 (1998): 903–30.

———. "Prices and Sanctions." *Columbia Law Review* 84 (1984): 1523–60.

Cordato, Roy E. *Welfare Economics and Externalities in an Open Ended Universe: A Modern Austrian Perspective*. Boston: Kluwer Academic Press, 1992.

Crane, Daniel A. "Lochnerian Antitrust." *NYU Journal of Law & Liberty* 1 (2005): 496–514.

Cummiskey, David. *Kantian Consequentialism.* New York: Oxford University Press, 1996.

Dancy, Jonathan. *Ethics Without Principles.* Oxford: Oxford University Press, 2004.

Darwall, Stephen L. *Impartial Reason.* Ithaca, NY: Cornell University Press, 1983.

———. "Scheffler on Morality and the Ideals of the Person." *Canadian Journal of Philosophy* 12 (1982): 247–55.

Davidson, Donald. *Essays on Actions and Events.* Oxford: Clarendon Press, 1980.

———. "How Is Weakness of Will Possible?" In *Essays on Actions and Events,* 21–42. Oxford: Clarendon Press, 1980.

Davis, John B. "Atomism, Identity Criteria, and Impossibility Logic." *Methodus* 4 (1992): 83–7.

———. "Collective Intentionality and Individual Behavior." In *Intersubjectivity in Economics: Agents and Structures,* edited by Edward Fullbrook, 11–27. London: Routledge, 2002.

———. "The Conception of the Socially Embedded Individual." In *The Elgar Companion to Social Economics,* edited by John B. Davis and Wilfred Dolfsma, 92–105. Cheltenham, UK: Edward Elgar, 2008.

———. "Identity and Commitment: Sen's Fourth Aspect of the Self." In *Rationality and Commitment,* edited by Fabienne Peter and Hans Bernhard Schmid, 313–35. Oxford: Oxford University Press, 2007.

———. "Identity and Individual Economic Agents: A Narrative Approach." In *Ethics and Economics: New Perspectives,* edited by Mark D. White and Irene van Staveren, 142–65. London: Routledge, 2009.

———. "The Normative Significance of the Individual in Economics." In *Ethics and the Market: Insights from Social Economics,* edited by Jane Clary, Wilfred Dolfsma, and Deborah Figart, 69–83. London: Routledge, 2006.

———. *The Theory of the Individual in Economics: Identity and Value.* London: Routledge, 2003.

Dolan, Paul, Richard Edlin, Aki Tsuchiya, and Allan Wailoo. "It Ain't What You Do, It's the Way That You Do It: Characteristics of Procedural Justice and Their Importance in Social Decision-Making." *Journal of Economic Behavior & Organization* 64 (2007): 157–70.

Doris, John M. *Lack of Character: Personality and Moral Behavior.* Cambridge: Cambridge University Press, 2002.

Dowell, Richard S., Robert S. Goldfarb, and William B. Griffith. "Economic Man as a Moral Individual." *Economic Inquiry* 36 (1998): 645–53.

Duff, R. A. *Punishment, Communication, and Community.* Oxford: Oxford University Press, 2001.

Dworkin, Gerald. "Autonomy and Behavior Control." *The Hastings Center Report* 6 (1976): 23–28.

———. *The Theory and Practice of Autonomy*. Cambridge: Cambridge University Press, 1988.

Dworkin, Ronald. "Hard Cases." In *Taking Rights Seriously*, 81–130. Cambridge, MA: Harvard University Press, 1977.

———. "Is Wealth a Value?" In *A Matter of Principle*, 237–266. Cambridge, MA: Harvard University Press, 1985.

———. *Law's Empire*. Cambridge, MA: Harvard University Press, 1986.

———. *Taking Rights Seriously*. Cambridge, MA: Harvard University Press, 1977.

———. "Why Efficiency?" In *A Matter of Principle*, 267–89. Cambridge, MA: Harvard University Press, 1985.

Elster, Jon, ed. *Addiction: Entries and Exits*. New York: Russell Sage Foundation, 1999.

———, ed. *The Multiple Self*. Cambridge: Cambridge University Press, 1986.

———. *Ulysses and the Sirens: Studies in Rationality and Irrationality*. Cambridge: Cambridge University Press, 1979.

———, and Ole-Jørgen Skog, eds. *Getting Hooked: Rationality and Addiction*. Cambridge: Cambridge University Press, 1999.

Engstrom, Stephen. "The Inner Freedom of Virtue." In *Kant's Metaphysics of Morals: Interpretative Essays*, edited by Mark Timmons, 289–315. Oxford: Oxford University Press, 2002.

———, and Jennifer Whiting, eds. *Aristotle, Kant, and the Stoics: Rethinking Happiness and Duty*. Cambridge: Cambridge University Press, 1996.

Epstein, Joseph. *Friendship: An Exposé*. Boston: Houghton Mifflin Company, 2006.

Epstein, Richard A. "Private Property and the Public Domain: The Case of Antitrust." In *Ethics, Economics, and the Law: NOMOS XXIV*, edited by J. Roland Pennock and John W. Chapman, 48–82. New York: New York University Press, 1982.

———. "Public Use in a Post-*Kelo* World." *Supreme Court Economic Review* 17 (2009), 151–71.

———. *Skepticism and Freedom: A Modern Case for Classical Liberalism*. Chicago: University of Chicago Press, 2003.

———. "A Theory of Strict Liability." *Journal of Legal Studies* 2 (1973): 151–204.

———. "Unconscionability: A Critical Appraisal." *Journal of Law and Economics* 18 (1975): 293–315.

Esheté, Andreas. "Virtue and Freedom." *Philosophy* 57 (1982): 495–513.

Etzioni, Amitai. "The Case for a Multiple Utility Conception." *Economics and Philosophy* 2 (1986): 159–83.

———. *The Moral Dimension: Toward a New Economics.* New York: Free Press, 1988.

———. "Toward a Kantian Socio-Economics." In *Economics, Ethics, and Public Policy,* edited by Charles K. Wilber, 139–49. Lanham, MD: Rowman & Littlefield, 1987.

Evensky, Jerry. *Adam Smith's Moral Philosophy: A Historical and Contemporary Perspective on Markets, Law, Ethics, and Culture.* Cambridge: Cambridge University Press, 2005.

Feinberg, Joel. *Harm to Self.* Oxford: Oxford University Press, 1986.

———. *Offense to Others.* Oxford: Oxford University Press, 1985.

Ferzan, Kimberly Kessler. "Some Sound and Fury from Kaplow and Shavell." *Law and Philosophy* 23 (2004): 73–102.

Fischer, Carolyn. "Read This Paper Even Later: Procrastination with Time-Inconsistent Preferences." Discussion Paper 99-20, Resources for the Future, April 1999.

———. "Read This Paper Later: Procrastination with Time-Consistent Preferences." *Journal of Economic Behavior & Organization* 46 (2001): 249–69.

Fleischacker, Samuel. *On Adam Smith's* Wealth of Nations. Princeton, NJ: Princeton University Press, 2004.

———. "Philosophy in Moral Practice: Kant and Adam Smith." *Kant-Studien* 82 (1991): 249–69.

———. *A Third Concept of Liberty: Judgment and Freedom in Kant and Adam Smith.* Princeton, NJ: Princeton University Press, 1999.

———. "Values Behind the Market: Kant's Response to the *Wealth of Nations.*" *History of Political Thought* 17 (1996): 379–407.

Fletcher, George P. *Basic Concepts of Legal Thought.* New York: Oxford University Press, 1996.

———. "Fairness and Utility in Tort Theory." *Harvard Law Review* 85 (1972): 537–73.

———. "A Transaction Theory of Crime?" *Columbia Law Review* 85 (1985): 921–30.

Foot, Philippa. *Virtues and Vices.* Oxford: Clarendon Press, 2002.

Frankena, William K. *Ethics.* 2nd ed. Englewood Cliffs, NJ: Prentice-Hall, 1973.

Frankfurt, Harry G. "Freedom of the Will and the Concept of a Person." *Journal of Philosophy* 68 (1971): 5–20.

———. *Necessity, Volition, and Love.* Cambridge: Cambridge University Press, 1999.

Frey, Bruno S. *Not Just for the Money: An Economic Theory of Personal Motivation.* Cheltenham, UK: Edward Elgar Publishing, 1997.

Frey, R. G., ed. *Utility and Rights.* Minneapolis: University of Minnesota Press, 1984.

Friedman, David. "Rational Criminals and Profit-Maximizing Police: The Economic Analysis of Law and Law Enforcement." In *The New Economics of Human Behavior*, edited by M. Tommasi and Kathryn Ierulli, 43-58. Cambridge: Cambridge University Press, 1995.

———. "Why Not Hang Them All: The Virtues of Inefficient Punishment." *Journal of Political Economy* 107 (1999): S259-69.

———, and William Sjostrom. "Hanged for a Sheep: The Economics of Marginal Deterrence." *Journal of Legal Studies* 12 (1993): 345–66.

Friedmann, Daniel. "The Efficient Breach Fallacy." *Journal of Legal Studies* 18 (1989): 1–24.

Frierson, Patrick R. *Freedom and Anthropology in Kant's Moral Philosophy.* Cambridge: Cambridge University Press, 2003.

Gaus, Gerald F. "The Limits of *Homo Economicus*: The Conflict of Values and Preferences." In *Essays on Philosophy, Politics & Economics: Integration and Common Research Projects*, edited by Christi Favor, Gerald Gaus, and Julian Lamont, 37–68. Stanford, CA: Stanford University Press, 2010.

———. "What Is Deontology? Part One: Orthodox Views." *Journal of Value Inquiry* 35 (2001): 27–42.

———. "What Is Deontology? Part Two: Reasons to Act." *Journal of Value Inquiry* 35 (2001): 179–193.

Gauthier, David. *Morals by Agreement.* Oxford: Oxford University Press, 1986.

George, David. *Preference Pollution: How Markets Create the Desires We Dislike.* Ann Arbor: University of Michigan Press, 2001.

Gilbert, Margaret. *Living Together: Rationality, Sociality, & Obligation.* Lanham, MD: Rowman & Littlefield, 1996.

———. *On Social Facts.* Princeton, NJ: Princeton University Press, 1989.

———. *Sociality and Responsibility: New Essays in Plural Subject Theory.* Lanham, MD: Rowman & Littlefield, 2000.

Gintis, Herbert. *The Bounds of Reason: Game Theory and the Unification of the Social Sciences.* Princeton, NJ: Princeton University Press, 2009.

———. "Strong Reciprocity and Human Sociality." *Journal of Theoretical Biology* 206 (2000): 169–79.

———, Samuel Bowles, Robert Boyd, and Ernst Fehr, eds. *Moral Sentiments and Material Interests: The Foundations of Cooperation in Economic Life.* Cambridge, MA: MIT Press, 2005.

Gjelsvik, Olav. "Addiction, Weakness of the Will, and Relapse." In *Addiction: Entries and Exits*, edited by Jon Elster, 47–64. New York: Russell Sage Foundation, 1999.

Glaeser, Edward. "Paternalism and Psychology," *University of Chicago Law Review* 73 (2006): 133–56.

Gold, Natalie, and Robert Sugden. "Theories of Team Agency." In *Rationality and*

Commitment, edited by Fabienne Peter and Hans Bernhard Schmid, 280–312. Oxford: Oxford University Press, 2007.

Goldfarb, Robert S., and William B. Griffith. "Amending the Economist's 'Rational Egoist' Model to Include Moral Values and Norms, Part 1: The Problem." In *Social Norms & Economic Institutions*, edited by Kenneth J. Koford and Jeffrey B. Miller, 39–57. Ann Arbor: University of Michigan Press, 1991.

———. "Amending the Economist's 'Rational Egoist' Model to Include Moral Values and Norms, Part 2: Alternative Solutions." In *Social Norms & Economic Institutions*, edited by Kenneth J. Koford and Jeffrey B. Miller, 59–84. Ann Arbor: University of Michigan Press, 1991.

Gordon, Robert W. "The Path of the Lawyer." *Harvard Law Review* 110 (1997): 1013–18.

Graaff, Johannes de V. *Theoretical Welfare Economics*. Cambridge: Cambridge University Press, 1957.

Granovetter, Mark. "Economic Action and Social Structure: The Problem of Embeddedness." In *The Sociology of Economic Life*, edited by Mark Granovetter and Richard Swedberg, 53–81. Boulder, CO: Westview Press, 1992.

Gregor, Mary J. *Laws of Freedom: A Study of Kant's Method of Applying the Categorical Imperative in the* Metaphysik der Sitten. Oxford: Basil Blackwell, 1963.

Griffin, James. *Well-Being: Its Meaning, Measurement, and Moral Importance*. Oxford: Clarendon Press, 1986.

Guyer, Paul. "Ends of Reason and Ends of Nature: The Place of Teleology in Kant's Ethics." *Journal of Value Inquiry* 36 (2002): 161–86.

———. *Kant on Freedom, Law, and Happiness*. Cambridge: Cambridge University Press, 2000.

———. "Kant on the Theory and Practice of Autonomy." In *Autonomy*, edited by Ellen Frankel Paul, Fred D. Miller, Jr., and Jeffrey Paul, 70–98. Cambridge: Cambridge University Press, 2003.

Hardin, Russell. "The Morality of Law and Economics." *Law and Philosophy* 11 (1992): 331–84.

Hargreaves Heap, Shaun P. "Individual Preferences and Decision-Making." In *The Elgar Companion to Social Economics*, edited by John B. Davis and Wilfred Dolfsma, 79–91. Cheltenham, UK: Edward Elgar, 2008.

———, Martin Hollis, Bruce Lyons, Robert Sugden, and Albert Weale. *The Theory of Choice: A Critical Guide*. Oxford: Blackwell, 1992.

Harris, John R. "On the Economics of Law and Order." *Journal of Political Economy* 78 (1970): 165-74.

Hart, H.L.A. *The Concept of Law*. 2nd ed. Oxford: Oxford University Press, 1961/1994.

————. *Punishment and Responsibility: Essays in the Philosophy of Law*. Oxford: Oxford University Press, 1968.

Hausman, Daniel M., and Michael S. McPherson. *Economic Analysis, Moral Philosophy, and Public Policy*. 2nd ed. Cambridge: Cambridge University Press, 2006.

Hausman, Daniel M., and Brynn Welch. "Debate: To Nudge or Not to Nudge." *Journal of Political Philosophy* 18 (2010): 123–36.

Hayek, Friedrich A. "Individualism: True or False." In *Individualism and Economic Order*, 1–32. Chicago: University of Chicago Press, 1948.

Heath, Joseph, and Joel Anderson. "Procrastination and the Extended Will." In *The Thief of Time: Philosophical Essays on Procrastination*, edited by Chrisoula Andreou and Mark D. White, 233–52. Oxford: Oxford University Press, 2010.

Heatherton, Todd F., and Roy F. Baumeister. "Self-Regulation Failure: Past, Present, and Future." *Psychological Inquiry* 7 (1996): 90–8.

Hegel, G.W.F. *The Philosophy of Right*. Translated by T. M. Knox. Oxford: Oxford University Press, 1952 (originally 1821).

Herman, Barbara. "Bootstrapping." In *Moral Literacy*, 154–75. Cambridge, MA: Harvard University Press, 2007.

————. "A Cosmopolitan Kingdom of Ends." In *Moral Literacy*, 51–78. Cambridge, MA: Harvard University Press, 2007.

————. "Making Room for Character." In *Aristotle, Kant, and the Stoics: Rethinking Happiness and Duty*, edited by Stephen Engstrom and Jennifer Whiting, 36–60. Cambridge: Cambridge University Press, 1996.

————. "Moral Improvisation." In *Moral Literacy*, 276–99. Cambridge, MA: Harvard University Press, 2007.

————. "Murder and Mayhem." In *The Practice of Moral Judgment*, 113–31. Cambridge, MA: Harvard University Press, 1993.

————. "Obligatory Ends." In *Moral Literacy*, 254–75. Cambridge, MA: Harvard University Press, 2007.

————. "On the Value of Acting from the Motive of Duty." In *The Practice of Moral Judgment*, 1–22. Cambridge, MA: Harvard University Press, 1993.

————. "The Practice of Moral Judgment." In *The Practice of Moral Judgment*, 73–93. Cambridge, MA: Harvard University Press, 1993.

————. "Responsibility and Moral Competence." In *The Practice of Moral Judgment*, 79–105. Cambridge, MA: Harvard University Press, 1993.

————. "The Scope of Moral Requirement." In *Moral Literacy*, 203–29. Cambridge, MA: Harvard University Press, 2007.

————. "The Will and Its Objects." In *Moral Literacy*, 230–53. Cambridge, MA: Harvard University Press, 2007.

Hicks, John R. *Value and Capital.* Oxford: Clarendon Press, 1939.

Hill, Claire A. "Anti-Anti-Anti-Paternalism." *NYU Journal of Law & Liberty* 2 (2007): 444–54.

Hill, Thomas E., Jr. "Autonomy and Benevolent Lies." In *Autonomy and Self-Respect*, 25–42. Cambridge: Cambridge University Press, 1991.

———. "Humanity as an End in Itself." In *Dignity and Practical Reason in Kant's Moral Theory*, 38–57. Ithaca, NY: Cornell University Press, 1992.

———. "Imperfect Duty and Supererogation." In *Dignity and Practical Reason in Kant's Moral Theory*, 147–75. Ithaca, NY: Cornell University Press, 1992.

———. "The Importance of Autonomy." In *Autonomy and Self-Respect*, 43–51. Cambridge: Cambridge University Press, 1991.

———. "The Kantian Conception of Autonomy." In *Dignity and Practical Reason in Kant's Moral Theory*, 76–96. Ithaca, NY: Cornell University Press, 1992.

———. "Kant's Anti-Moralistic Strain." In *Dignity and Practical Reason in Kant's Moral Theory*, 176–95. Ithaca, NY: Cornell University Press, 1992.

———. "Kant on Punishment: A Coherent Mix of Deterrence and Retribution?" In *Respect, Pluralism, and Justice*, 173–99. Oxford: Oxford University Press, 2000.

———. "Kant on Wrongdoing, Desert, and Punishment." In *Human Welfare and Moral Worth*, 310–39. Oxford: Oxford University Press, 2002.

———. "Moral Dilemmas, Gaps, and Residues." In *Human Welfare and Moral Worth*, 362–402. Oxford: Oxford University Press, 2002.

———. "Promises to Oneself." In *Autonomy and Self-Respect*, 138–54. Cambridge: Cambridge University Press, 1991.

———. "Punishment, Conscience, and Moral Worth." In *Human Welfare and Moral Worth*, 340–61. Oxford: Oxford University Press, 2002.

———. "Self-Regarding Suicide: A Modified Kantian View." In *Autonomy and Self-Respect*, 85–103. Cambridge: Cambridge University Press, 1991.

———. "Self-Respect Reconsidered." In *Autonomy and Self-Respect*, 19–24. Cambridge: Cambridge University Press, 1991.

———. "Social Snobbery and Human Dignity." In *Autonomy and Self-Respect*, 155–72. Cambridge: Cambridge University Press, 1991.

———. "Wrongdoing, Desert, and Punishment." In *Human Welfare and Moral Worth: Kantian Perspectives*, 310–39. Oxford: Oxford University Press, 2002.

———. "Weakness of Will and Character." In *Autonomy and Self-Respect*, 118–37. Cambridge: Cambridge University Press, 1991.

Hodgson, Geoffrey M. "Meanings of Methodological Individualism." *Journal of Economic Methodology* 14 (2007): 211–26.

Hoffman, David A., and Michael P. O'Shea. "Can Law and Economics Be Both

Practical and Principled?" *Alabama Law Review* 53 (2002): 335–417.

Hollis, Martin, and Robert Sugden. "Rationality in Action." *Mind* 102 (1993): 1–35.

Holmes, Oliver Wendell, Jr. "The Path of the Law." *Harvard Law Review* 10 (1897): 457–78.

Holtman, Sarah. "Autonomy and the Kingdom of Ends." In *The Blackwell Guide to Kant's Ethics*, edited by Thomas E. Hill, Jr., 102–17. Chichester, UK: Wiley-Blackwell, 2009.

Holton, Richard. "How Is Strength of Will Possible?" In *Weakness of Will and Practical Irrationality*, edited by Sarah Stroud and Christine Tappolet, 39–67. Oxford: Oxford University Press, 2003.

———. *Willing, Wanting, Waiting*. Oxford: Oxford University Press, 2009.

Hume, David. *A Treatise of Human Nature*. Buffalo, NY: Prometheus Books, 1992. (originally 1739-40.)

Hurd, Heidi M. "The Moral Magic of Consent." *Legal Theory* 2 (1996): 121–46.

Hursthouse, Rosalind. *On Virtue Ethics*. Oxford: Oxford University Press, 1999.

Hurtado, Jimena. "Jeremy Bentham and Gary Becker: Utilitarianism and Economic Imperialism." *Journal of the History of Economic Thought* 30 (2008): 335–57.

Ikeda, Sanford. "Market Process." In *The Elgar Companion to Austrian Economics*, edited by Peter J. Boettke, 23–9. Cheltenham, UK: Edward Elgar, 1994.

Irwin, Terence. "Kantian Autonomy." In *Agency and Action*, edited by John Hyman and Helen Steward, 137–64. Cambridge: Cambridge University Press, 2004.

Jolls, Christine, Cass R. Sunstein, and Richard Thaler. "A Behavioral Approach to Law and Economics." *Stanford Law Review* 50 (1998): 1471–1550.

Kahneman, Daniel, and Amos Tversky. "Prospect Theory: An Analysis of Decision Under Risk." *Econometrica* 47 (1979): 263–91.

Kant, Immanuel. "An Answer to the Question: What Is Enlightenment?" In *Kant: Political Writings*, 2nd ed., edited by H. S. Reiss and translated by H. B. Nisbet, 54–60. Cambridge: Cambridge University Press, 1991 (originally 1784).

———. *Anthropology from a Pragmatic Point of View*. Translated by Victor Lyle Dowdell. Carbondale: Southern Illinois University Press, 1978 (originally 1798).

———. *Critique of Practical Reason*. Translated by Lewis White Beck. Upper Saddle River, NJ: Prentice Hall, 1993 (originally 1788).

———. *Critique of Pure Reason*. Translated by Norman Kemp Smith. New York: St. Martin's Press, 1929 (originally 1781/1787).

———. *Grounding for the Metaphysics of Morals*. Translated by James W. Ellington. Indianapolis, IN: Hackett Publishing Company, 1993 (originally 1785).

———. "Idea for a Universal History with a Cosmopolitan Intent." In *Perpetual Peace and Other Essays*, translated by Ted Humphrey, 29–40. Indianapolis, IN: Hackett Publishing Company, 1983 (originally 1784).

———. *The Metaphysics of Morals.* Translated and edited by Mary J. Gregor. Cambridge: Cambridge University Press, 1996 (originally 1797).

———. "On a Supposed Right to Lie Because of Philanthropic Concerns." In *Grounding for the Metaphysics of Morals*, translated by James W. Ellington, 63–7. Indianapolis, IN: Hackett Publishing Company, 1993 (originally 1799).

———. "On the Proverb: That May Be True in Theory, But Is of No Practical Use." In *Perpetual Peace and Other Essays*, translated by Ted Humphrey, 61–92. Indianapolis, IN: Hackett Publishing Company, 1983 (originally 1793).

———. *Religion Within the Boundaries of Mere Reason (and Other Writings).* Translated and edited by Allen Wood and George di Giovanni. Cambridge: Cambridge University Press, 1998 (originally 1793).

Kaplow, Louis, and Steven Shavell. "Any Non-Welfarist Method of Policy Assessment Violates the Pareto Principle." *Journal of Political Economy* 109 (2001): 281–6.

———. *Fairness Versus Welfare.* Cambridge, MA: Harvard University Press, 2002.

Kapur, Neera Badhwar. "Why It Is Wrong to Be Always Guided by the Best: Consequentialism and Friendship." *Ethics* 101 (1991): 483–504.

Katz, Leo. "Choice, Consent, and Cycling: The Hidden Limitations of Consent." *Michigan Law Review* 104 (2006): 627–70.

Kersting, Wolfgang. "Kant's Concept of the State." In *Essays on Kant's Political Philosophy*, edited by Howard Lloyd Williams, 143–65. Chicago: University of Chicago Press, 1992.

Kim, Jeong-Yoon. "Hyperbolic Discounting and the Repeated Self-Control Problem." *Journal of Economic Psychology* 27 (2006): 344–59.

Kipnis, Kenneth. "Criminal Justice and the Negotiated Plea." *Ethics* 86 (1976): 93–106.

Kirzner, Israel M. *Market Theory and the Price System.* Princeton, NJ: Van Nostrand, 1963.

Kitcher, Patricia. "Kant on Self-Identity." *Philosophical Review* 91 (1982): 41–72.

———. "Kant's Philosophy of the Cognitive Mind." In *The Cambridge Companion to Kant and Modern Philosophy*, edited by Paul Guyer, 169–202. Cambridge: Cambridge University Press, 2006.

Klevorick, Alvin. "The Economic Analysis of Crime." In *Criminal Justice: Nomos XXVII*, edited by J. R. Pennock and J. W. Chapman, 289–344. New York: New York University Press, 1985.

———. "Legal Theory and the Economic Analysis of Torts and Crimes." *Columbia Law Review* 85 (1985): 905–20.

Klick, Jonathan, and Gregory Mitchell. "Government Regulation of Irrationality: Moral and Cognitive Hazards." *Minnesota Law Review* 90 (2006): 1620–63.

Kneller, Jane. "Introducing Kantian Social Theory." In *Autonomy and Community: Readings in Contemporary Kantian Social Philosophy*, edited by Jane Kneller and Sidney Axinn, 1–14. Albany, NY: SUNY Press, 1998.

Kornhauser, Lewis A. "The Normativity of Law." *American Law and Economic Review* 1 (1999): 3–25.

Korobkin, Russell B., and Thomas S. Ulen. "Law and Behavioral Science: Removing the Rationality Assumption from Law and Economics." *California Law Review* 88 (2000): 1051–1144.

Korsgaard, Christine M. "Creating the Kingdom of Ends: Reciprocity and Responsibility in Personal Relations." In *Creating the Kingdom of Ends*, 188–221. Cambridge: Cambridge University Press, 1996.

———. "Personal Identity and the Unity of Agency: A Kantian Response to Parfit." In *Creating the Kingdom of Ends*, 363–97. Cambridge: Cambridge University Press, 1996.

———. "The Right to Lie: Kant on Dealing with Evil." In *Creating the Kingdom of Ends*, 133–58. Cambridge: Cambridge University Press, 1996.

———. *Self-Constitution: Agency, Identity, and Integrity*. Oxford: Oxford University Press, 2009.

———. *The Sources of Normativity*. Cambridge: Cambridge University Press, 1996.

Kronman, Anthony T. "Wealth Maximization as a Normative Principle." *Journal of Legal Studies* 9 (1980): 227–42.

Kubara, Michael. "Acrasia, Human Agency and Normative Psychology." *Canadian Journal of Philosophy* 5 (1975): 215–52.

Kupfer, Joseph H. *Autonomy and Social Interaction*. Albany, NY: SUNY Press, 1990.

Laffont, Jean-Jacques. "Macroeconomic Constraints, Economic Efficiency and Ethics: An Introduction to Kantian Economics." *Economica* 42 (1975): 430–37.

Lawson, Gary. "Efficiency and Individualism." *Duke Law Journal* 42 (1992): 53–98.

Leff, Arthur Allen. "Economic Analysis of Law: Some Realism About Nominalism." *Virginia Law Review* 60 (1974): 451–82.

Leiter, Brian. "Holmes, Economics, and Classical Realism." In The Path of Law and Its Influence: The Legacy of Oliver Wendell Holmes, Jr., edited by Steven J. Burton, 285–325. Cambridge: Cambridge University Press, 2000.

Little, I.M.D. *A Critique of Welfare Economics*. 2nd ed. Oxford: Oxford University Press, 1957.

Loewenstein, George. "Willpower: A Decision-Theorist's Perspective." *Law and Philosophy* 19 (2000): 51–76.

———, and Emily Haisley. "The Economist as Therapist: Methodological Ramifications of 'Light' Paternalism." In *The Foundations of Positive and Normative Economics: A Handbook*, edited by Andrew Caplin and Andrew Schotter, 210–45. Oxford: Oxford University Press, 2008.

Louden, Robert. *Kant's Impure Ethics: From Rational Beings to Human Beings*. Oxford: Oxford University Press, 2000.

———. "Kant's Virtue Ethics." *Philosophy* 61 (1986): 473–89.

Lutz, Mark A. *Economics for the Common Good: Two Centuries of Social Economic Thought in the Humanistic Tradition*. London: Routledge, 1999.

———. "The Utility of Multiple Utility: A Comment on Brennan." *Economics and Philosophy* 9 (1993): 145–54.

———, and Lux, Kenneth. *Humanistic Economics: The New Challenge*, New York: Bootstrap Press, 1988.

Lynne, Gary D. "Divided Self Models of the Socioeconomic Person: The Metaeconomics Approach." *Journal of Socio-Economics* 28 (1999): 267–88.

———. "Toward a Dual Motive Metaeconomic Theory." *Journal of Socio-Economics* 35 (2006): 634–51.

MacIntyre, Alasdair. *After Virtue: A Study in Moral Theory*. Notre Dame, IN: Notre Dame University Press, 1981.

Mackensie, Catriona, and Kim Atkins, eds. *Practical Identity and Narrative Agency*. New York: Routledge, 2008.

Markel, Dan. "Are Shaming Punishments Beautifully Retributive? Retributivism and the Implications for the Alternative Sanctions Debate." *Vanderbilt Law Review* 54 (2001): 2157–2242.

McCloskey, Deirdre N. "Adam Smith, the Last of the Virtue Ethicists." *History of Political Economy* 40 (2008): 43–71.

———. *The Bourgeois Virtues: Ethics for an Age of Commerce*. Chicago: University of Chicago Press, 2006.

———. *How to Be Human (Though an Economist)*. Ann Arbor: University of Michigan Press, 2000.

McFall, Lynne. "Integrity." *Ethics* 98 (1987): 5–20.

McKeever, Sean, and Michael Ridge. *Principled Ethics: Generalism as a Regulative Ideal*. Oxford: Oxford University Press, 2006.

Mele, Alfred. *Effective Intentions: The Power of Conscious Will*. Oxford: Oxford University Press, 2009.

Mercuro, Nicholas, and Steven G. Medema. *Economics and the Law: From Posner to Post-Modernism and Beyond*. 2nd ed. Princeton, NJ: Princeton University Press, 2006.

Mill, John Stuart. *On Liberty*. Edited by David Spitz. New York: W. W. Norton, 1975 (originally 1859).

Minkler, Lanse. *Integrity and Agreement: Economics When Principles Also Matter*. Ann Arbor: University of Michigan Press, 2008.

———. "The Problem with Utility: Toward a Non-Consequentialist/Utility Theory Synthesis." *Review of Social Economy* 57 (1999): 4–24.

———, and Thomas J. Miceli. "Lying, Integrity, and Cooperation." *Review of Social Economy* 62 (2004): 27–50.

Minow, Martha. "The Path as Prologue." *Harvard Law Review* 110 (1997): 1023–7.

Mitchell, Gregory. "Libertarian Paternalism Is an Oxymoron." *Northwestern University Law Review* 99 (2005): 1245–77.

———. "Taking Behavioralism Too Seriously? The Unwarranted Pessimism of the New Behavioral Analysis of Law." *William & Mary Law Review* 43 (2002): 1907–2021.

Moore, Michael S. "Justifying Retributivism." *Israel Law Review* 27 (1993): 15–49.

———. "Torture and the Balance of Evils." *Israel Law Review* 23 (1989): 280–344.

Morris, Herbert. "The Decline of Guilt." *Ethics* 99 (1988): 62–76.

Munzel, G. Felicitas. *Kant's Conception of Moral Character: The "Critical" Link of Morality, Anthropology, and Reflective Judgment*. Chicago: University of Chicago Press, 1999.

Muraven, Mark, and Roy F. Baumeister. "Self-Regulation and Depletion of Limited Resources: Does Self-Control Resemble a Muscle?" *Psychological Bulletin* 126 (2000): 247–59.

Murphy, Jeffrie G. "Does Kant Have a Theory of Punishment?" *Columbia Law Review* 87 (1987): 509–32.

———. *Kant: The Philosophy of Right*. Macon, GA: Mercer University Press, 1994 (originally 1970).

———. "Marxism and Retribution." *Philosophy and Public Affairs* 2 (1973): 217–43.

———, and Jules L. Coleman. *The Philosophy of Law: An Introduction to Jurisprudence*. Rev. ed. Boulder, CO: Westview Press, 1990.

Nozick, Robert. *Anarchy, State, and Utopia*. New York: Basic Books, 1974.

———. "Coercion." In *Socratic Puzzles*, 15–44. Cambridge, MA: Harvard University Press, 1997.

———. *Philosophical Explanations*. Cambridge, MA: Harvard University Press, 1981.

Nussbaum, Martha C. "Flawed Foundations: The Philosophical Critique of (a Particular Type of) Economics." *University of Chicago Law Review* 64 (1997): 1197-1214.

O'Donoghue, Ted, and Matthew Rabin. "Choice and Procrastination." *Quarterly Journal of Economics* 116 (2001): 121–60.

———. "Doing It Now or Later." *American Economic Review* 89 (1999): 103–24.

———. "Incentives for Procrastinators." *Quarterly Journal of Economics* 114 (1999): 769–816.

———. "Procrastination on Long-Term Projects." *Journal of Economic Behavior & Organization* 66 (2008): 161–75.

O'Neill, Onora. "Between Consenting Adults." In *Constructions of Reason: Explorations of Kant's Practical Philosophy*, 105–25. Cambridge: Cambridge University Press, 1989.

———. "Kant After Virtue." In *Constructions of Reason: Explorations of Kant's Practical Philosophy*, 145–61. Cambridge: Cambridge University Press, 1989.

———. "Kant: Rationality as Practical Reason." In *The Oxford Handbook of Rationality*, edited by Alfred R. Mele and Piers Rawling, 93–109. Oxford: Oxford University Press, 2004.

Oshana, Marina A. L. "Autonomy and Free Agency." In *Personal Autonomy: New Essays on Personal Autonomy and Its Role in Contemporary Moral Philosophy*, edited by James Stacey Taylor, 183–204. Cambridge: Cambridge University Press, 2005.

———. "The Autonomy Bogeyman." *Journal of Value Inquiry* 35 (2001): 209–26.

———. "Wanton Responsibility." *Journal of Ethics* 2 (1998): 261–76.

O'Shaughnessy, Brian. *The Will: A Dual Aspect Theory*, vol. 1. Cambridge: Cambridge University Press, 1980.

Otteson, James R. *Actual Ethics*. Cambridge: Cambridge University Press, 2006.

Page, Talbot. "Responsibility, Liability, and Incentive Compatibility." *Ethics* 97 (1986): 240–62.

Pareto, Vilfredo. *Manual of Political Economy*. New York: Augustus M. Kelley, 1906.

Parisi, Francesco, and Vernon L. Smith. *The Law and Economics of Irrational Behavior*. Stanford, CA: Stanford University Press, 2005.

Parfit, Derek. "Later Selves and Moral Principles." In *Philosophy and Personal Relations*, edited by Alan Montefiore, 137–69. London: Routledge and Kegan Paul, 1973.

Paton, H. J. *The Categorical Imperative: A Study in Kant's Moral Philosophy*. Philadelphia: University of Pennsylvania Press, 1947.

———. "Kant on Friendship." In *Friendship: A Philosophical Reader*, edited by Neera Kapur Badhwar, 133–54. Ithaca, NY: Cornell University Press, 1993.

Pears, David. *Motivated Irrationality*. Oxford: Clarendon Press, 1984.

Peil, Jan, and Irene van Staveren, eds. *Handbook of Economics and Ethics*. Cheltenham, UK: Edward Elgar, 2009.

Pigou, Arthur C. *The Economics of Welfare*. 4th ed. London: Macmillan and Co., 1932.

Pincione, Guido. "Welfare, Autonomy, and Contractual Freedom." In *Theoretical*

Foundations of Law and Economics, edited by Mark D. White, 214–33. Cambridge: Cambridge University Press, 2009.

Plato. *The Republic.* Translated by Desmond Lee. London: Penguin Classics, 2007.

Posner, Richard A. *Antitrust Law.* 2nd ed. Chicago: University of Chicago Press, 2001.

———. "The Concept of Corrective Justice in Recent Theories of Tort Law." *Journal of Legal Studies* 10 (1981): 187–206.

———. *Economic Analysis of Law.* 6th ed. New York: Aspen Publishers, 2003.

———. "The Economic Approach to Law." *Texas Law Review* 53 (1975): 757–82.

———. "An Economic Theory of the Criminal Law." *Columbia Law Review* 85 (1985): 1193–1231.

———. *The Economics of Justice.* 2nd ed. Cambridge, MA: Harvard University Press, 1983.

———. "The Ethical and Political Basis of the Efficiency Norm in Common Law Adjudication." *Hofstra Law Review* 8 (1980): 487–507.

———. "The Ethical Significance of Free Choice: A Reply to Professor West." *Harvard Law Review* 99 (1986): 1431–48.

———. "Rational Choice, Behavioral Economics, and the Law." *Stanford Law Review* 50 (1998): 1551–75.

———. "Retribution and Related Concepts of Punishment." *Journal of Legal Studies* 9 (1980): 71–92.

———. "Strict Liability: A Comment." *Journal of Legal Studies* 2 (1973): 205–21.

———. "The Value of Wealth: A Comment on Dworkin and Kronman." *Journal of Legal Studies* 9 (1980): 243–52.

Pugmire, David. "Motivated Irrationality." *Proceedings of the Aristotelian Society* 56 (1982): 179–96.

Rawls, John. *A Theory of Justice.* Cambridge, MA: Harvard University Press, 1971.

———. "Two Concepts of Rules." *Philosophical Review* 64 (1955): 3–32.

Reath, Andrews. "Legislating for a Realm of Ends: The Social Dimension of Autonomy." In *Agency and Autonomy in Kant's Moral Theory*, 173–95. Oxford: Oxford University Press, 2006.

Reiss, Hans J. "Introduction." In *Kant: Political Writings*, 2nd ed., edited by Hans J. Reiss and translated by H. B. Nisbet, 1–40. Cambridge: Cambridge University Press, 1991.

Ripstein, Arthur. *Force and Freedom: Kant's Legal and Political Philosophy.* Cambridge, MA: Harvard University Press, 2009.

———. "Kant on Law and Justice." In *The Blackwell Guide to Kant's Ethics*, edited by Thomas E. Hill, Jr., 161–78. Chichester, UK: Wiley-Blackwell, 2009.

Rizvi, S. Abu Turab. "Adam Smith's Sympathy: Towards a Normative Economics."

In *Intersubjectivity in Economics: Agents and Structures*, edited by Edward Full-brook, 241–53. London: Routledge, 2002.

Ross, Don. "Economic Models of Procrastination." In *The Thief of Time: Philosophical Essays on Procrastination*, edited by Chrisoula Andreou and Mark D. White, 28–50. Oxford: Oxford University Press, 2010.

———. *Economic Theory and Cognitive Science: Microexplanation*. Cambridge, MA: MIT Press, 2005.

Rossi, Philip J., S.J. "Public Argument and Social Responsibility: The Moral Dimensions of Citizenship in Kant's Ethical Commonwealth." In *Autonomy and Community: Readings in Contemporary Kantian Social Philosophy*, edited by Jane Kneller and Sidney Axinn, 63–85. Albany, NY: SUNY Press, 1998.

Roth, Timothy P. *Equality, Rights and the Autonomous Self: Toward a Conservative Economics*. Cheltenham, UK: Edward Elgar, 2004.

———. *The Ethics and the Economics of Minimalist Government*. Cheltenham, UK: Edward Elgar, 2002.

Ryle, Gilbert. *The Concept of Mind*. Chicago: University of Chicago Press, 1949.

Sabini, John, and Maury Silver. "Emotion, Character, and Responsibility." In *Responsibility, Character, and the Emotions: New Essays in Moral Psychology*, edited by Ferdinand Schoeman, 165–75. Cambridge: Cambridge University Press, 1987.

Sager, L. G. "Pareto Superiority, Consent, and Justice." *Hofstra Law Review* 8 (1980): 913–37.

Sagoff, Mark. "Should Preferences Count?" *Land Economics* 70 (1994): 127–44.

———. "Values and Preferences." *Ethics* 96 (1986): 301–16.

Sandbu, Martin E. "Valuing Processes." *Economics and Philosophy* 23 (2007): 205–35.

Scheffler, Samuel, ed. *Consequentialism and Its Critics*. Oxford: Oxford University Press, 1988.

———. "Ethics, Personal Identity, and Ideals of the Person." *Canadian Journal of Philosophy* 12 (1982): 229–46.

———. *The Rejection of Consequentialism*. Oxford: Oxford University Press, 1982.

Schelling, Thomas C. *Choice and Consequence*. Cambridge, MA: Harvard University Press, 1984.

Schmid, Hans Bernhard. "Rationalizing Coordination: Towards a Strong Conception of Collective Intentionality." In *Economics and the Mind*, edited by Barbara Montero and Mark D. White, 159–79. London: Routledge, 2007.

Schulte-Ostermann, Katinka. "Agent Causation and Collective Agency." In *Concepts of Sharedness: Essays on Collective Intentionality*, edited by Hans Bernhard Schmid, Katinka Schulte-Ostermann, and Nikos Psarros, 191–208. Piscataway, NJ: Transaction Books, 2008.

Searle, John. *Rationality in Action.* Cambridge, MA: MIT Press, 2001.

Seidler, Michael. "Kant and the Stoics on the Emotional Life." *Philosophy Research Archives* 7 (1981): 1–56.

Seligman, Martin. *What You Can Change . . . and What You Can't: The Complete Guide to Successful Self-Improvement.* New York: Alfred A. Knopf, 1993.

Sen, Amartya K. "Choice, Orderings and Morality." In *Choice, Welfare and Measurement,* 74–83. Cambridge, MA: Harvard University Press, 1982.

———. "Evaluator Relativity and Consequential Evaluation." *Philosophy and Public Affairs* 12 (1983): 113–32.

———. "Foreword." In *Economics, Values, and Organization,* edited by Avner Ben-Ner and Louis Putterman, vii–xiii. Cambridge: Cambridge University Press, 1998.

———. "The Impossibility of a Paretian Liberal." In *Choice, Welfare and Measurement,* 285–90. Cambridge, MA: Harvard University Press, 1982.

———. "Liberty, Unanimity and Rights." In *Choice, Welfare and Measurement,* 291–326. Cambridge, MA: Harvard University Press, 1982.

———. "Maximization and the Act of Choice." In *Rationality and Freedom,* 158–205. Cambridge, MA: Belknap Press, 2002.

———. *On Ethics and Economics,* Oxford: Blackwell, 1987.

———. "Rational Fools: A Critique of the Behavioural Foundations of Economic Theory." In *Choice, Welfare and Measurement,* 84–106. Cambridge, MA: Harvard University Press, 1982.

———. *Rationality and Freedom.* Cambridge, MA: Belknap Press, 2002.

———. "Rights and Agency." *Philosophy and Public Affairs* 11 (1982): 3–39.

———. "Utilitarianism and Welfarism." *Journal of Philosophy* 76 (1979): 463–89.

———, and Bernard Williams, eds. *Utilitarianism and Beyond.* Cambridge: Cambridge University Press, 1982.

———, and Bernard Williams. "Introduction: Utilitarianism and Beyond." In *Utilitarianism and Beyond,* edited by Amartya K. Sen and Bernard Williams, 1–21. Cambridge: Cambridge University Press, 1982.

Shackle, G.L.S. *Decision Order and Time in Human Affairs.* Cambridge: Cambridge University Press, 1961.

Shavell, Steven. *Economic Analysis of Accident Law.* Cambridge, MA: Harvard University Press, 1987.

Shaw, Patrick. "The Pareto Argument and Inequality." *Philosophical Quarterly* 49 (1999): 353–68.

Sherman, Nancy. *The Fabric of Character: Aristotle's Theory of Virtue.* Oxford: Clarendon Press, 1989.

———. *Making a Necessity out of Virtue: Aristotle and Kant on Virtue.* Cambridge: Cambridge University Press, 1997.

———. "The Place of Emotions in Kantian Morality." In *Identity, Character, and Morality,* edited by Owen Flanagan and Amélie Oksenberg Rorty, 149–70. Cambridge, MA: MIT Press, 1990.

———. "The Virtues of Common Pursuit." *Philosophy and Phenomenological Research* 53 (1993): 277–99.

Shiffrin, Seana V. "Paternalism, Unconscionability Doctrine, and Accommodation." *Philosophy and Public Affairs* 29 (2000): 205–50.

Shoemaker, David. "Utilitarianism and Personal Identity." *Journal of Value Inquiry* 33 (1999): 183–99.

Simon, Herbert A. "A Behavioral Model of Rational Choice." *Quarterly Journal of Economics* 69 (1955): 99–118.

Singer, Peter. "Famine, Affluence, and Morality." *Philosophy and Public Affairs* 1 (1972): 229–43.

Slote, Michael. "Some Advantages of Virtue Ethics." In *Identity, Character, and Morality,* edited by Owen Flanagan and Amélie Oksenberg Rorty, 429–48. Cambridge, MA: MIT Press, 1990.

Smart, J.J.C., and Bernard Williams. *Utilitarianism: For and Against.* Cambridge: Cambridge University Press, 1973.

Smith, Adam. *An Inquiry into the Nature and Causes of the Wealth of Nations.* Edited by R. H. Campbell and A. S. Skinner. Indianapolis, IN: Liberty Fund, 1982 (originally 1776).

———. *The Theory of Moral Sentiments.* Edited by D. D. Raphael and A. L. Macfie. Indianapolis, IN: Liberty Fund, 1982 (originally 1759).

Somin, Ilya. "Controlling the Grasping Hand: Economic Development Takings After *Kelo.*" *Supreme Court Economic Review* 15 (2007): 183–271.

Steedman, Ian, and Ulrich Krause. "Goethe's *Faust,* Arrow's Possibility Theorem and the Individual Decision-Taker." In *The Multiple Self,* edited by Jon Elster, 197–231. Cambridge: Cambridge University Press, 1986.

Stocker, Michael. "The Schizophrenia of Modern Ethical Theories." *Journal of Philosophy* 73 (1976): 453–66.

Strotz, Robert H. "Myopia and Inconsistency in Dynamic Utility Maximization." *Review of Economic Studies* 23 (1955–56): 165–80.

Stroud, Sarah. "Is Procrastination Weakness of Will?" In *The Thief of Time: Philosophical Essays on Procrastination,* edited by Chrisoula Andreou and Mark D. White, 51–67. Oxford: Oxford University Press, 2010.

———, and Christine Tappolet, eds. *Weakness of Will and Practical Irrationality.* Oxford: Clarendon Press, 2003.

Sugden, Robert. "Capability, Happiness, and Opportunity." In *Capability and Happiness*, edited by Luigino Bruni, Flavio Comim, and Maurizio Pugno, 299–322. Oxford: Oxford University Press, 2008.

———. "Why Incoherent Preferences Do Not Justify Paternalism." *Constitutional Political Economy* 19 (2008): 226–48.

Sullivan, Roger J. *Immanuel Kant's Moral Theory*. Cambridge: Cambridge University Press, 1989.

———. *An Introduction to Kant's Ethics*. Cambridge: Cambridge University Press, 1994.

Sunstein, Cass R. *Behavioral Law and Economics*. Cambridge: Cambridge University Press, 2000.

———. "On the Psychology of Punishment." In *The Law and Economics of Irrational Behavior*, edited by Francesco Parisi and Vernon L. Smith, 339–57. Stanford, CA: Stanford University Press, 2005.

———, and Richard H. Thaler. "Libertarian Paternalism Is Not an Oxymoron." *University of Chicago Law Review* 70 (2001): 1159–1202.

Taylor, Charles. *Sources of the Self: The Making of Modern Identity*. Cambridge, MA: Harvard University Press, 1989.

Ten, C. L. *Crime, Guilt, and Punishment*. Oxford: Oxford University Press, 1987.

Thaler, Richard H., and H. M. Shefrin. "An Economic Theory of Self-Control." *Journal of Political Economy* 89 (1981): 392–406.

Thaler, Richard H., and Cass R. Sunstein. "Libertarian Paternalism." *American Economic Review Papers and Proceedings* 93 (2003): 175–9.

———. *Nudge: Improving Decisions About Health, Wealth, and Happiness*. New Haven, CT: Yale University Press, 2008.

Thomson, Judith Jarvis. *The Realm of Rights*. Cambridge, MA: Harvard University Press, 1990.

———. "The Trolley Problem." In *Rights, Restitution and Risk*, edited by William Parent, 94–116. Cambridge, MA: Harvard University Press, 1986.

Trout, J. D. "Paternalism and Cognitive Bias." *Law and Philosophy* 24 (2005): 393–434.

Tuomela, Raimo. *The Importance of Us: A Philosophical Study of Basic Social Notions*. Stanford, CA: Stanford University Press, 1995.

Usher, Dan. "Theft as a Paradigm for Departures from Efficiency." *Oxford Economic Papers* 39 (1987): 235–52.

van Staveren, Irene. "Beyond Utilitarianism and Deontology: Ethics in Economics." *Review of Political Economy* 19 (2007): 21–35.

———. *The Values of Economics: An Aristotelian Perspective*. London: Routledge, 2001.

Veblen, Thorstein. "Why Economics Is Not an Evolutionary Science." *Quarterly Journal of Economics* 12 (1898): 373–97.

Veljanovski, Cento G. "Wealth Maximization, Law and Ethics—On the Limits of Economic Efficiency." *International Review of Law and Economics* 1 (1981): 5–28.

Velleman, J. David. "Love as a Moral Emotion." *Ethics* 109 (1999): 338–74.

———. "The Self as Narrator." In *Self to Self: Selected Essays*, 203–23. Cambridge: Cambridge University Press, 2006.

———. "What Happens When Someone Acts?" *Mind* 101 (1992): 461–81.

Vohs, Kathleen D., et al. "Making Choices Impairs Subsequent Self-Control: A Limited-Resource Account of Decision Making, Self-Regulation, and Active Initiative." *Journal of Personality and Social Psychology* 94 (2008): 833–98.

Waldron, Jeremy. "Locating Distribution." *Journal of Legal Studies* 32 (2003): 277–302.

Walker, Arthur F. "The Problem of Weakness of Will." *Noûs* 23 (1989): 653–76.

Wallace, R. Jay. "Addiction as Defect of the Will: Some Philosophical Reflections." In *Normativity of the Will: Selected Essays on Moral Psychology and Practical Reason*, 165–89. Oxford: Oxford University Press, 2006.

———. "Normativity, Commitment, and Instrumental Reason." In *Normativity of the Will: Selected Essays on Moral Psychology and Practical Reason*, 82–120. Oxford: Oxford University Press, 2006.

———. "Three Conceptions of Rational Agency." In *Normativity of the Will: Selected Essays on Moral Psychology and Practical Reason*, 43–62. Oxford: Oxford University Press, 2006.

Walsh, Vivian. *Rationality, Allocation, and Reproduction*. Oxford: Clarendon Press, 1996.

Ward, Keith. "Kant's Teleological Ethics." *Philosophical Quarterly* 21 (1971): 337–51.

Watson, Gary. "Free Agency." *Journal of Philosophy* 72 (1975): 205–20.

———. "Skepticism About Weakness of Will." *Philosophical Review* 86 (1977): 316–39.

Wattles, Jeffrey. *The Golden Rule*. Oxford: Oxford University Press, 1996.

Wegner, Daniel. *The Illusion of Conscious Will*. Cambridge, MA: MIT Press, 2003.

Weinrib, Ernest J. "Corrective Justice in a Nutshell." *University of Toronto Law Journal* 52 (2002): 349–56.

———. *The Idea of Private Law*. Cambridge, MA: Harvard University Press, 1995.

Wennberg, Mikko. "Modeling Hypothetical Consent." *Rechtstheorie* 35 (2004): 71–86.

Wertheimer, Alan. *Coercion*. Princeton, NJ: Princeton University Press, 1987.

West, Robin. "Authority, Autonomy, and Choice: The Role of Consent in the Moral and Political Visions of Franz Kafka and Richard Posner." *Harvard Law Review* 99 (1985): 384–428.

Whitman, Douglas Glen, and Mario J. Rizzo. "Paternalist Slopes." *NYU Journal of Law & Liberty* 2 (2007): 411–43.

Wight, Jonathan B. "Adam Smith and Greed." *Journal of Private Enterprise* 21 (2005): 46–58.

———. "Adam Smith's Ethics and the 'Noble Arts.'" *Review of Social Economy* 64 (2006): 155–80.

Wittman, Donald. "Punishment as Retribution." *Theory and Decision* 4 (1974): 209–37.

Wolfelsperger, A. "Sur l'Existence d'une Solution 'Kantienne' du Problème des Biens Collectifs." *Revue Économique* 50 (1999): 879–901.

Wood, Allen W. *Kantian Ethics.* Cambridge: Cambridge University Press, 2008.

———. *Kant's Ethical Thought.* Cambridge: Cambridge University Press, 1999.

Wright, Richard W. "Right, Justice, and Tort Law." In *Philosophical Foundations of Tort Law*, edited by David G. Owen, 159–82. Oxford: Oxford University Press, 1995.

Yuengert, Andrew. *The Boundaries of Technique: Ordering Positive and Normative Concerns in Economic Research.* Lanham, MD: Lexington Books, 2004.

Young, Jeffrey T. *Economics as a Moral Science: The Political Economy of Adam Smith.* Cheltenham, UK: Edward Elgar, 1997.

Zaibert, Leo. *Punishment and Retribution.* Aldershot, UK: Ashgate, 2006.

Zamir, Eyal, and Barak Medina. *Law, Economics, and Morality.* Oxford: Oxford University Pres, 2010.

Zerbe, Richard O., Jr. and Howard EMcCurdy. "The Failure of Market Failure." *Journal of Policy Analysis and Management* 18 (1999): 558–78.

Zwirn, Gregor. "Methodological Individualism or Methodological Atomism: The Case of Friedrich Hayek." *History of Political Economy* 39 (2007): 47–80.

Index